THE PERSIAN GULF
IN THE TWENTIETH CENTURY

By the same author

REBELLION IN PALESTINE

ANGLO-EGYPTIAN RELATIONS 1800–1953

THE PURITAN TRADITION IN ENGLISH LIFE

THE SEAT OF PILATE

ARAB NATIONALISM AND BRITISH IMPERIALISM

THE PERSIAN GULF IN THE TWENTIETH CENTURY

By John Marlowe

FREDERICK A. PRAEGER, *Publisher*

NEW YORK

BOOKS THAT MATTER

Published in the United States of America in 1962
by Frederick A. Praeger, Inc., Publisher
64 University Place, New York 3, N. Y.

Library of Congress Catalog Card Number: 62-13490

Printed in Great Britain by
Western Printing Services Ltd. Bristol

RR 12-4-85

In Memory of
IRENE SMIT

Contents

Maps
(following page 278)

THE PERSIAN GULF

COUNTRIES BORDERING THE PERSIAN GULF

CHAPTER ONE

The Historical Background

THE PERSIAN GULF is one of the two arms of the Indian Ocean—the other being the Red Sea—stretching north-westwards towards the Mediterranean which have, throughout historical time, been channels of trade between the Indies and the Mediterranean.

'The Gulf', as considered in this book, consists (a) of the Persian Gulf proper, stretching from the mouth of the Shatt-al-Arab in the north-west in the latitude of 30 degrees N. and the longitude of 48 degrees E. to the Strait of Hormuz in the south-east in the latitude of 26 degrees N. and the longitude of 56 degrees E. and covering an area of some 97,000 square miles, and (b) of the Gulf of Oman stretching south-east from the Strait of Hormuz to Ras-al-Hada at the eastern tip of the Arabian Peninsula. From the mouth of the Shatt-al-Arab to the Strait of Hormuz is some 500 miles; from the Strait of Hormuz to the ocean is some 300 miles. The breadth of the Gulf varies from 180 miles at its widest to 25 miles at the Strait of Hormuz. The two great rivers of Mesopotamia, the Tigris and the Euphrates, now converging into the single stream of the Shatt-al-Arab some 150 miles from the sea, discharge into the headwaters of the Persian Gulf.

On the east the Persian Gulf is bounded by the great plateau of Iran, rising precipitously to a mean height of 5,000 feet above sea-level within a few miles of the coast. On the west it is bounded by the plateau of Arabia rising more gently and to a lesser altitude from a wide and mostly desert coastal plain.

The climate of the Persian Gulf is hot and mostly humid for about seven months of the year with shade temperatures rising to as much as 120 degrees F. During the months November to April inclusive the mean shade temperature varies from 40 degrees to 60 degrees F. according to locality. Rainfall is low, ranging from a maximum of 11 inches per annum on the

B

Iranian coast to a minimum of about 2½ inches on the Arabian side.

The waters of the Persian Gulf proper are extremely shallow —not more than 50 fathoms maximum; beyond the Strait of Hormuz in the Gulf of Oman the sea floor falls rapidly to a maximum depth of about 1,800 fathoms. There are few natural harbours (Musqat in the Gulf of Oman is the best) but numerous creeks suitable for small vessels. The Shatt-al-Arab is navigable for large ocean-going vessels as far as Basra.

The Assyrians, the Babylonians and, to a lesser extent, the Persians in Achaemenian times, all used the Gulf as a channel of trade between Mesopotamia and Southern Arabia, the Horn of Africa and, possibly, India. There is some evidence of trade having been carried on by the Phoenicians between the Indies and the Mediterranean via the Persian Gulf and the Euphrates Valley. But the first known sea voyage from India to the head of the Persian Gulf was made in 326–325 B.C. by Nearchus who, under the orders of Alexander the Great, paralleled Alexander's return land march from the Indus to Mesopotamia through Baluchistan and Persia by sailing a fleet from the mouth of the Indus through the Gulf of Oman, into the Persian Gulf to the mouth of the Tigris. But it was not until the occupation of Egypt and Syria by Rome in the latter half of the first century B.C. that there was regular trading between the Indies and the Mediterranean, and this passed almost entirely by way of the Red Sea and thence either along the great caravan route through Petra or via the port of Myos Hormos to the Nile Valley and so to Alexandria. The endemic hostility between Rome and Persia, and the fact that Mesopotamia was usually, if precariously, in the hands of whoever was ruling Persia, inhibited the use of the Persian Gulf route as a channel of communication between East and West.

The rise of Islam, the Arab conquest of Mesopotamia and Persia, and the establishment of the Abbasid Caliphate in Baghdad in the eighth century A.D. made the Persian Gulf the principal channel of communication between the exotic markets of the East and the two richest and most powerful empires on earth. This was the Golden Age of the Arabian Nights, the heyday of the port of Basra, and the time of those great merchant adventurers, epitomized by Sinbad the Sailor, who set out from

Basra to experience fantastic adventures and to purchase rich and rare cargoes for the delectation of the great cities of the Abbasid and Byzantine Empires.

From about the twelfth century onwards Western Europe, cut off from Asia for upwards of five centuries, first by the fall of the Roman Empire in the West, and then by the rise of Islam in the East, once more, by way of the Crusades, returned to the shores of the Levant and thereby revived the old trading relationships with the East via the Fertile Crescent.

The Eastern goods principally and increasingly in demand in the markets of Europe were spices and silks. Spices were needed to preserve and to season meats in days when refrigeration was unknown and winter feeding for animals precarious, making it necessary to slaughter cattle in advance for winter consumption. Silks were increasingly demanded for clothes by the upper classes of western Europe who were gradually rediscovering, from the Saracens, the amenities of an almost forgotten civilization. These Eastern goods were exchanged for cloth and metals. At first, the principal intermediaries in this trade were the Venetians, who traded with the East both by sea from depots in Egypt and by land from a trading station established at Aleppo.

The expulsion of the Crusaders from the Levant, the rise of the Ottoman Turks and, finally, the capture of Constantinople by the Ottomans in 1453, had the effect of putting the eastern trade under the control, and at the mercy, of the Ottoman Turks. But the European demand for Eastern goods, shortly to be stimulated by the tremendous influx of gold and silver from the New World, was not to be denied. The discovery of the New World by Columbus was made incidentally in the course of a voyage in an attempt to reach the Indies from the west; hence the name West Indies given to the islands he discovered off what proved to be the mainland of the American continent. In 1497, at about the same time as Columbus's voyage, Vasco da Gama made his great voyage from Lisbon round the Cape of Good Hope to India, thus laying the foundations of the Portuguese Empire in the East and establishing the Cape route as the principal channel of trade between Europe and the East for the next 350 years.

Within a few years of Vasco da Gama's voyage the Portuguese had established a trading station at Goa, on the west coast of

India, and were pushing farther east to the Spice Islands (Indonesia and Malaya) to establish, for the next hundred years, a monopoly of the spice trade with Europe, based on the great trading station which they founded at Malacca. The first Portuguese incursion into the Persian Gulf took place in 1506 when Affonso da Albuquerque, who had sailed round the Cape to the Indian Ocean with a fleet under the command of Tristan da Cunha to protect the Portuguese India trade from Egyptian and Venetian rivals operating from the Red Sea, attacked and occupied the island of Hormuz, in the Strait of that name, after having previously occupied the island of Socotra, at the entrance to the Gulf of Oman, and Musqat, which he pillaged and burnt.

The brief but brilliant splendour of Hormuz is one of the most remarkable episodes in the long history of the Persian Gulf. After the decline of the Abbasid Caliphate had destroyed the previous pre-eminence of the port of Basra, the centre of the Persian Gulf trade had moved successively to Siraf (the modern Tahiri), to the island of Qais, and then to 'Old' Hormuz, situated up a creek on the Persian shore of the Strait of Hormuz near where Bandar Abbas is now. At the beginning of the fifteenth century, for some reason now unknown, but probably connected with the Mongol invasions, the inhabitants of 'Old' Hormuz moved themselves and their goods *en bloc* to the tiny island, subsequently to be known as Hormuz, situated some five miles off the Persian shore of the twenty-five-mile strait between Persia and Arabia. A less promising location for intensive human habitation could hardly be imagined. Only about six square miles in extent, the island had no water, no trees and no cultivation. Food, water, building material, everything, had to be brought from the mainland. The climate was unhealthy and incredibly hot. Nevertheless, within a very few years, a trading community was established which, in the years of its glory, became proverbial throughout the world for its opulence and for its elegance, giving rise to a saying, widely current in those times, of which the English version is, 'Were the world a ring, Hormuz would be the jewel in it'. The rulers of Hormuz, nominally subject to the Shahs of Persia, established a dominion on both sides of the Gulf, which at one time included much of the province of Fars on the Persian, and Musqat and Bahrain on the Arabian, side.

The origin of the prosperity of Hormuz was the position of the old mainland settlement at the seaward terminus of the great caravan route from China and India which followed the present road from Meshed through Birjand and Kerman to the sea. Later, it became an entrepot for the sea trade between China, India and the Spice Islands on the one hand and the Mediterranean and Western Europe on the other. Until the coming of the Portuguese the trade westward was mainly by way of the Red Sea in Arab or Venetian ships. The grand design of Albuquerque was to create a monopoly for the Portuguese Eastern trade via the Cape of Good Hope, first by the capture and control of Hormuz and then by a blockade of the Red Sea, for which the capture and occupation of Aden would probably have been necessary. The first design succeeded, the second did not. For just over 100 years Hormuz continued to flourish under the Portuguese who used the strategic position of the island to control all movements of traffic in and out of the Persian Gulf. This Portuguese dominance came to an end in the early years of the seventeenth century as a result both of the rise of the Safavi dynasty in Persia and of the arrival of the English in Eastern waters.

All through the second half of the sixteenth century, England, emerging under Tudor rule as a great maritime and a major European Power, had been seeking ways and means of obtaining access to, and challenging the Portuguese monopoly of, the valuable Eastern trade. The abortive attempts to find a northeast and a north-west passage through the Arctic to the East were inspired by this motive. Attempts were made by various English merchants to establish a trade route to and from Persia via Archangel, the Volga and the Caspian. Eventually, in 1600, the East India Company was incorporated by Royal Charter for the purpose of trading with the East Indies. In the first twelve years of its existence the Company sent a fleet every year to the Indies via the Cape of Good Hope, and, in 1608 they established a trading station at Surat, on the west coast of India, not far distant from the Portuguese colony of Goa.

In 1615 a mission was sent to Persia by the East India Company from Surat which obtained from the great Shah Abbas a Firman for the Company to trade in Persia. The Company's principal object in penetrating the Persian Gulf was to sell

English woollens in Persia in exchange for Persian silk. For this purpose it was necessary to set up agencies in the interior of Persia. In 1617 such an agency was opened at Shiraz and in the following year at Isfahan. Up to that time, most of the Persian silk trade with Europe had passed overland through the Ottoman dominions, and some had been sold to the Portuguese. Shah Abbas appears to have regarded the coming of the English as an opportunity to strike a blow at the influence of the Turks and the Portuguese. His first contacts with the English had been some years earlier. (In 1598 the two brothers, Anthony and Robert Sherley, had arrived at the Shah's Court on a semi-official mission to encourage the Shah to hostility against Turkey in the interest of the Christian Powers of Europe. One brother, Robert, was engaged in training the Shah's army for, and participating with the Shah's army in, various campaigns against the Turks, while the other brother, Anthony, spent most of his time in more or less unsuccessful diplomatic voyages to Europe in connexion with these hostilities.) It was probably with a view to obtaining the assistance of the East India Company against what amounted to a maritime blockade of Persia by the Portuguese that the Shah, in 1618, agreed to grant to the Company's mission a monopoly for the export of silk from Persia. In 1619, probably as a consequence of this agreement, the Company opened a trading station at Jask, which has been chosen as the most suitable port from which to trade with Persia. (In fact, Jask could not have been very suitable and the decision was probably taken because the presence of the Portuguese at Hormuz virtually blocked access to and egress from the Persian Gulf proper by other foreign merchant vessels.)

This activity on the part of the English Company was bound, as was no doubt intended by Shah Abbas, sooner or later to embroil the English with the Portuguese. In 1618 they had already tried to intercept the Company's vessel *James*, the first English vessel to trade in the Gulf, on its way from Surat to Jask. By the beginning of the seventeenth century the Portuguese had been in the Gulf for nearly 100 years and had made themselves masters of the principal ports on both sides of the Gulf—of Hormuz on the Persian side and of Musqat and Bahrain on the Arabian side. They used their position as far as possible to prevent any other foreign ships from trading in the Gulf. The rise of Shah Abbas was a threat to the Portuguese position. In 1602 Bahrain, in 1615 Gombrun (now Bandar Abbas) and in 1619 Ras al Kheima were captured by the Persians from the Portuguese. The arrival of the English in the Indian Ocean was a bigger threat still. Almost from the beginning of the establishment of Surat trading station by the East India Company, there had been intermittent forays between the English and the Portuguese in Indian waters and, on two occasions at least, in 1612 and 1615, Portuguese attempts to attack Surat from the sea had been defeated.

This double threat to the Portuguese position from the Persians and from the English culminated, in 1621, in a successful joint attack on Hormuz by Persian troops supported by English ships of the East India Company, as a result of which Hormuz was taken and sacked. That was the end of Hormuz after 200 years of greatness.

The capture of Hormuz was the beginning of the end of Portuguese supremacy in the Gulf. In 1640 they lost Basra to the Turks and in 1650 they lost Musqat, their last stronghold, to the Sultan of Oman. Meanwhile the English East India Company who, after the capture of Hormuz, had transferred their headquarters from Jask to Bandar Abbas, were meeting with serious commercial competition from the Dutch. After the end of the Spanish rule over the Netherlands in 1595, the Dutch had begun to develop as a great maritime and commercial people. By the time of the formation of the Dutch East India Company in 1602 they had already established themselves as the principal rivals of the Portuguese in the Far Eastern spice trade. In 1625, three years after the capture of Hormuz, they appeared in the Persian Gulf, opened a trading station at Bandar Abbas (where the English had just established themselves) and proceeded to dispute the rather precarious English monopoly of the silk trade, as well as the English Customs franchise at Bandar Abbas which had been granted to the English Company by the Shah in recognition of their assistance over the capture of Hormuz. At first the Dutch proved much more commercially successful than the English, partly because of the lapsing of the English silk monopoly on the death of Shah Abbas in 1629, partly because of the Dutch ability to trade spices from the Far East, to which trade the English Company had not yet obtained any access, but mainly because of the support which the Dutch Company obtained from their home government as compared with the English Company. For the Dutch, the eastern trade was an important matter of national policy; for the English it was still a matter of private enterprise.

The English-Dutch war in Europe which broke out in 1652 resulted in several reverses for the English at the hands of the Dutch in the Gulf, and, by about 1680, the°Dutch were firmly established both at Bandar Abbas and Basra and were almost as powerful in the Gulf as the Portuguese had been a century before. But the very support from the home government, and the consequent ability to use armed force to an extent denied to the English, which had assisted the Dutch towards predominance over the English, was a major cause of their subsequent decline. Their violent methods, evidenced *inter alia* in their forcible seizure of Qishm from the Persians in 1645, built up a great deal of resentment which expressed itself in action whenever either the Persians or the Turks were in a position to retaliate. Furthermore, the decline of the power of metropolitan Holland during the eighteenth century diminished both the material support and the moral prestige which the Dutch had, during most of the seventeenth century, enjoyed in eastern waters. In 1759 they were compelled to abandon their station at Bandar Abbas; already, in 1753, they had transferred their station at Basra to the island of Kharg, near the head of the Gulf. Kharg, in its turn, was abandoned in 1765 and, with its abandonment, Dutch influence in the Gulf came to an end.

Meanwhile the British (as we must now call them since the Union with Scotland in 1707) had been learning and applying some lessons from their earlier lack of success. Up to the closing years of the seventeenth century the East India Company had been a purely commercial enterprise. But successful trading in the East at that time demanded both the assumption of political and military responsibilities and the support and encouragement of the home government. An agreement between the British Government and the Company in 1688 by which the island of Bombay, recently evacuated by the Portuguese, was made over by the Crown to the Company together with permission to raise troops and maintain civil administration, marks the beginning of a change in the Company's status from that of

8

The Historical Background

private traders to that of administrators acting, in effect if not formally, on behalf of the Crown. At the same time the head-quarters of the Company in the East were transferred from Surat to Bombay. In 1708 the trading position of the Company was strengthened by its amalgamation with various rival societies of British merchants trading with the East, and its political position fortified by the appointment of a British Ambassador to the Court of the Grand Mogul.

In spite of this increased status and strength, the Company's affairs in the Persian Gulf during the eighteenth century were not universally prosperous, mainly as a result of unsettled con-ditions on both sides of the Gulf. In Persia, the Safavi dynasty, which had given the country over a century of comparative stability and, during the reign of Shah Abbas, a few years of greatness, came to an end in 1722 with an invasion from the Afghans and the consequent abdication of Shah Husain, the last of his line. The Afghans were expelled in 1730 by Tahmasp Quli, a great soldier and adventurer, who came to the throne as Nadir Shah in 1736 and ruled for eleven years until his assassina-tion in 1747. Thereafter the country relapsed into deepening chaos from which it did not emerge until the advent of the Qajar dynasty at the end of the century.

On the Arabian side of the Gulf the Arabs of Musqat and Ras al Kheima, taking advantage of Persian weakness and profiting both from European rivalries and the lack of any adequate European naval force in the Gulf, occupied many of the Persian offshore islands and almost brought maritime trade in the Gulf to a standstill by determined and successful piracy.

These deterrents to successful trading were increased by the outbreak of the Seven Years War between France and Britain in 1756. During the course of hostilities, which were to a large extent concerned with an Anglo-French struggle for mastery in India, the British station at Bandar Abbas was attacked and almost destroyed by a French naval squadron. This event preci-pitated the removal, in 1763, of the British Company's head-quarters in the Gulf from Bandar Abbas to Basra, in Ottoman territory. At about the same time an agreement was arrived at with the Persian ruler, Karim Khan, for the establishment of another station at Bushire which was afterwards, until the middle of the twentieth century, to become the headquarters of

B*

the Chief British Political Resident in the Gulf. The Firman under which the Bushire station was established gave to the British Company a monopoly of the import of woollens into Persia, freedom from all taxes, either on imports or exports, and a promise that no other European nation would be allowed to establish a trading station at Bushire as long as the British remained there. This grant, comparatively unimportant as it seemed at the time, owing to the political instability of Persia, was nevertheless an indication of the predominant position which Britain, among European nations, had attained in the Gulf as a result of the decline, first of Portuguese and then of Dutch influence, and can be said to mark the beginning of that long period, lasting for nearly 200 years, of British political and commercial supremacy in the Gulf.

For its first fifteen years the new station had a turbulent existence as the result of war between Persia and the Ottoman Empire. In 1769 it was temporarily abandoned, and staff and merchandise transferred to Basra. But in 1775 Basra was occupied by the Persians and soon afterwards, in 1778, the Company returned to Bushire and made it their headquarters in the Gulf.

It was during this period of the Persian-Turkish war that, for the first time, ships of the Royal Navy were called upon to intervene in the Persian Gulf in defence of the Company's interests, which were continually menaced by the unpredictable behaviour of Karim Khan, the then ruler of Persia. The first of these interventions appears to have been in 1775 when the *Seahorse*, a ship of twenty guns (on which, incidentally, Nelson was a midshipman at the time) arrived in the Gulf from the East Indies Squadron with orders to assist the Company 'where the Company had any settlement or factory or it was requested by the Company's servants'.

From about the end of the Seven Years War (1763) onwards, the emphasis of British activity in the Gulf became less purely commercial and more distinctively political. Although this political activity was, as will be seen, at first directed primarily towards the protection of British commerce, it soon assumed a less exclusive aspect and became directed, in appearance and in intention, towards the establishment, maintenance and policing of a British zone of influence covering the western land and sea approaches to, and for the protection of, the British possessions in India, of which sub-continent Great Britain had become the paramount Power as a result of the conquests of the Seven Years' War.

This change in the emphasis of British policy resulted in a series of further changes in the status of the East India Company. In 1784 an Act of Parliament was passed by which a Board of Control was created as a Department of Government responsible for the political, military, and financial supervision of the British possessions in India, where the Crown was subsequently represented by a Governor-General. In 1833 another Act of Parliament deprived the East India Company of its commercial monopoly. Finally, in 1857, after the Indian Mutiny, the East India Company ceased to exist and its remaining functions were taken over by the Government of India which was directly responsible to the Crown, through the India Office. These changes had their repercussions on the British position in the Gulf where British interests had always been, and continued until well into the twentieth century to be, administered from India.[1] After the lease of Bombay to the East India Company in 1688, and the concurrent right given to the Company to raise military and naval forces, the East India Company developed the small fleet of armed vessels with which they had previously protected their trading vessels from piracy into a larger force, known first as the Bombay Marine and afterwards as the Indian Navy. This force lasted until 1863 and many of the operations in the Persian Gulf against pirates and slave traders which will now be described were undertaken by the Indian Navy, reinforced to an ever-increasing extent from the East Indies Squadron of the Royal Navy which, on the disbandment of the Indian Navy, took over entire responsibility for policing the waters of the Persian Gulf.

As in most unpoliced narrow waters through which trade passes, piracy was endemic in the Persian Gulf and flourished at all those times when neither any of the littoral States nor any European naval power was sufficiently strongly established to discourage it. The Kings of Hormuz who, in the plenitude of their power, occupied Musqat and what was later known as the Pirate Coast between Oman and Qatar, as well as much of the Persian mainland opposite Hormuz, were apparently more or less able to keep piracy under control during the fifteenth century.

Thereafter, first the Portuguese, then the Safavi dynasty in Persia, then the Dutch and English, seem to have exercised a more or less effective policing. But, towards the end of the seventeenth century two circumstances combined to encourage piracy and so to endanger lawful shipping in the Gulf. First the absence of any strong central authority in Persia; secondly, the advent, in Central Arabia, of the fanatical and xenophobic creed of Wahhabism, and the invasion by its warlike and predatory devotees of many of the littoral Sheikhdoms on the Arabian side of the Gulf.

Between the peninsula of Qatar, standing out due north from the Arabian coast south-east of Bahrain, and Ras Musandam on the Arabian shore of the Strait of Hormuz, there lie some 400 miles of flat coastline, broken at numerous intervals by creeks. Authority on this coast was, and still is, wielded by a number of petty tribal Sheikhs, usually at feud with each other who, whatever their nominal suzerainty, in fact enjoyed an independent status except at such times as their lawlessness combined with their weakness to circumscribe that independence. It was on the eastern half of this coast, from Abu Dhabi in the south-west to Ras Musandam in the north, that piracy, incited by the Wahhabis, and encouraged both by the weakness of Persia and the absence of any strong fleet of foreign warships in the vicinity, became a principal way of life for most of the inhabitants during the last years of the eighteenth century.

It fell to the British, as the only naval power in the area, to deal with this piracy and so, in effect, to embark on their long career as international policemen for the waters of the Gulf. At that time there was nobody to challenge the British in the performance of that role. The Egyptian ruler, Mohamed Ali, in his campaign against the Wahhabis, undertaken on behalf of his nominal suzerain, the Sultan of Turkey, did not reach the Gulf until about 1816; the Dutch, after the abandonment of Kharg in 1765, had, as we have seen, ceased to be a force in the Gulf; the French, having lost India, and soon to be in the throes of a revolution, were temporarily disinterested.

Nothing very effective was done until about 1808, by which date the principal pirate bands, under the temporary and precarious leadership of Sultan bin Saqar, the Sheikh of Sharja, had become more than usually powerful and well organized, attacking and plundering British, as well as Arab and Persian, shipping, with something like impunity. In 1807 a combined British and Musqati force (since 1793 Musqat and most of the coast of Oman has passed from the rule of the Imams of Oman and had become an independent State, with which the Bombay Government had come to an agreement in 1798 providing for mutual assistance in matters of common interest) attacked and defeated a pirate force which had occupied the island of Qishm. In 1809 a naval force sent by the Government of Bombay, in co-operation with the Ruler of Musqat, passed over to the offensive and attacked and destroyed Ras al Kheima, the principal pirate stronghold on the Arabian coast of the Gulf, and Lingeh, a port on the Persian coast which had fallen into pirate hands. This expedition was only momentarily discouraging to the pirates, and by 1816 it was necessary once more to mount an expedition which once more attacked and destroyed Ras al Kheima and other pirate strongholds. On this occasion, naval operations were followed by negotiations with the various Sheikhs of the Pirate Coast, as a result of which a Treaty was concluded, under the terms of which these Sheikhs, as well as the Sheikh of Bahrain, who was a party to the Treaty, bound themselves to refrain from piracy against third parties (but not yet against each other). From this time on a British naval force was stationed in the Gulf, first at Ras al Kheima and then at the island of Qishm, to supervise the observance of this and subsequent treaties. The 1820 treaty was followed by various other agreements, including one in 1835 by which the Sheikhs bound themselves not to make war against each other by sea, until, in 1853 a 'Treaty of Peace in Perpetuity' was signed under British auspices by which, in effect, the rulers of the Pirate Coast recognized the existence of a British protectorate over their Sheikhdoms. From that time onwards the old 'Pirate Coast' ceased to deserve its name and became known as the Trucial Coast, by which it is known to this day.

Some time before this matter of piracy had been settled, the British Government had become deeply concerned with the question of the slave trade in the Gulf. As a result of the development of humanitarian sentiment in England, the British Government and successive British Parliaments had for some time been increasingly conscious of the cruelties and injustices associated

13

with slave owning and slave trading. (British public opinion was slower to recognize and to correct profitable cruelties such as child labour prevalent nearer home.) In 1807 it became illegal for any vessel to clear for slaves from any port in the British Dominions. In 1808 it became illegal to land slaves in a British colony; in 1811 slave trading by a British subject became a felony. Finally, in 1833, ownership of slaves was prohibited, throughout the British Dominions.

Up to that time opinion in Great Britain had been almost entirely concerned with the trading of West African slaves to, and the ownership of these slaves in, the British colonies in the West Indies. Having put their own house in order, the British turned their attention to the flourishing trade in slaves carried on by Arab slave merchants in East Africa. Every year, slave hunts organized by these merchants set out into the interior from East African ports, and every year the fruits of these hunts were shipped by sea from these East African ports across the Indian Ocean to the markets of Arabia, Persia and Turkey. The British were determined to use their developing naval power in the Indian Ocean to suppress this traffic. The 1820 piracy agreement, which has already been referred to, classed slave trading with piracy as forbidden activities by the signatories. Between 1822 and 1845 a series of agreements was made with the Ruler of Musqat who, since 1798, had been in alliance with Great Britain and who was also, until 1856 the Ruler of Zanzibar as well, progressively restricting and finally prohibiting the export of slaves from Zanzibar and the import of slaves into Musqat, and giving the British the right of stopping and seizing Omani ships suspected of infringing these prohibitions. Similar agreements regarding the control of the slave trade were entered into with the Trucial Sheikhs in 1838 and 1847, with the Sheikh of Bahrain in 1861, and with the now separate Sultanates of Musqat and Zanzibar in 1874. In 1851 a Convention was concluded between Great Britain and Persia by which the Persian Government undertook to prohibit the import of African slaves by sea into Persia and giving British warships the right to search Persian merchant vessels for slaves. In 1880 a similar agreement was arrived at between Great Britain and the Ottoman Empire.

The policing of these agreements was not at first entirely effective, owing to lack of enthusiasm on the one side and lack of adequate naval forces on the other. But gradually, under the pressure not so much of public opinion in Britain as that of the patient persistence of the naval officers on the spot, control became more and more effective until, by the end of the century, slave trading was as rare as piracy in the waters of the Gulf. (By then these two activities had been largely superseded by gun-running which remained for some years a serious problem, aggravated by the fact that some of the most skilful practitioners were Europeans.)

The anti-slavery measures which have just been described referred almost entirely to slave trading. Little attempt was made to interfere with the ownership of domestic slaves in Moslem countries, many of whose economies were inextricably bound up with slavery. This was in accordance with what was to become a general objective of British policy in the Gulf, which was to secure acceptance of British naval paramountcy in the area by enforcing conditions of law and order at sea and so providing safe trading and navigation for all, without interfering in local politics or domestic customs.

As we shall see, during the course of the nineteenth century, this objective was more and more rarely attained as far as domestic politics were concerned. As from the second half of the eighteenth century onwards, the grand design of British policy in the Gulf was to provide for the defence of British possessions in India by mounting guard on their western approaches. So long as no other European power was interested, this principally involved securing the sea approaches to these possessions from the west. Hence the campaign against piracy. (The campaign against the slave trade appears to have been one of the few genuinely altruistic acts of policy in imperial history. So far from being advantageous to any imperial interest, the suppression of the slave trade irritated and mystified many potential friends of British imperialism, and provided opportunities for mis-representation and vilification on the part of many of its actual enemies.) But other European Powers became more interested; this interest resulted in British diplomacy by land being called in to supplement the resources of the British Navy at sea, and led to the development of those increasingly intimate relationships between Great Britain and the various littoral States of the Gulf which will now be described.

The loss by the French of most of their possessions in India as a result of the Seven Years War had by no means extinguished French interest in the affairs of the Indian Ocean, where they were, in the course of the nineteenth century, to develop a new Empire based on Indo-China and Madagascar. Immediately, however, their most important possession was the rich sugar island of Mauritius, which was lost to the British in 1810, during the Napoleonic wars. In the Gulf French interest became principally concentrated on a series of attempts to establish what would have amounted to a French protectorate over the State of Musqat, which would have given them a valuable trading port, naval base and *point d'appui* generally commanding the entrance to the Gulf.

As has been related, Musqat became independent of the Imamate of Oman in 1793. In 1798 when, it is to be remembered, Great Britain and France were at war, an agreement, directed specifically against the French, was entered into between Britain and Musqat by which the Ruler of Musqat agreed to be guided in matters of foreign policy by the British, to deny any concessions to France within his domains (which included Zanzibar) as long as a state of war existed between Great Britain and France, to expel any French nationals then in his service, to exclude French vessels from any ports under his jurisdiction, and generally to assist the British against the French in any hostilities between them in adjacent waters. In 1800 a British Political Agent was appointed to Musqat. In 1807 the then Ruler of Musqat was assassinated and the rulership usurped by one Sayyid Said. From then on British relations with Musqat were almost consistently good. On the one hand the Ruler received British assistance against, first Wahhabi and, later, after Mohamed Ali had defeated the Wahhabis, against Egyptian attempts to encroach on his dominions. On the other hand, as we have seen, the Ruler of Musqat co-operated with the British in the measures taken against piracy and the slave trade. In 1839 a Commercial Agreement, and in 1846 a Customs Agreement, were concluded between Great Britain and Musqat. In 1854 the islands of Kuria Muria, off the south coast of Arabia, were presented by the Ruler to the British Crown (probably as a means of forestalling their occupation by the French, who had been unwearying in their attempts to displace, or at all events to offset, British influence in Musqat, sometimes even to the extent of providing the protection of the French flag to Omani vessels engaged in the slave trade). In 1856 Sayyid Said, who had been a firm friend of the British throughout his long reign, died, and the Musqati dominions were divided between his two sons, one taking Zanzibar and the other Musqat itself. (From that time on, the Rulers of Musqat and Zanzibar were each styled 'Sultan' instead of the previous title 'Sayyid' by which the Rulers of Musqat had been known.) In 1862 the long rivalry between Britain and France was mitigated, but not settled, by an Anglo-French Declaration in which each of the two great powers bound themselves to respect the independence of Musqat and Zanzibar. (Some thirty years later, Zanzibar was annexed, without protest either from the British or French, by the Germans, who subsequently exchanged it with the British for the North Sea island of Heligoland.)

British relations with Musqat continued to develop after the death of Sayyid Said. In 1864 the British intervened to protect Musqat from renewed incursions by the Wahhabis, in alliance with the Imam of Oman. (This was the first of a long series of hostilities between the Sultans of Musqat and the Imams of Oman. Perhaps the principal value of the British connexion to the Sultans of Musqat was the assistance they were thereby afforded against the Imams of Oman.) In the same year an agreement was made between the British and Sultan Thwaini, Said's successor, for the use of Musqat as a terminus for a submarine telegraph cable. (The British were at that time in process of constructing a land and submarine telegraph system from Great Britain to India via the Euphrates Valley and the Persian Gulf.) In 1891 a Treaty of Friendship, Commerce and Navigation was concluded which, besides reaffirming the provisions of the 1839 and 1846 agreements with Sayyid Said, provided for British control over imports into and exports from Musqat.

During the 1890's, the French, who had never entirely relinquished their interest in Musqat, deriving principally from a desire to secure the sea approaches to their newly-acquired possessions in Indo-China and Madagascar, and who at this time were, as a result of their alliance with Russia, jointly interested with Russia in diminishing British influence in the

Gulf, established a Consulate in Musqat, with the scarcely concealed intention of combating British interests there. The long and confused intrigue which then developed, during which a complicated Franco-British dispute over the alleged behaviour of French-protected subjects in the Sultanate was referred to the Hague Tribunal, only came to an end as one of the beneficent results of the Anglo-French Entente of 1904 when this, together with other fruitful sources of discord between Great Britain and France in various parts of the world, was allowed to lapse into a state of innocuous desuetude.[2]

We must now return to the beginning of the nineteenth century and briefly trace the course of events in Persia after the accession of the Qajar dynasty in 1796. After a short period of chaos following the assassination of Nadir Shah in 1747, Persia returned to comparative internal stability, although involved in almost continual war with Turkey, under the rule of Karim Khan Zand, who reigned until 1779. There followed nearly twenty years of continual civil war from which emerged, in 1796, the soldier-eunuch, Agha Mohamed Khan, the founder of the Qajar dynasty, who was proclaimed Shah in that year. In 1797 he was assassinated—the usual fate of rulers of Persia at that time—and was succeeded by his nephew, Fath Ali Shah.

During the fifty years which had elapsed since the death of Nadir Shah, Persian influence in the Gulf, which had been restored by that monarch almost to the level which had existed during the great days of the Safavis, had declined almost to zero. Bahrain had been lost in 1783 to the Utubi Arabs from the Arabian mainland. Pirate bands were in possession of most of the off-shore islands and many of the mainland ports. So far from being able successfully to invade her neighbours the Persians were, as was soon to be demonstrated, unable to defend their own frontiers.

By the beginning of the nineteenth century, Russia was already turning her eyes to the possibilities of colonizing Central Asia and of securing a warm water port in the Persian Gulf. The state of Persia at the time presented an obvious temptation to the furtherance of these two ambitions, both of which were viewed with great apprehension by the British, as embodying the unwelcome prospect of Russian expansion, both by land and by sea, in the direction of India. It may be said, without serious exaggeration, that, from the beginning of the nineteenth century, British policy in Persia and the Persian Gulf was conditioned principally by the existence of this apprehension.

During the wars with France, however, the British were more concerned with the immediate French, than with the potential Russian, menace, and the first mission of Sir John Malcolm to Persia in 1799, sent thither by the Governor-General of India to conclude a Treaty with the Shah, was intended principally, in the words of Malcolm himself, 'to counteract the possible attempts of those villanous but active democrats, the French' themselves to conclude such a Treaty. But, although Malcolm succeeded in concluding a Treaty, the Shah was principally interested in obtaining European assistance against the apparent imminence of a Russian invasion of his Caucasian provinces. Failing to receive such assistance from the British the Shah, in 1807, denounced the Malcolm Treaty and concluded with France the Treaty of Finkenstein, in which Russia was stated to be 'equally an enemy of the kings of Persia and of France', and by the terms of which a French Military Mission (the first of a long succession of European Military Missions to Persia), was sent to Persia to help train the Persian army. But the Treaty of Finkenstein was shortly followed by the Treaty of Tilsit between Napoleon and the Czar, and no effective French help was forthcoming for Persia when, in 1812, occurred the first of two wars between Persia and Russia which, by 1833, had lost Persia all of her Caucasian provinces to Russia.

In 1833, when the Treaty of Unkiar Skelissi between Russia and Persia, confirming these conquests, was signed, Napoleon was dead, and the French menace to British India had been extinguished, never seriously to be revived. From henceforward, and until the closing years of the century, Russia was regarded by the British as the great potential enemy in the East, and British policy in Persia was conditioned by that fact.

After her Caucasian conquests, which brought the Russo-Persian frontier southward to the river Aras where it is today, the Russians embarked on the colonization of Transcaspia. By 1844 the Russians had reached the Aral Sea. The Crimean War momentarily halted the process of expansion, but in 1868 Samarkand, in 1873 Khiva, and in 1884 Merv, were occupied by the Russians. By 1890 Russia had a common frontier with

Persia stretching eastwards to Afghanistan. The conquest of Persia's north-easterly neighbours, the Turcomans, by the Russians gave stability to a region from which northern Persia had frequently been harrassed by tribal raids, but at the price of a Russian dominance over Persia which has, ever since, been a major factor in Persian political life.[3]

The concept of the Concert of Europe, which was born during the Congress of Vienna, which survived until the last quarter of the nineteenth century, and which dominated relationships between the Great Powers during its lifetime, provided that the rivalries of these powers in the Middle East— that is to say in the Ottoman Empire and in Persia—were pursued by the indirect methods of diplomacy and intrigue rather than by the more direct ones of bombardment and invasion. It is within this context that the Anglo-Russian struggle for power in nineteenth-century Persia must be viewed.

The great British design in the Persian Gulf (executed by the Government of India which, up to towards the middle of the twentieth century, was responsible for British policy in the Gulf)[4] was to uphold the independence of and territorial integrity of Persia and Afghanistan as buffer States between India and the expanding Russian dominions in Asia. In accordance with the diplomatic convention established by the Concert of Europe, this independence and integrity could not openly be challenged by Russia who, after having annexed the Caucasian provinces in the early part of the century, signed, in 1834, with Great Britain, an agreement, which was reaffirmed in 1888, and broken by both parties in 1907, by which both parties bound themselves to respect the independence and territorial integrity of Persia.

While the Russians used their lengthening common land frontier with Persia and propinquity to the principal Persian cities to develop commercial relations in Northern Persia, the British used their, by now, almost unchallenged maritime control of the Gulf to develop similar relationships in South Persia, the two Powers thus establishing respective spheres of influence for themselves which were eventually to be formalized in the Anglo-Russian Agreement of 1907.

Naturally, the pull of British and Russian influence in Persia ebbed and flowed with circumstances—with the proclivities of the reigning monarch, with the skill or otherwise of their respective diplomats, and so on. From the time of the death of Fath Ali Shah in 1834 until 1857 there was continual dispute, and two wars, between Great Britain and Persia over Afghanistan. Fearful lest Afghanistan might fall totally under Russian influence in the event of a similar lot befalling Persia, the British were determined to keep Afghanistan as an independent buffer state between Persia and India and regarded any Persian attack on Afghanistan as an unfriendly act. The Persians, on the other hand, were inclined to regard Afghanistan not only as a troublesome neighbour, which she was, but also as a Persia Irredenta, which had once been part of Persia, and which ought again to become part of Persia. In 1838 Mohamed Shah, who had succeeded Fath Ali Shah, launched an expedition against Herat, whereupon the British occupied Kharg Island and continued to do so until the Persians retreated from Afghanistan. In 1856 there was again war between Great Britain and Persia over Herat. British forces from India, operating from Bushire (where, as a result of the 1763 agreement previously referred to, Great Britain had a Political Residency enjoying extra-territorial privileges) again occupied Kharg, and also Mohammerah (now Khorramshahr), at the confluence of the Shatt-al-Arab and the Karun rivers. This second war was terminated in 1857 by a Treaty under which Persia undertook to abstain from all future interference in Afghanistan. After that, relations between Great Britain and Persia tended to improve, the object of Nasr-ed-Din Shah, who had succeeded Mohamed Shah in 1846, being to balance as far as possible Russian pressure from the north by conniving at British penetration from the south. This meant an even distribution of his favours between the two.

An account of the further development of the rivalry between Great Britain and Russia, its repercussions on the affairs of the Persian Gulf, and the way in which this rivalry merged and dissolved in the menacing pattern of international rivalries which eventually exploded into the First Great War, is best reserved for the next chapter. Before turning to these events it will be appropriate, in this chapter, to give some brief account of the nineteenth-century history of those desert Principalities on the Arabian shore of the Gulf whose oil deposits were, during the twentieth century, destined to bring so many riches to themselves and so much renewed importance to the Persian Gulf.

We have already given some description of events in Musqat and on the Slave, or Trucial, Coast. Immediately north of the Trucial Coast is the Qatar Peninsula, about 90 miles long and about 60 miles wide at its broadest point. This land, sparsely inhabited, arid and unattractive, now an independent Sheikhdom with its capital at Doha, on the east coast of the peninsula, has little independent history of any importance. At the end of the eighteenth century the Wahhabis occupied Qatar, and the ruling family and most of the inhabitants profess the Wahhabi faith to this day. In 1871 Qatar, together with the littoral district of al-Hasa to the north-west, was occupied by the Turks, who appointed the head of the ruling family as their Deputy-Governor. In 1913, after the Ruler of Nejd had occupied al-Hasa, the Turks also withdrew from Qatar, which was thereupon regarded as an independent Sheikhdom by the British who, in 1916, signed a treaty with the Ruler similar to the existing treaties concluded with the Sheikhs of the Trucial Coast.

The Bahrain archipelago, a group of islands lying in the acute angle formed by the west coast of Qatar and the coast of al-Hasa, has had a more eventful history. Possessed of copious supplies of spring water, and being the only cultivable area on the whole Arabian side of the inner Gulf, these islands had naturally been the prey of invaders from the mainland since the earliest times. For some time prior to the sixteenth century it appears to have been independent and prosperous and to have been possessed of much of the adjacent mainland in what is now the province of al-Hasa. In 1551 it was attacked by the Turks from Basra and relieved from Hormuz by the Portuguese, who subsequently occupied it. The Portuguese remained there for about eighty years, when it was captured from them and occupied by the Persians, who retained it until 1717, when it fell to the Imam of Oman. It was recaptured by the Persians during the reign of Nadir Shah, and lost again, this time to the Utubi Arabs from the mainland (the present dominant tribe on the archipelago), in 1783. During the next fifty years it was variously threatened or attacked by the Omanis and by the Wahhabis, who drove the Sheikhs of Bahrain out of al-Hasa. By the middle of the nineteenth century Bahrain, deprived of its mainland possessions, was maintaining a precarious independence under the rule of an Utubi Sheikh. By that time the Ruler of Bahrain had already been concerned with the British in connexion both with piracy and the slave trade and had been associated with the various treaties and agreements on these matters made between Great Britain and the Trucial Sheikhdoms.

The principal threat to the independence of the archipelago came from the rival claims put forward to its possession by the Turks and by the Persians. (Iran to this day claims that Bahrain is part of Iran on the strength of the previous Persian occupation terminating in 1783.)[5] In 1861, mainly on account of this dual threat, the Sheikh of Bahrain entered into a Protectorate Treaty with Great Britain by the terms of which, in return for the support of the British Government against external aggression, he promised to abstain from 'the prosecution of war, piracy and slavery by sea', undertook to recognize the jurisdiction of the British Resident in the Gulf over British subjects in Bahrain, and agreed to permit British subjects to reside and trade in his dominions. (The British Resident in the Persian Gulf was a Political Officer in the service of the Government of India, whose Residency was at Bushire.)

In 1871, when the Turks occupied al-Hasa, this British protection, conferred by the agreement of 1861, had the effect of securing Bahrain's continued independence. In 1880 and 1892 the British position in Bahrain was further consolidated by two agreements, known respectively as the First Exclusive Agreement and Final Exclusive Agreement by which the Sheikh bound himself not to permit the establishment of other than British Consulates, diplomatic posts or coaling stations in his territory, and not to part with any of his territory by gift, sale, lease or otherwise to any foreign Power except Great Britain. In 1895 an attempted Turkish-inspired invasion of Bahrain from Qatar caused the Sheikh once more to invoke British protection; in 1905 internal disorders on the islands resulted in British intervention to restore order and to impose some internal reforms.[6] Bahrain had become, to all intents and purposes, a British colony. A British Political Agent was appointed there by the Government of India in 1900.

British influence never spread to the province of al-Hasa, whose coastline stretches from the borders of Qatar on the south

23

to the borders of Kuwait on the north. Al-Hasa has had a chequered history. The Utubi Arabs who captured Bahrain from the Persians in 1783 came originally from al-Hasa, as, probably, did the Kuwaitis. Up to the end of the eighteenth century Bahrain and al-Hasa had usually been under a single rule, exercised either from the archipelago or the mainland. At the end of the eighteenth century the Wahhabis occupied al-Hasa but failed to occupy Bahrain. Some twenty years later al-Hasa was temporarily occupied by the Egyptians in the course of Mohamed Ali's victorious campaign against the Wahhabis. In 1871 al-Hasa was occupied by the Turks and incorporated into the Ottoman Empire until 1913, when it was annexed by the Amir of Nejd, later to become famous as Abdul Aziz ibn Saud.

The Sheikhdom of Kuwait consists of the port of Kuwait, situated on the southern shore of a small bay near the head of the Gulf, and a small area of desert land surrounding it. It is bounded on the south by the province of al-Hasa (now part of Saudi Arabia), on the west by Saudi Arabia and on the north by Iraq. It appears originally to have been settled by Utubi Arabs of the same tribe which occupied Bahrain in 1783. It played no important part in the life of the Gulf until towards the end of the eighteenth century when a number of Arab merchants from nearby Basra settled there at the time of the Persian occupation of Basra from 1776 to 1779, and diverted to Kuwait some of Basra's overland trade via Baghdad and Aleppo. During the nineteenth century the Kuwaitis became famous in the Gulf as sailors and boat builders and Kuwait became of some importance as a port for central Arabia. The Principality was ruled by a line of hereditary Sheikhs under the suzerainty of the Sultan of Turkey. It came under British influence in 1898 when Sheikh Mubarak as Subah, who had usurped the Sheikhdom the year before, fearing annexation by Turkey, appealed for British protection. There was at that time a British reluctance to provoke the Porte by encroaching on Turkish preserves, and this appeal was not taken up until a year later when, in 1899, it appeared both that Russian agents were negotiating with the Porte for a coaling station at Kuwait and that German interests were considering Kuwait as a possible terminus for the 'Berlin–Baghdad Railway' which was to become one of the principal features of the German 'Drang Nach Osten' policy. Thereupon the British, through the Government of India and their Chief Political Agent in the Gulf, made an agreement with the Sheikh of Kuwait similar to those which had already been made with Bahrain and the Trucial Sheikhdoms, and which made of the Sheikhdom a virtual British Protectorate. (Although, up to the Turkish declaration of war against the Allies in October 1914 Kuwait remained formally subject to Ottoman Suzerainty.)[7]

The headwaters of the Gulf, between Kuwait and Persia, consisting of the mouth of the Shatt-al-Arab and the great port of Basra, had for the most part been in Turkish occupation since the Ottoman conquest of Iraq in the sixteenth century. The boundary between Turkey and Persia at the head of the Gulf was a fluctuating one. Once, in 1776, the Persians had occupied Basra; more often the Turks were in possession of Mohammerah (now Khorramshahr) and other towns on the east bank of the Shatt. It was not until just before the 1914–18 war that the boundary was established along the low water line of the Shatt on the Persian side, leaving the control of the navigation of the Shatt up to Basra in Turkish hands.[8]

Basra, in Abbasid times the greatest port in the Gulf, regained much of its former importance after the rise of the Ottoman Empire in the sixteenth century, in spite of the opening of the Cape of Good Hope sea route, and the competition of the Red Sea route, as being the terminus of the Euphrates Valley route leading to Aleppo, Smyrna, Constantinople and the Mediterranean. The Portuguese, British and Dutch trading stations established farther down the Gulf, on the Persian side, during the sixteenth, seventeenth and eighteenth centuries were largely actuated, on the part both of the Persians and the European merchants, by a desire to divert from the Euphrates route the flow of trade, controlled by the Turks, in and out of the port of Basra. Both the British and Dutch, for a time, themselves established trading stations at Basra when the weakness of Persia *vis-à-vis* Turkey made it impracticable to divert the bulk of the trade from the Euphrates route anyway.

During the nineteenth century the British showed considerable interest in developing the Euphrates route as a means of rapid communication with India until, in 1882, the British occupation of Egypt conferred on Great Britain control of the

Suez Canal route, opened up as a result of the completion of the Suez Canal in 1869. In 1835 a British expedition, jointly financed by the British and Indian Governments, investigated the possibilities of navigation on the Tigris and the Euphrates, and in 1861 a service of British steamers was inaugurated on the Tigris plying between Basra and Baghdad. (Later, in 1888, this service was expanded by the establishment of a service of steamers on the lower Karun, plying between Mohammerah (now Khorramshahr), at the confluence of the Karun and the Shatt, and Ahwaz, the capital of Arabistan (now Khuzistan) province.)[9] More importantly, the British, between 1858 and the end of the century, established telegraphic communication with India (after the original scheme for a cable system via the Red Sea had failed) by means of a land-line between Constantinople and Fao (at the mouth of the Shatt-al-Arab) and thence by a series of submarine cables running down the eastern coasts of the Persian Gulf and the Gulf of Oman to Karachi. Owing to the uncertain security conditions prevailing between Baghdad and Basra, part of the land line was duplicated by means of a land line running eastward from Baghdad into Persian territory and thence via Kermanshah, Hamadan, Tehran, Isfahan and Shiraz, connecting with the submarine line at Bushire. This land line, which was constructed and operated by British engineers as the result of a series of agreements made between Persia and the Government of India during the 1860's, was an important means by which the British were able to extend their influence from the Persian shores of the Gulf into the interior of Persia and so, to some extent, to offset the growing Russian influence in Persia.[10]

This particular British interest in the Euphrates route to the Persian Gulf and India, although to some extent modified by British control over the Suez Canal route, was sufficiently important for Great Britain to feel serious concern over the German 'Drang Nach Osten', which appeared to aim at the creation of a German presence in the Gulf by way of a German-owned railway down the Euphrates Valley to the headwaters of the Gulf.[11] (Just before the outbreak of the 1914–18 war an amicable agreement was arrived at between Great Britain and Germany which provided for a British interest in the proposed railway.) This German threat, as it was regarded, to the British position in India

26

(it must be repeated here that, by this time, British interests in the Gulf were viewed almost, if not quite, entirely in their relationship to the security of India) played its part in that dramatic Great Power realignment during the opening years of the twentieth century which put an end, for the time being, to the endemic rivalries between Great Britain and Russia, and between Great Britain and France, which converted the traditional friendship between Great Britain and Turkey into a state of potential hostility, and which formed a prelude to the 1914–18 war. This changing alignment, in so far as it affected the politics of the Persian Gulf, will be the principal theme of the next chapter.

CHAPTER TWO

The Impending Storm

THE GRADUAL DISSOLUTION of the Concert of Europe which, apart from the Crimean War, and the Franco-Prussian War, prevented overt hostilities between any major European Powers for 100 years, came about as a result of the rise of Prussia and the amalgamation of the German States into the German Empire under Prussian leadership. The three great stages in Prussia's aggressive rise to hegemony in Germany and their threatened domination of Europe are the Prussian rape of Slesvig-Holstein in 1862, the Prussian defeat of Austria at Sadowa in 1866 and the Prussian defeat of France at Sedan in 1870. Thereafter, for some twenty years, the realistic statesmanship of Bismarck was concerned to try and secure by diplomacy a fitting place for the new German Empire within the Concert of Europe. This design was frustrated, partly by French chauvinism and desire for revanche after the Franco-Prussian War, but mainly by the idiotic megalomania of Kaiser Wilhelm II, who dismissed Bismarck from office soon after his accession to the German throne in 1890.

With Germany entering on her now familiar role of the bully of Europe, the old European alignments began to dissolve. Revolutionary France and autocratic Russia came together into an alliance against the Central European Triple Alliance between Germany, Austria-Hungary and Italy. Between these two great groupings Great Britain held the balance of power. During the nineties, successive British Governments, partly as a result of traditional enmities against France and Russia, partly as the result of a calculated determination to lean over towards the supposedly weaker side in order to preserve the balance, had tended towards support of the Triple as against the Dual Alliance. But the growing power of Germany, its increasingly aggressive competition in British export markets, its colonial expansion and its naval construction programme, combined with the petulant arrogance of the Kaiser's public attitudes, slowly but surely brought Great Britain into the opposite camp. The signature of the Anglo-French Agreement (the Entente) in 1904, while it did not make Great Britain a full member of the Dual Alliance, was a clear indication that Great Britain had come off the fence and a clear, if unheeded, warning to Berlin and Vienna.

One important effect of the new alignment, and an all-important effect for the Persian Gulf, was the developing friendship between Germany and Turkey. The German aim in this friendship was to wean Turkey from her now almost traditional tolerance of British influence in her dominions and to provide for Germany a corridor for the expansion of her influence towards South-West Asia. The Turkish aim in this friendship was to obtain military and technical assistance from Germany for the improvement of her armed forces. German ambitions in South-West Asia were principally expressed in the form of a plan, which matured during the nineties, for the construction, by means of German capital and German technicians, of a railway (the Berlin–Baghdad railway as it was popularly known) which would extend the European railway system through Asia Minor and down the Euphrates Valley to the Persian Gulf. We have already seen that rumours of a German intention to use Kuwait as a terminus for this railway had, in 1899, resulted in the assumption of a British Protectorate over Kuwait.

These German attempts to win Turkish friendship came to their full fruition after 1908, the year of the Young Turk revolution, when a group of young army officers, mostly German-trained and full of admiration for German ideas and methods, seized and held the reins of government in Constantinople.

In the Gulf these developments had the effect of suspending those Anglo-Russian and Anglo-French rivalries which had been such a feature of international politics during almost the whole of the nineteenth century. There was a tacit acceptance by the French of the British position in Musqat which, as we have seen, was a source of Anglo-French discord during the nineties. Much more importantly, it led, in 1907, to an Anglo-Russian Agreement over Persia.

We have already seen how Russia, first by means of her Caucasian conquests between 1813 and 1833, and subsequently as a result of her colonization of Transcaspia between 1836 and 1880, had established herself as a powerful and menacing neighbour to Persia, with her frontiers within striking distance of most of the principal cities of Persia. This menacing proximity had necessarily resulted in great attention being paid to Russian wishes by the Persian Government in Tehran. Meanwhile, the British in the south had not been backward in the advancement of their own interests in Persia. The electric telegraph concessions obtained by Great Britain from Persia during the sixties have already been referred to, as has the establishment of a British line of steamers on the lower Karun. In 1872 Baron Julius de Reuter, a naturalized British subject, obtained from the Shah a remarkably comprehensive concession covering the exploitation of all minerals throughout Persia, for the establishment of a Bank and for the construction of a railway. Not surprisingly, this concession was soon annulled as a result of Russian pressure. In 1889 the Baron was partially compensated for his disappointment by a concession for a Bank, to be called the Imperial Bank of Persia. This concession was upheld, but another British concession for a tobacco monopoly, foolishly granted by Nasr-ed-Din Shah in 1890, was cancelled as a result of popular clamour and large compensation was paid to the concessionaires in lieu. In 1887, rumours of a British scheme to construct a railway from the Persian Gulf to Tehran resulted, on Russian insistence, in an agreement by the Persian Government not to give any concession for railway construction to a foreign company without previous consultation with Russia. (This agreement had the effect of retarding railway construction in Persia by about forty years.) And so the process of rivalry went on, Russia relying on her massive presence on Persia's northern frontiers, Britain continually probing for an extension of her influence from her *point d'appui* on the Persian Gulf.

In 1896 Nasr-ed-Din Shah was assassinated after a reign of nearly fifty years and was succeeded by Muzaffar-ed-Din, who soon made the discovery that his predecessor's personal extravagances had brought the Treasury to bankruptcy. An international loan was solicited, and the Customs revenue offered as security for the loan. Russia was quicker than Great Britain to seize the opportunity; two loans of 32½ million roubles and 10 million roubles respectively were granted by Russia in 1900 and 1901 on conditions which gave to Russia almost entire control over the Persian Customs tariffs, which were in consequence adjusted so as to give the maximum advantage to Russian and the maximum disadvantage to British goods.

On the whole, by the beginning of the twentieth century, the Russians were having the best of it in the Anglo-Russian struggle for power in Persia, and Russian agents had already been observed in the Gulf surveying possible sites for coaling stations. It was probably as a result of this diminishing British influence that Lord Curzon, the Viceroy of India, paid a State visit to the Gulf in 1903, accompanied by the East India Squadron of the Royal Navy. Lord Curzon was intensely interested in the affairs of the Gulf; some twelve years previously, as a private individual, he had made a long journey through Persia, mostly on horseback, and as a result of his travels, had published a two-volume account of Persia which, *inter alia*, dealt exhaustively with British trade in Persia, with Anglo-Russian rivalry and with the strategic position of Persia in relation to that rivalry. The Persian Gulf visit was undoubtedly made as a result of that special interest and knowledge and led to a considerable increase in the establishment of British Political and Consular officers in the Gulf.[1]

In 1904–5 the Russo-Japanese War, and the defeat of Russia by the Japanese, had a profound psychological effect on the Persians in their relations with Russia. Russia had been defeated by an Asiatic Power; Russia had been publicly humiliated in the eyes of the world; Russia was no longer all-powerful.

Meanwhile, domestic affairs in Persia were in a state of ferment. At the beginning of the twentieth century Persia was an absolute monarchy in which the Shah had the power of life and death over all his subjects. His word was the supreme law, against which there was no appeal. The business of his Ministers, who could be dismissed at will by him, was to carry out the Shah's wishes irrespective of any other consideration. Such a system could only survive given three conditions; a reasonably efficient administration; a strong and loyal army; a complete isolation of the country from outside influences. None of these conditions existed in Persia at the beginning of the twentieth century. The country was bankrupt and the new Shah was neither greatly feared nor much respected. During the nineteenth century an increasing number of upper-class Persians had had a European education and knowledge of European ways and European politics was spreading. The pan-Islamic propaganda of Jamal-ed-Din Afghani had a great deal of influence among religious people. (Today, when official Islam is synonymous with reaction, it is not easy to recall that the Islamic Modernist Movement, of which Afghani was the leader, was a reformist movement which had a great deal of influence on contemporary political attitudes in Turkey, Egypt and, perhaps more than anywhere else, Persia.) In those days the immediate objective of reform was the granting of a Constitution which, it was believed from the teachings of the political philosophers of the west who had such a profound influence on the revolutionary movements of the Middle East, would subject the Ruler and his Government to the rule of laws drawn up by the representatives of the people instead of leaving them to make and break their own laws as they went along. In a country and age where the very word 'law' has something oppressive and sinister about it, it is instructive to recall that Muzaf-ar-ed-Din Shah regarded the Persian word Qanun, meaning law, as almost a synonym for revolution. One of the reasons for Jamal-ed-Din Afghani's expulsion from Persia was his alleged advocacy of a system of fixed laws, and the principal subversive newspaper published (in London) by the Persian reformers was called 'Qanun'.

In 1905 there were anti-Government riots in Tehran led by a group of merchants and mullahs. (Here again it is odd to find that those who are, at the present day, the stoutest upholders of reaction were at that time in the vanguard of the agitation for reform.) As a result of these disturbances promises were made by the Shah, none of which were kept, to dismiss his Chief Minister Ayn-ed-Dowla, who had made himself particularly obnoxious by his tyranny and corruption, and to institute Courts of Justice, a Code of Laws, and a Council to consider the question of administrative reforms. In the following year, with none of the Shah's promises fulfilled and with Ayn-ed-Dowla still in office, there were further serious disturbances, during which some of the ringleaders, mostly merchants and bankers, took sanctuary in the British Legation compound in Tehran.[2] This time the Shah issued a Decree conceding an elected National Assembly and granting an amnesty to all those who had taken part in the disturbances. Subsequently, elections were held and the first Assembly, or Majlis, met in October 1906. The Majlis drew up a Constitution which was ratified in 1907 by Muzaffar-ed-Din who thereupon, incontinently, departed this life, being succeeded by his son Mohamed Ali Shah. The new Ruler immediately set to work to undermine the new Constitution. He made an abortive attempt at a *coup d'état* in December 1907 and only retained his throne as the result of intervention by Great Britain and Russia who, during the course of the year, had come to an agreement to partition Persia into 'spheres of influence' between them.

This Agreement, which was a clear violation of the Anglo-Russian Agreement of 1834, by which both Powers bound themselves to respect the territorial integrity and the independence of Persia, derived from the Anglo-French Entente of 1904 by which Great Britain had, in effect, aligned herself with the Dual Alliance of France and Russia against the growing menace of the Central Powers. In the Middle East this menace was most clearly seen in the increasing friendliness between Germany and Turkey, and in Germany's obvious intention to use Turkey as a means of furthering her ambitions in South-West Asia. In view of all this, it was natural for Great Britain and Russia to compose their rivalries over Persia; it was also, perhaps, inevitable that these rivalries should be composed at the expense of Persia. The text of the Agreement, as presented to the Persian Government in September 1907, was as follows:

'Desiring to avoid any cause of conflict between their respective interests in certain regions of Persia, on the one hand, contiguous with or in the neighbourhood of the Russian frontier, and on the other, of the frontier of Baluchistan and Afghanistan, the Governments of Great Britain and of Russia have signed a friendly Arrangement on the subject.

'The two Governments mutually agree to the strict independence and integrity of Persia by that Agreement, and testify that they sincerely desire not only the permanent establishment of equal advantages for the industry and commerce of all other nations, but also the pacific development of that country. Further, each of the two States binds itself to seek no Concession of any kind whatsoever in these regions which are coterminous with or in the neighbourhood of the frontier of the other.

'In the Arrangement the above-mentioned regions are clearly defined in order that, in the future, misunderstandings may be avoided, and in order to avoid creating a state of things which might, in any respect whatever, place the Persian Government in an embarrassing situation. The Russian and British Governments recognize, in mentioning the revenues affected to the loans concluded with the Discount and Loan Bank, and with the Imperial Bank, by the Persian Government, that, in the future, these loans will be affected to the same purpose as in the past; and in the case of irregularities in the amortization or in the payment of interest on the loan above-mentioned, the two Governments engage equally, in order by common agreement to determine the measures of control which it would be necessary to take, to enter on a friendly exchange of views, and to avoid all interference which would not be in accordance with the principles laid down in that arrangement.

'The two States have, in signing the Arrangement, steadfastly kept the fundamental principle in view that the independence and integrity of Persia should be respected absolutely. The sole object of the Arrangement is the avoidance of any cause of misunderstanding on the ground of Persian affairs between the Contracting Parties. The Shah's Government will be convinced that the Agreement concluded between Russia and Great Britain cannot fail to promote the prosperity, security and ulterior development of Persia in the most efficacious manner.'

The two 'spheres of influence' in the Agreement were defined as follows:

'Starting from Kasr-i-Shirin, the Russian line crosses and includes Isfahan, Yezd and Kakh, ending at that point on the Persian frontier where the Russian and Afghan frontiers intersect. Going from the Afghan frontier via Gazik, Birjand, Kerman, the British line ends at Bandar Abbas.'

34

The Agreement,[3] which was an Agreement between Great Britain and Russia imposed on Persia, and in no sense an agreement made by Great Britain and Russia with Persia, was generally resented in Persia and particularly resented by the Constitutionalists who had, only the year before, regarded the British Government as their patron in the struggle against despotism. Thus the popularity of Great Britain, which had been very high among the Constitutionalists at the beginning of 1907, had sunk to zero by the end of the year. Although it had not always been the case, Great Britain, in the course of the agitations of the previous few years, had given the general impression that she supported the Constitutionalists against the Court, while Russia was regarded as having supported the Court against the Constitutionalists. The essence of the British betrayal, as the Constitutionalists saw it, was that Great Britain had now joined Russia in the support of the Shah in his determination to suppress such precarious liberties as has been granted under the Constitution. In fact, Great Britain was manoeuvred into precisely this position as a result of the inevitable opposition of the Constitutionalists to the Agreement, and as a result of the Shah's willingness to accept the Agreement as a means of procuring Anglo-Russian support against the Constitutionalists. Thus that apparent identity between British imperialism and despotism which had been established in Egypt as a result of the British occupation in 1882 was now duplicated in Persia as a result of the 1907 Agreement.

At the end of 1907, as has been related, Great Britain and Russia intervened to save the Shah from probable deposition. In June 1908 the Shah made a second attempt to overthrow the Constitution which resulted in civil war. After a year of fighting, during which Russia openly sided with the Shah and the British ostentatiously refrained from assisting the Constitutionalists, Mohamed Ali Shah was deposed in July 1909 and succeeded by his son, a boy of 12, with an elderly and respected Qajar, Azud-al-Mulk, acting as Regent. The Constitution appeared to have passed successfully through its baptism of fire. But Azud-al-Mulk died soon afterwards and everything turned to confusion. Morgan Shuster, an American financial expert engaged by the Government to try and disentangle Persia's disordered finances, managed to embroil the Government with the Russians, as a result of which Russia sent troops into Persia and bombarded the city of Meshed, damaging the holy Shrine there. This action did not add to the popularity of the Anglo-Russian Agreement. There was trouble with the powerful Bakhtiari tribe who, having assisted the Constitutionalists in the civil war, now claimed, and for a time obtained, a dominant share in the Government, until they were expelled from power by Salar-ed-Dowla, who had succeeded Azud-al-Mulk as Regent.

In the midst of all this political flurry something was taking place in south Persia which, although it passed almost unnoticed at the time, was to revolutionize the politics, economics and strategic importance of the whole Persian Gulf area. In 1901 an Australian named William Knox d'Arcy had obtained from the Persian Government a concession to explore for oil anywhere in southern Iran. After a long and apparently unrewarding search oil was struck in commercial quantities in 1908 at Mesjid-i-Suleiman, in the foothills of the Zagros Mountains, about 150 miles from the head of the Persian Gulf. A year later, the Anglo-Persian Oil Company was formed to take over the concession from d'Arcy. By 1912 Mesjid-i-Suleiman was linked by pipeline to Abadan, an island in the Shatt-al-Arab, where a refinery had been built, and the export of oil started. In 1913 the British Admiralty, at that time in the charge of Winston Churchill, purchased on behalf of the British Government a controlling share in the Anglo-Persian Oil Company as a means of securing supplies of oil fuel for the British Fleet which was beginning to turn over from coal to oil firing. Although, in 1914, production of oil from the new Persian field was still very small by present-day standards, the existence of this British-owned oil, and its potential importance to the British Navy, was a major factor in determining the course of British wartime operations in the Persian Gulf.

As war approached, the Anglo-Russian position in Persia, as it existed after the 1907 Agreement, could be regarded as strategically satisfactory but politically much less so. Strategically, the British Navy was in secure command of the whole of the Persian Gulf and the Russian Army was in a position immediately to occupy the whole of North Persia and to hold it against any domestic insurrection or likely foreign invasion. Such a foreign invasion was only likely to come from Turkey who, by this time seemed committed to enter the war, when it came, on the side of the Central Powers. The old state of endemic warfare between the Ottoman Empire and Persia had more or less come to an end by the beginning of the nineteenth century. By the beginning of the twentieth century a common religion and a common hostility towards Russia had, in spite of endemic frontier violations by the Turks, done much to diminish the traditional hostility between the two countries, and there was very little likelihood that a Turkish alliance with Germany against Great Britain and Russia would have any effect in stimulating Persian support for the latter. Just before the outbreak of war a Boundary Commission, in which both British and Russian representatives participated, delineated the vague and disputed frontier between Persia and Turkey, a boundary which was to be violated soon afterwards by all the governments represented on the Commission, except for the Persian Government.

Politically, both British and Russians were extremely unpopular in Persia. Constitutionalism, such as it was, had lost most of its attraction owing to the venality and inefficiency of the constitutional régime, which was regarded as having been achieved in spite of Anglo-Russian support for the previous despotism, and whose inefficiency was generally ascribed to Anglo-Russian interference. Although Persia was to remain formally neutral, most educated Persians quite openly wished for a German victory which would, they hoped, enable them to get rid of both the British and the Russians. In the South the tribes, of whom the Bakhtiari and the Qashgai were the most important, were disloyal to the Government and resentful of the British and were, as events proved, to be a rich field for the German 'cloak and dagger' work during the war, and an endemic menace to the security of the new oilfield.

The Germans, since the beginning of the nineties, had been becoming more and more conspicuous in the Gulf, their activities taking the time-honoured form of trade which, as so often, preceded rather than followed the flag. In 1896 the German trading firm of Wonckhaus opened a branch at Lingeh on the Persian shore of the Gulf and started trading in a small way in mother-of-pearl. In 1897 a German Vice-Consulate was opened at Bushire. In 1900 a German mission arrived at Kuwait to try and negotiate a lease of land intended to serve as a terminus for the 'Berlin–Baghdad Railway'. During the next few years the firm of Wonckhaus opened branches in Bahrain, Basra and Bandar Abbas. Attempts by this firm to secure pearl fishing concessions from the Sheikhs of Bahrain and Sharja were foiled by British insistence on the exclusive treaties concluded by these Sheikhs with Great Britain. In 1906 the German Hamburg–Amerika shipping line started a service of steamers to the Gulf and built up a considerable trade with the port of Basra.[4] At the same time German trade with the interior of Persia was being assiduously developed, particularly in connexion with German aniline dyes, which had begun to replace the old indigenous vegetable dyes in the manufacture of Persian carpets. Politically, it was not difficult, and by no means illegitimate, for German diplomacy to take advantage of current British and Russian unpopularity to point the contrast in favour of Germany.

On the Arabian side of the Gulf little of immediate, though something of potential, importance had been happening during the first years of the twentieth century. In 1891 the Amir of Nejd,[5] Abdul Rahman ibn Saud, together with his son Abdul Aziz, had had to leave his Nejdi capital of Riadh and to seek refuge with the Sheikh of Kuwait following on the successful invasion of his dominions by ibn Rashid, the Ruler of Shammar, in the north of the Arabian Peninsula, and at that time the most powerful of the Rulers of Arabia. Father and son remained as guests of the Sheikh of Kuwait until 1900, when Abdul Aziz, now grown to manhood, collected a handful of his followers and set off to recapture his desert inheritance. Within a few years he had not only reconquered Nejd, but had, in 1913, annexed the Turkish province of al-Hasa[6] on the shore of the Gulf, and was waging successful war against the ibn Rashid of Shammar who had turned his family out of their dominions some twenty years before.

The rising importance of the young Amir of Nejd was recognized by the Government of India (who at the time of the outbreak of war was still responsible for British policy in the Arabian Peninsula as well as in the Persian Gulf) and immediately before the outbreak of war they sent the Political Agent at Kuwait, Major Shakespeare, as their envoy to Riadh. Unfortunately, Major Shakespeare was killed early in 1915 in the course of a foray against the Banu Rashid, whither he had accompanied the Amir of Nejd. If he had lived to represent the cause of ibn Saud to the British Government as eloquently as the cause of the Sherif of Makka was represented by the not always objective arabophiles of the Arab Bureau, the subsequent course of history in the Middle East might have been different.

That part of the Ottoman Empire enclosed by the lower waters of the Tigris and Euphrates known to the world as Mesopotamia was divided administratively into the Vilayets of Basra and Baghdad. Bounded on the east by Persia and on the north by the Vilayet of Mosul, the western and southern boundaries were indeterminate and, during the early years of the twentieth century, formed a frequent subject of dispute with the Sheikh of Kuwait and with the rising Amir of Nejd, both of which Rulers, although nominally under Ottoman suzerainty, were not under direct Turkish administration.

The British regarded themselves as enjoying a special position of privilege in the Vilayets of Basra and Baghdad conferred by their paramount position in the Persian Gulf as a whole. They maintained a Political Resident and Consul-General in Baghdad who, like the Chief Political Resident Persian Gulf at Bushire, was usually a member of the Indian Political Service. There was also a British Consul at Basra, and a British-Indian Post Office which enjoyed extra-territorial rights in the two Vilayets.

During the first decade of the twentieth century British relationships with the Ottoman Empire over the affairs of the Persian Gulf were concentrated on three objectives: (*a*) a measure of control over the concession given by the Ottoman Empire to the German-owned Anatolian Railway Company for the construction of the so-called 'Berlin–Baghdad Railway': (*b*) Ottoman recognition of British naval supremacy in the Persian Gulf; (*c*) Ottoman recognition of the Treaties concluded by H.M.G. with the various Arab Sheikhdoms in the Persian Gulf. The Ottoman Government proved to be reasonably compliant over all these three matters. In 1912, an agreement was reached between the two Governments by which (*a*) Turkey agreed not to extend the 'Berlin–Baghdad Railway' beyond Basra to the headwaters of the Gulf without British consent (the British protectorate over Kuwait had been declared as the result of a

German-inspired attempt to make Kuwait the terminus of the projected railway), and agreed that two British representatives should sit on the Board of the Railway (a simultaneous agreement was arrived at with Germany in the same sense; and (*b*) Turkey recognized the British right to light, buoy and police the waters of the Persian Gulf and agreed that Great Britain should have unrestricted rights of navigation on the Shatt-al-Arab and a share in the control of the port of Basra. In the following year this agreement was translated into a Convention which also provided for Ottoman recognition of the British Treaties with Kuwait and Bahrain. This Convention was never ratified owing to the outbreak of war between Great Britain and Turkey in October 1914. It is noteworthy that, in this Convention, a distinction was made between the status of Bahrain and that of Kuwait. Whereas, by the terms of the Convention, Turkey renounced all claims to sovereignty over Bahrain, the Sheikhdom of Kuwait was, under the Convention, recognized by H.M.G. as part of the Ottoman dominions. (Simultaneously with the signature of the Convention, the British status in Bahrain was underlined by the issue of a 'Bahrain Order in Council' which, in effect, defined Bahrain's status as that of a British colony, with the Chief Political Resident Persian Gulf having much the same powers over Bahrain as a Colonial Governor. The importance attached to Bahrain by H.M.G. clearly arose from Bahrain's eminent suitability as a naval base in the Persian Gulf, should the establishment of such a base be deemed necessary by H.M.G. In the event Bahrain was used in October 1914 as a point of assembly for the Indian Expeditionary Force on its way to Mesopotamia, and a permanent British Naval Base was established there in 1935.)

Turkey's principal interest in the Persian Gulf before 1914 lay in free access to and egress from the port of Basra. By the terms of the Treaty of Erzerum with Persia in 1847 the border between Turkey and Persia had been fixed along the low-water mark of the Shatt on the Persian side—that is to say, the navigation channel by which Basra had access to the Persian Gulf was inside Turkish territory. The terms of the Convention referred to above seemed to confirm British acceptance of this frontier, which was re-confirmed by an international Boundary Commission in 1914. This Boundary Commission also established the long-disputed land boundary between Turkey and Persia from the Shatt in the south to Mount Ararat in the north.

War came to the Persian Gulf in October 1914, when Turkey threw in her lot with the Central Powers and declared war on the Allies. On 6 November 1914 a British-Indian expeditionary force landed at Fao, at the mouth of the Shatt-al-Arab. The subsequent course of the war in the Persian Gulf will be outlined in the next chapter.

CHAPTER THREE

The First World War

W HEN, IN AUGUST 1914, war broke out between Great Britain and Germany, British authority in the Persian Gulf was a matter of dual control exercised by the Foreign Office and by the Government of India, with the India Office acting as liaison between the two. The Home Government was responsible for relations with the Ottoman Empire; the British Minister in Tehran was under the Foreign Office, as were the various British Consuls-General and Consuls in Persia and Mesopotamia, and the British Consul in Musqat. The Chief Political Resident Persian Gulf, stationed at Bushire, and the various Political Agents in the Arab Sheikhdoms, and at Mohammerah in Persia, were appointed by and responsible to the Government of India, which was generally responsible for political relations with all Rulers, other than the Persian and Ottoman Governments, in the Persian Gulf and Arabian Peninsula.[1] The Chief Political Officer at Bushire, who was also Consul-General for Fars and Khuzistan, as well as several of the Political Agents, who also held consular appointments, thus had to serve two masters, the Government of India and the British Foreign Office.[2]

The advent of war, and the increasing probability that Turkey would enter the war on the side of Germany, presented the British and Indian Governments with urgent problems concerning the defence of British interests in the Persian Gulf. Perhaps the most immediate problem was the defence of the British-owned oilfield and refinery in South Persia and the pipeline connecting the two. The British also had an obligation both of interest and honour to protect the Sheikhs in Treaty or other friendly relationship with Great Britain, whose independence, property, freedom, and even lives would be endangered in the event of Turkey entering the war against Great Britain. Of these, the most immediately threatened would be Sheikh Mubarak of Kuwait who, although in treaty relationship with Great Britain on terms which made of his Sheikhdom a British protectorate, was still under Ottoman suzerainty, and Sheikh Khazaal of Mohammerah. Sheikh Khazaal, although nominally a subject of the Shah of Persia, was *de facto* ruler of the Persian province of Khuzistan. It was from him that part of the island of Abadan had been leased for the Anglo-Persian Oil Company refinery and it was to him that the Company and the British authorities looked (in return for a subsidy) for the maintenance of order in the area of the Company's operations. In the event of war Sheikh Khazaal's position (and that of the Company) would be threatened, not only by the Turks from over the other side of the Shatt-al-Arab, where the Sheikh had both followers and property, but by the Bakhtiari tribesmen from the Zagros Mountains to the north-east of Khuzistan, with whom he was continually at variance, whose depredations had been a thorn in the side of the Company and who would certainly use the opportunity of a general war to create trouble both for Sheikh Khazaal and the Company. The position of the other British-protected Sheikhdoms farther down the Gulf was to some extent safeguarded by the rise of the Amir of Nejd in the interior, who acted as a buffer between them and the Turks and whose benevolent intent towards the various littoral Sheikhdoms was more or less guaranteed by the unofficial relationships between him and the British which had, over the years, been cultivated by the Chief Political Resident.

More generally it was necessary to consider the defence of the British position in the Gulf as a whole in relation to the defence of India. This involved the safeguarding of British naval supremacy in the Gulf in the event of German penetration to the headwaters of the Gulf and some attempt, probably in conjunction with Russia, to block the possibility of a German-Turkish advance eastwards through Persia, and across the Caspian, towards India, Afghanistan and Central Asia.

The gravity of the situation imposed the necessity for the closest co-operation between the Home and Indian Governments and, to some extent, the subordination of the Government of India's views to those of the Home Government. The most delicate problem, in the early days of the war with

Germany, was that of relations with Turkey. So long as Turkey's decision about war was still in the balance it was obviously desirable to avoid any provocative action which might help to precipitate that decision in the direction of war. On the other hand it was also desirable to anticipate the possibility of war against Turkey. The first consideration precluded the possibility of any formal Treaty with the Amir of Nejd who had not only, a year before, seized the province of al-Hasa from his nominal suzerain but who was also engaged in war with his northern neighbour and a Turkish protégé, ibn Rashid of Shammar. All that was done, as has been related, was to despatch a Political Officer, Major Shakespeare, to the Amir's court at Riadh to maintain friendly contact. The second consideration resulted, early in October, in a decision to send an Indian Army Brigade from India, which, it was intended, would land at Abadan to protect British oil interests and to assure local rulers of British support in the event of a Turkish attack. (The despatch of this force was a decision imposed on the Government of India by the British Cabinet.) By the time that this force arrived at the head of the Gulf on 5 November, Great Britain and Turkey were at war and the necessity for diplomacy, as far as the Ottoman Empire was concerned, had disappeared.

Persia had declared herself neutral in the war which had broken out, but she was in no position to enforce or to defend that neutrality. North-west Persia soon became a battleground between the Russians, operating from the Caucasus, and the Turks, operating from Asia Minor. During 1915 and 1916, the tribes of south-west Persia, mainly as a result of the activities of Wassmuss, the 'German Lawrence', succeeded in making much of that area into a battle-front against the British.

As has been related, the Germans in Iran, in the immediate pre-war years, had been assiduous in developing their commercial interests and in cultivating contacts with the Persians. When war broke out they were in a favourable position for subversive activities against the Allies in Persia. Since Persia was neutral they still had their diplomatic, consular and commercial representation. The unpopularity of the Russians and British was enhanced by the fact that both countries violated Persian neutrality within a few weeks of the outbreak of war. (Although this was to some extent offset by the fact that the Turks, the allies

44

of Germany, did the same.) At the end of 1914 a German Mission, consisting of Wassmuss, who had been German Consul in Bushire before the war, and several other German orientalists, arrived in Baghdad with the intention of organizing subversive operations in Persia. One scheme, which miscarried, was to enter Afghanistan through Persia and there try and persuade the Amir Habibullah to side with Germany. Another scheme was to try and raise the Kurds of north-west Persia against the British. But the most successful operations were those led by Wassmuss in south-west Persia, which were directed against the oil installations, the British *pied-à-terre* at Bushire and British interests in south-west Persia generally. Wassmuss had already, during his time as Consul at Bushire, made many useful contacts among the tribes in south-west Persia, particularly among the Tangestanis and the Qashgais, and to a lesser extent among the Bakhtiaris, the tribe in the best geographical position to operate against the oil installations. But he was never able to achieve the same ascendancy over the Bakhtiaris as he achieved over the Tangestanis and the Qashgais. Wassmuss succeeded for a time in besieging the British Residency in Bushire together with the small British-Indian force which had landed there. He also, for a time, occupied Shiraz, where he took over the branch of the British Imperial Bank and imprisoned the whole British colony. From towards the end of 1916 his activities were progressively curtailed as a result of the formation of the South Persia Rifles, a British-officered mobile force raised and commanded by Sir Percy Sykes, who had previously had long service in Persia as a Consul. After the Armistice Wassmuss went into hiding; in March 1919 he was arrested by the Persians and handed over to the British, who sent him back to Germany.

Wassmuss's exploits, which were performed with very little money and with no direct military assistance, were aided by the presence of German diplomatic and consular representatives in Persia, by the presence of many German nationals, by the non-existence (until the formation of the South Persia Rifles) of any Persian military force in the area, by the pro-German proclivities of the Swedish-officered Persian Gendarmerie, and by the weakness of the Central Government. His greatest achievement lay in the effect on the British of the threat presented to them by his presence. According to Christopher Sykes,[3] the threat to

Bushire presented by Wassmuss at the beginning of 1916 was such that troops were diverted to Bushire from Mesopotamia who could otherwise have been used for the relief of Kut.

Meanwhile, the Indian Expeditionary Force,[4] with the assistance of sloops and minesweepers of the Royal Navy, had landed at Fao, at the mouth of the Shatt-al-Arab, and begun to advance on Basra, which was occupied on 21 November. On 5 December troops of the I.E.F., which had by this time been brought up to division strength, occupied Kurna, at the junction of the Tigris and Euphrates. Here for the time being the advance stopped. By this time Khuzistan had been invaded, and Persian neutrality violated, by the Turks. In order to protect the oil installations from this threat, British troops from the I.E.F. advanced up the lower Karun, in Persian territory, to Ahwaz.

The landing of the expedition and the establishment of a bridgehead extending inland as far as Kurna and Ahwaz provided for the immediate problems of protecting the oil installations, of safeguarding the Sheikhs of Kuwait and Mohammerah, and of forestalling a possible Turkish-German advance to the headwaters of the Gulf. It was now necessary to decide on future action, both military and political. On the political side, was it intended to bid for the support of the Arabs of Mesopotamia and elsewhere by promising them liberation from the Turks? This involved a political decision not to treat with the Turks on terms which would leave them in possession of their Arab provinces, and a military decision to press on with all speed to Baghdad and possibly beyond. On the military side there were two principal decisions to be taken. (a) What was the best line to advance from the point of view of the security of the Persian oil installations? (b) considering the campaign in its relation to the Turco-Russian front further north (where the Russians were advancing from the Caucasus on Trebizond and Erzerum and Lake Van), what British action in Mesopotamia was desirable in order to sustain their allies and so diminish the risk of a Turco-German thrust eastwards through Persia? (At about this time a British force under General Malleson, known as the East Persian Line of Communications—or East Persian Cordon—had landed in Persia and taken up position along the Indian and Afghanistan frontiers from the sea to Birjand, linking up with Russian forces north of Birjand with the object of checking gun-running and subversive communications.) Both these decisions had to be taken with reference to the number of troops and the amount of supplies available. Politically, in deference to the susceptibilities of allies and the general uncertainties of war, it was decided to make no promises to the Arabs and thus for the time being to forego the possibility of active assistance from the Arabs. Militarily, it was decided immediately to occupy the whole of Basra Vilayet and to clear the Turks from the neighbourhood of Ahwaz and the oil installations. The latter objective was attained as a result of the battle of Shaiba in April 1915 which forced the Turks to evacuate their troops from Persia in order to avoid being cut off there; the former objective was attained as a result of the capture of Nasiriya on the Euphrates in July 1915. It was then considered necessary to advance up the Tigris as far north as Kut in order to block further Turkish raids in the direction of the oil installations. Kut was captured at the end of September and the British Cabinet then authorized the Commander-in-Chief (Sir John Nixon) to advance on Baghdad. The only valid reason for this decision, seeing that the political objective of Arab liberation had been declined (with the consequent forfeiture of active Arab support in the campaign), and seeing that the safety of the oil installations, as far as the possibility of a Turkish attack was concerned, had been secured by the capture of Kut, appears to have been to support the Russian advance from the Caucasus. Whatever the reason, the result was disastrous. Whether this was due to inadequate leadership, inadequate supplies, or both, cannot be discussed here. In November 1915, General Townshend with three infantry brigades, who had advanced as far as Azizia, 60 miles north of Kut, set out towards Baghdad. Three days later he was defeated by a superior Turkish force at Ctesiphon, between Azizia and Baghdad, and forced to retreat to Kut, with the Turks in pursuit. Townshend and his force were besieged in Kut and eventually, after enduring a five months seige, surrendered with nearly 12,000 officers and men. Thus ended the first phase of the Mesopotamian campaign.

While Townshend and his men were locked up in Kut important moves were being made in the sphere of British-Arab relations. In Cairo the British authorities had, since the beginning of the war, been in negotiation with the Sherif of Makka with a view to financing him and provisioning him for a projected revolt against his Ottoman suzerain. Towards the end of 1915 these negotiations seemed on the point of reaching some fruitful end and it was desirable that some arrangement should be made with the Amir of Nejd, who was no friend of the Sherif of Makka, to ensure that he would view benevolently any action taken by the Sherif in alliance with the British. There were other reasons too, from the British point of view, for some friendly understanding with ibn Saud. To the north-east his dominions marched with the territories of the powerful Aneiza group of tribes on the borders of Iraq, with whose paramount Sheikh, Fahad, ibn Saud was on friendly terms. The friendship, or at all events, the neutrality, of the Aneiza would be an important asset for the British lines of communication in Mesopotamia, and the assistance of ibn Saud could be a powerful influence in this direction. It will be remembered that, before the war, the possibility of some formal treaty relationship with ibn Saud had been excluded because of the British desire to avoid giving offence to Turkey. This reason was, of course, no longer valid; ibn Saud, for his part, whose war with the Shammar was not at that moment going particularly well, and who was nervous about the possible effect on his position of a British alliance with the Sherif, was more than willing to accept British protection, British guarantees and the consequent prospect of a British subsidy. So, in December 1915, Sir Percy Cox, the Chief Political Resident in the Persian Gulf, and Chief Political Officer to the I.E.F., negotiated on behalf of H.M.G. a Treaty (known as the Treaty of Darin) with ibn Saud which provided for (*a*) British recognition of ibn Saud and his descendants as independent rulers of Nejd and al-Hasa; (*b*) British assistance to ibn Saud in the event of external aggression; (*c*) British control of the Amir's foreign relations; (*d*) a promise by the Amir not to cede any of his territories to any foreign power without British consent; (*e*) a promise by the Amir to keep the pilgrim routes in his dominions open; (*f*) a promise by the Amir to refrain from any interference with or aggression on the territories of the Sheikhs of Kuwait, Bahrain, Qatar, and the Trucial Sheikhdoms. (It is noteworthy that the Treaty contains no pledge by ibn Saud not to attack the territories of the Sherif of Makka.) Later, in September 1916, ibn Saud, at Cox's request, met

Sheikh Jabir of Kuwait (Sheikh Mubarak had died in 1915), Sheikh Khazaal of Mohammerah, and Shiekh Fahad of the Aneiza in a meeting convened by Cox at Basra. At this meeting ibn Saud's intervention with Sheikh Fahad on behalf of the British resulted in his receiving from the British an annual subsidy of £60,000 (later to be increased to £100,000) and a gift of 3,000 rifles and four machine guns.

It is necessary at this point to make some reference to the differences of opinion which grew up over matters of Arab policy between the Arab Bureau in Cairo and the Government of India who, with the limitations indicated at the beginning of this chapter, were responsible for British-Arab relations in the Persian Gulf and the Arabian Peninsula. (The Arab Bureau was a body of Arab experts formed at British Military Headquarters in Cairo which conducted political relations with those areas under the operational control of British Military Headquarters in Cairo—that is to say, Syria and the Hijaz.) These differences were partly due to departmental rivalries, partly to clashes of personality, but mainly perhaps to different conceptions of policy. The Arab Bureau, which tended to think of British-Arab relations mainly in terms of prospective post-war Great Power rivalries, formulated, in the course of their activities, a policy which aimed at the setting up of 'an Arab State or Confederation of States' (to quote the words of the famous McMahon pledge) under British protection which would, in the first place, circumscribe French ambitions in the Levant and, in the second place, safeguard the 'imperial life line' to the Indian Ocean. The Government of India, which tended to view Arab relations solely in terms of the security of India, was thinking in terms of a Mesopotamia, consisting of the Vilayets of Basra and Baghdad, administered on British Indian lines and buttressed by a number of British-protected Sheikhdoms whose relations with the Government of India would be similar to those of the Indian Princes. They were scornful of the whole conception of Arab unity and apprehensive of the effects, both in the Persian Gulf and in Mesopotamia, of British encouragement of the pretensions of the Sherif of Makka to leadership of the Arab world. Put in the crudest terms, the Arab Bureau visualized Mesopotamia and the Persian Gulf as the eastern extremity of a new British Empire ruled from Cairo, while the Government of

India saw Mesopotamia and the Persian Gulf as the western extremity of an older British Empire ruled from New Dehli.

To return to the Mesopotamia war front. In February 1916 control of operations was transferred from New Delhi to the War Office in London. In August 1916, three months after the fall of Kut, General Lake (who had succeeded General Nixon) was relieved as C.-in-C. by General Maude. After some discussion with London about the future course of the campaign (during which a withdrawal south was advocated by General Roberston the C.I.G.S.) an offensive was decided on with Baghdad as the objective. This decision was probably made as the result of events in Persia. In March 1916, soon after the fall of Kut, the Turks had launched an offensive against the Russians in Persia which brought them down to a line Qazvin-Hamadan-Kermanshah-Qasr-e-Shirin. A threat to the oil installations appeared again to have developed. As a result of the British offensive towards Baghdad the Turks withdrew from most of Persia in February 1917. The British advance started on Christmas Day 1916. Kut was retaken in February 1917 and on 11 March British troops entered Baghdad, exactly one week before the beginning of the Russian Revolution. From Baghdad British forces began to fan out northwards into Mosul Vilayet.

By the time of the Revolution, the Russians, in the course of their Caucasus campaign against the Turks, had occupied Persian Azerbaijan (which the Turks had attempted to invade at the beginning of war in order to get to the Russian oilfields at Baku) and Turkish Armenia and occupied a line extending south-east from Trebizond through Erzerum, Van and across the Persian frontier to Kermanshah. When the British occupied Baghdad therefore the gap between the allies had almost been closed[5] and the Turks in Mosul Vilayet would soon have found themselves occupying a dangerous salient. After the March (Kerensky) Revolution Russian pressure on the Turks slackened, and after the November (Bolshevist) Revolution the Russian front rapidly disintegrated, until, in December 1917, the Bolshevist Government signed an armistice with Turkey, under the terms of which Russian forces withdrew from Asia Minor and north-west Persia, which was promptly reoccupied by the Turks, who remained there until the Mudros Armistice in October 1918. By March 1918, when the Bolshevist Government made peace with Germany at the Treaty of Brest-Litovsk, there was no effective Russian presence south of the Caucasus. In Transcaucasia three 'independent' republics—Armenia, Georgia and Azerbaijan—had been proclaimed by anti-Bolshevik elements. Of these, Armenia was mostly occupied by the Turks and Georgia by the Germans. Moslem Azerbaijan was well-disposed towards the Turks and, by the beginning of 1918, the way seemed to be clear for a combined Turkish and German advance from Armenia and Georgia across Azerbaijan to Baku and the Russian oilfields. The town of Baku had been seized and was, for the time being, held by a Bolshevist Committee, the one outpost of Red authority south of the Caucasus.

In these deteriorating circumstances, some attempt at British intervention in Transcaucasia was clearly desirable. In January 1918 a small force was organized at Khanaqin, on the Persian-Mesopotamian border, known as Dunsterforce,[6] after its Commander, Major-General Dunsterville, with the mission of proceeding across Persia to the Caspian port of Enzeli (now Bandar Pahlevi) via Hamadan and Qazvin, and from there to Baku and Tiflis with the object of trying to rally the three newly-formed republics against German, Turkish and Bolshevik penetration. But events were moving too fast. Moreover, Dunsterville was hampered in his move across Persia by the activities of the Jangali rebels, under Kuchik Khan, who had been in rebellion against the Persian Government since 1915 and whose area of activities lay across Dunsterville's lines of communication. Nevertheless, by a shrewd mixture of fighting and accommodation, Dunsterville opened the route between Khanaqin and Enzeli and, in August 1918, on hearing news that the Red Committee in Baku had been overthrown by a group of White Russians, sailed with his force from Enzeli to Baku. By this time, however, the Turks were advancing on Baku in greatly superior strength, and Dunsterville evacuated Baku a few days after landing there and returned to Enzeli. The Turks entered Baku, but their occupation was short-lived. After the Mudros Armistice at the end of October, Turkish forces were withdrawn from Transcaucasia, closely followed by the Germans. Whereupon the British force at Enzeli, now commanded by General Thompson, returned to Baku and proceeded to stimulate resistance throughout the three republics, this time

51

against the Bolsheviks. A British naval detachment also arrived to patrol the Caspian.

It is convenient at this point to run ahead of our story and outline the subsequent history of these three Transcaucasian republics to its melancholy conclusion. Their independence was precarious and its maintenance depended on the continued presence of British troops. When, early in 1920, as a result of a British Cabinet decision to cease active intervention on behalf of counter-revolutionary forces in Russia, British troops began to be withdrawn from Transcaucasia, the fate of the three republics was sealed. In April 1920, within days of the British evacuation of Baku, Bolshevist forces landed and the Soviet Socialist Republic of Azerbaijan was proclaimed. In March 1921, the Bolshevist Government, after signing a Treaty with Kemalist Turkey adjusting (in favour of Turkey) their common frontier in Transcaucasia, and so safeguarding themselves from possible Turkish interference, sent Red forces to occupy Georgia and Russian Armenia and proclaimed Soviet Socialist Republics in Tiflis and Erivan. The counter-revolution in Transcaucasia was at an end, and the authority of a Government controlled from Moscow was once more established on the north-west frontier of Persia.

Meanwhile the Bolsheviks were establishing their rule in the Russian colonies in Central Asia. After the November Revolution, the Amirs of Khiva and Bokhara had asserted their independence and counter-revolutionary régimes had been set up in Turkestan and, further east, at Kokand. But at Tashkent the Bolsheviks had succeeded in setting up an Administration, and it was from this Tashkent nucleus that the whole of Transcaspia was eventually recovered for Bolshevism. In February 1918 the Kokand régime was overthrown. In November 1918 an abortive attempt was made to overthrow the Amir of Bokhara. This was followed by a successful move against the Amir of Khiva and the establishment of the Soviet Socialist Republic of Khiva in June 1919. Bokhara was not finally subdued until September 1920 when the Soviet Socialist Republic of Bokhara was proclaimed. In the spring of 1919 the East Persian Cordon under General Malleson,[7] to which reference has been made, and which were still in south-east Persia, moved north to Ashkabad to assist the counter-revolutionary régime in Turkestan against the Bolsheviks. In August 1919 this force moved eastward from Ashkabad and occupied the oasis of Merv. They were ejected from Merv in October by the Reds who went on to occupy Ashkabad. By February 1920 the Reds had occupied Krasnovodsk on the Caspian and counter-revolutionary resistance in Central Asia was almost at an end. Malleson's force withdrew into Persia. In August 1920 they evacuated the province of Khorassan and by the end of the year they had been disbanded.

To return to the Mesopotamian front. After the capture of Baghdad the gradual defection of Russia and the demands of other Allied fronts precluded the possibility of any more major offensive operations. But the advance up the Tigris continued into the Vilayet of Mosul which, by the time of the armistice in October 1918 had been almost entirely occupied by the British.[8] In Baghdad political problems began to loom larger than military ones. A Civil Administration had to be set up and maintained in a large and (as a result of further military advances) expanding area from which all the Turkish officials had been withdrawn and in which the Arab notables and officials, still uncertain of the outcome of the war, and aware of the possibility of a Turkish return, either by arrangement with or in spite of the British, were naturally at best unco-operative and at worst actively hostile. This meant that a very large and comparatively inexperienced body of British administrators, mostly seconded from the armed forces, had to be recruited and sent out to learn their jobs, mainly by a process of trial and error. At the outset matters were not improved by continual friction between Sir Percy Cox, the Chief Political Officer (who became Civil Commissioner soon after the capture of Baghdad) and General Maude, the Commander-in-Chief (Maude died of typhoid in October 1917 and was replaced by General Marshall). Also, as the Government of India gloomily noted, the Sherifian propaganda of the Arab Bureau had produced among Iraqi notables a mood of ambitious restlessness which was the precursor of serious future trouble.

CHAPTER FOUR

The Aftermath of War

THE ARMISTICE BETWEEN the Allies and Turkey[1] was signed at Mudros on 31 October 1918. It provided, *inter alia*, for the surrender of all Turkish garrisons in the various theatres of war to the local Allied Military Commanders, for the withdrawal of the Turks from north-west Persia which they had occupied after the Russo-Turkish armistice in December 1917, and for the occupation by Allied troops of all Turkish territory in their possession at the time of the Armistice, as well as Constantinople and other Turkish cities and towns which had not been captured during hostilities. It was also provided that the Allies should occupy the oil ports of Batum and Baku, previously part of Russia, but in Turkish occupation at the time of the Armistice.

On the Mesopotamian front the M.E.F. found themselves, immediately after the Armistice, occupying the whole of the Vilayets of Basra, Baghdad and Mosul.[2] In addition to these areas, which they had occupied during the course of hostilities, they had had to take on two further responsibilities. With north-west Persia evacuated by the Turks, H.M.G. thought it desirable to keep lines of communication going through Persia from Mesopotamia to the Caspian in order to sustain the various counter-revolutionary movements in Transcaucasia and Transcaspia. Thus, that part of Persia north and west of a line drawn from Khanaqin to Enzeli became in effect a zone of British occupation. This was a considerable burden in several respects. First, because much of the area had been mercilessly plundered by the Turks and needed large relief supplies to keep the inhabitants from starvation. Secondly, it involved British responsibility for the succour of the Armenian and Assyrian communities in the area, who had been uprooted from their homes by the Turks. And thirdly because of the activities of the Jangali rebels,

54

led by Kuchik Khan, who threatened communications and public security generally in the northern part of the area. The other additional responsibility arose in the north-west, up the Euphrates Valley towards Deir ez Zor. As a result of armistice arrangements on the Palestine front an area, bounded on the west by the river Jordan and the Lebanon and Ansarieh mountain ranges and including the cities of Amman, Damascus, Homs, Hama and Aleppo, was placed under an Arab administration centred on Damascus and responsible to the British C.-in-C. (General Allenby). This area was left undefined on the east and there was consequently a 'no man's land' along the upper Euphrates Valley in which it was not clear whether administrative authority was exercised by the Arab administration in Damascus or by the British administration in Iraq.[3] This led to a great deal of friction between the Sherifian officials of the Damascus Administration and the British Civil Administration in Baghdad which was to persist until the fall of the Arab Government in Damascus in June 1920 after the award of the Syrian Mandate to France.

In Persia the position immediately following the Armistice was one of considerable confusion. During the war Persia, although officially neutral, had had the whole of her north-west area fought over and largely devastated by the Turks and Russians. The valley of the lower Karun had been invaded and occupied by the British. In the Province of Fars a guerilla force had been raised by a German agent. Largely to counteract the ravages of this guerilla force a British force had been maintained at Bushire and a British-raised force, the South Persia Rifles, had been operating throughout Southern Persia for the last two years of the war. Further north, along the line Khanaqin-Hamadan-Qazvin-Enzeli British lines of communication had been established at the beginning of 1918 and at the time of the Armistice were being held in strength. In East Persia a British Indian force was strung out along the main road from Bandar Abbas on the Persian Gulf to Meshed in the north-east of Persia. In the north-west, in the area between Qazvin and Resht, the Jangalis, led by Kuchik Khan, had, since 1915, been in successful revolt against the Central Government. The Cossack Brigade, the only efficient military formation in the Persian Army, was doubtfully loyal to the Central Government.

The Persian Treasury was bankrupt. The inhabitants of the previous battle areas in the north-west were starving. Civil war between White and Red Russians was raging on Persia's north-east and north-west frontiers. In the probable event (failing effective Allied support for the White Russians) of the Bolshevist Government establishing its authority over the Tsarist Russian territories in Transcaucasia and Transcaspia, it seemed likely that the influence of communism would spread to Persia's northern provinces of Azerbaijan, Gilan, Mazanderan, Asterabad and Khorassan. The only stable element amid all these varied troubles besetting Persia appeared to be the British with their armed forces, with their money, with the prestige conferred on them by victory, and with their apparent ambitions for hegemony over Persia.

If, to some Persians, the British seemed to represent a possible salvation, to some Englishmen, and particularly to Lord Curzon the Foreign Secretary and Chairman of the British Cabinet's Eastern Committee, the position in Persia appeared to afford a matchless opportunity. In September 1918 Sir Percy Cox, one of the greatest of the British Proconsuls, who was at that time Civil Commissioner in Baghdad and Chief Political Officer in the Persian Gulf, was sent to Tehran by Lord Curzon to replace Sir Charles Marling as British Minister in Persia. Immediately after the Armistice, the new Minister's principal task was to deal with the insistent Persian demand for representation at the Peace Conference. The Persian Government felt that Persia, in view of her manifold sufferings during the war and in view of the extent to which Persian territory had been used by the Allies for their own purposes, was entitled to a seat. This was, however, denied them, although an unofficial Persian delegation was present in Paris during the Conference. Meanwhile, through the spring and summer of 1919, Cox, on behalf of the British Government, was negotiating with the Persian Government, for the conclusion of a Treaty which would, had it been ratified, have reduced Persia almost to the status of a British protectorate. The main provisions of the Anglo-Persian Treaty, which was signed in August, were as follows: (*a*) Abrogation of the Anglo-Russian Agreement of 1907; (*b*) Appointment of British advisers to reorganize the Persian army and Persian finances; (*c*) A British loan of £2,000,000 at 7 per cent; (*d*) Anglo-Persian co-operation over rail and road construction in Persia; (*e*) Revision of the Persian Customs tariff (which, it will be remembered, had been revised by the Russians some twenty years before when the Customs revenues were pledged as security for a Russian loan). It was also agreed in the Treaty that the British would (*a*) press Persia's claim for war damage committed by the enemy on Persian soil; and (*b*) refrain from claiming from Persia for the cost of British forces sent to Persia during the war 'owing to the inability of the Persians to defend their neutrality' in return for Persia agreeing not to make any claim on H.M.G. for damages alleged to have been committed by British troops.

This Treaty, if it had ever become effective, would have been one of the corner stones of that grand design mapped out by Curzon and others by which, as a result of the British victory in the war, a vast accretion to the British Empire would have been created, stretching from the Nile to the Indus, from the Taurus Mountains to the Indian Ocean, linking up at its eastern end with the great British Indian Empire. It would, in the eyes of Lord Curzon and of those who thought like him, have been the culmination of all those patient years of Empire-building, on the Nile, in the Red Sea, on the Persian Gulf, and a decisive refutation of any suggestion that the British Empire was falling into decay or the British race into decadence. With this scheme for a virtual Protectorate over Persia was linked the idea of Iraq as a Crown Colony, of Egypt and the Sudan as a future British Dominion, and of an Arab State or Confederation of States stretching from Aleppo to Aden in a treaty relationship with H.M.G. similar to that of the Sheikhdoms of the Persian Gulf. It was a brave conception which the events of the next two years were substantially to modify. The Anglo-Persian Treaty was never ratified and was eventually denounced by a new Persian Government. In Iraq, after a serious rebellion, the attainment of immediate self-government and the promise of eventual independence was conceded. In Syria the British protégé, Feisal, was expelled and a French administration set up. In Egypt, after two years of intermittent rioting, the British Protectorate was abolished. Of Great Britain's wartime acquisitions in the Middle East, only the Bedouin State of Transjordan and the terrible inheritance of Palestine remained securely in British hands. The paramount British influence which survived in the area was conferred, not by a *pax britannica* bringing peace and relative prosperity to a previously troubled and poverty stricken area, but by a chain of British garrisons whose increasingly resented presence conferred neither justice nor the prospect of economic or social progress. So far as British influence went, these garrisons were a wasting asset. From the point of view of the local inhabitants they were, apart from some incidental and limited economic benefits, a nuisance. They embodied all the evils of imperialism without any of its redeeming features; they represented all the prudential selfishness of imperialism without any of its idealism or enterprise.

Why did this ambitious and not altogether ignoble conception falter and fail? Partly no doubt because it was an anachronism, inappropriate to the twentieth century. But the historian must seek for more immediate reasons. First, there was a failure of will among British rulers and people. They were prepared to supply neither the necessary men nor the necessary money. The war had not long been over before there was a strong, and perhaps natural, feeling in Great Britain in favour of financial retrenchment, particularly in the Middle East. There was an equally strong and equally natural demand for accelerated demobilization and for 'bringing the boys home'. There was a considerable objection to incurring British casualties on duty in countries in which the bulk of the British public were not remotely interested, either financially or otherwise. There were the commercial considerations which attached more importance to the oil of Mosul than to the keeping of faith with allies. There was Anglo-French rivalry and the assumed necessity, in view of France's major share and enormous sacrifices in the war effort, to compensate her in the Middle East. All these feelings, particularly relevant to the future British position in Persia, were demonstrated in the growing British reluctance to continue the limited British involvement in armed intervention against the Bolshevist régime, which resulted, during 1920 and 1921, in the withdrawal of British troops from Transcaucasia, Transcaspia and from Persia itself. (One of the principal arguments advanced by British imperialists of the Curzon school was the necessity of creating a strong, British protected cordon in the Middle East against the future possibility of Bolshevist expansion in the direction of India and Africa.)

The Anglo-Persian Treaty soon ran into trouble both in Persia and abroad. The French and Americans were both hostile—the French because they always on principle opposed any British expansionist move in the Middle East, the Americans because they regarded the Treaty as an infringement of the 'Open Door' principle which they had invented and on which, generally, they were able to insist, as a means of ensuring that they would collect a share of any of the spoils of war which might have been garnered by their allies. (We shall hear of the 'Open Door' again in connexion with oil.) In Persia there was little enthusiasm and enough opposition to prevent the Prime Minister, Vossuq ed Dowleh, from submitting the Treaty to the Majlis for ratification. But what really killed the Treaty in the eyes of the Persians was the British failure, during the course of 1920, to show any determination to protect Persia from the developing threat from Russia. Persian opinion had already been unfavourably impressed by the fiasco of Dunsterville's arrival at and speedy evacuation from Baku in the late summer of 1918. This unfavourable impression had to some extent been redeemed by the British reoccupation of Baku early in 1919. But, from the beginning of 1920 onwards, British troops started to withdraw from Transcaucasia and from Transcaspia. In April 1920, a few weeks after the British evacuation of Baku, the Soviet Socialist Republic of Azerbaijan was set up in a region of which the southern part was in Persian territory. Soon afterwards, a Red force, pursuing a remnant of Denikin's[4] defeated army, which had left Baku by sea to place itself under the protection of the small British force at Enzeli, arrived at Enzeli by sea, bombarded it, landed and compelled the withdrawal of the British force, which shortly afterwards evacuated Persia. The Red force thereupon, with the co-operation of the Jangali rebel Kuchik Khan, set up a Soviet Socialist Republic in the Persian province of Gilan, at about the same time as the last British troops were leaving Persia. This evidence of British unwillingness or inability to protect Persia from Soviet Russia killed any remnant of enthusiasm for the Treaty which might have existed in Persia.

Contemporaneously with these hostile activities (which Moscow attributed to the action of the independent state of Azerbaijan over which they had no control), the Bolshevist

Government had been making overtures to the Persian Government which were eventually to result in a Treaty which is still (1961) in force and which still has an important influence on Irano-Soviet relations. In January 1918 the Soviet Government addressed a Note to the Persian Government repudiating all privileges previously possessed by Tsarist Russia in Persia which were contrary to Persian sovereignty and offering assistance to Persia in expelling Turkish troops from that country. The Note also repudiated the 1907 Anglo-Russian Agreement (thus getting in ahead of the British Government by some months). Eighteen months later, in June 1919, when the Soviet Government had an unofficial representative in Tehran, a more detailed Note was delivered in which (*a*) all Persian debts to Tsarist Russia were declared cancelled; (*b*) the privileged position possessed by the Tsarist régime in respect of the Persian Customs, Post and Telegraphs was declared ended; (*c*) all Tsarist public and private concessions were renounced; (*d*) the Capitulations were declared null and void as far as Russian subjects were concerned; and (*e*) all public property in Iran belonging to the Russian State was handed over to the Persian Government. None of this meant very much, as all these privileges had lapsed anyway since the Russian Revolution and Soviet Russia was in no position to insist on them. Moscow was therefore endeavouring to make a virtue out of necessity. The Persian Government, apparently unimpressed by these evidences of Russian generosity, advanced, through the unofficial Persian delegation to the Peace Conference, the most preposterous claims to Russian territory in the Caucasus and in Transcaspia. However, neither the Russians nor anyone else, including the majority of Persians, took any notice of these claims and Soviet Russia continued to press on with attempts to secure friendly relations with Persia. In November 1920 diplomatic relations were established, and in February 1921 a Treaty between U.S.S.R. and Persia was signed (and subsequently ratified) which, apart from confirming the declarations made in the Note of June 1919, confirmed the pre-war boundaries between Russia and Persia, mutually renounced interference in each other's internal affairs,[5] mutually agreed not to permit organizations hostile to the one on the territory of the other, and regulated the rights of the two States with regard to fishing and other matters on the Caspian. It was further provided in the Treaty that none of the Russian concessions in Persia renounced under the Treaty would be ceded to any other foreign Power. But the most important clause in the Treaty was the one which permitted Russia to send her armed forces into Persia in the event of Persia becoming a base for any third party's attack on Russia. By their agreement to this clause the Persian Government had already clearly abandoned any idea of British protection against Russia. The Treaty was signed on 26 February 1921 and was followed almost immediately by the repudiation of the unratified Anglo-Persian Treaty.

Five days before the signature of the Russian Treaty the government of Moshir ed Dowleh had been overthrown in a bloodless coup engineered by Sayyid Zia-ed-Din Tabatabai, a young liberal politician who had a reputation for being pro-British, and Reza Khan, the Commander of the Cossack Brigade. Although the Persians did not know it at the time, they had found a new master and a new protector, this time an indigenous one. After the coup Zia-ed-Din became Prime Minister and Reza Khan Commander-in-Chief of the Army. Within a few months Reza Khan demonstrated that he was the real master. In May 1921, Zia-ed-Din, having quarrelled with Reza Khan, was forced to flee the country. Reza Khan now became Minister of War as well as C.-in-C. In 1923 he became Prime Minister in name as well as in fact. His first few years of power were devoted to restoring Persian sovereignty within Persian territory. He broke the power of the rebel Kuchik Khan and hanged him. He put an end to the Soviet Republic in Gilan. He suppressed Soviet-assisted separatist movements in Persian Azerbaijan and in Khorassan. In 1924, in spite of British protests, he arrested and imprisoned Sheikh Khazaal of Mohammerah who had for so long, under British protection, been the real ruler of Khuzistan. He then started to tame the great southern tribes—the Lurs, the Bakhtiari, the Tangestani and the Qashgai, who had for so long regarded themselves as independent of the central government. In 1925 he took the final step in his rapid rise to power; at his instance the Majlis deposed Ahmed Shah, the last of the Qajar sovereigns and proclaimed Reza Khan as Shahanshah. Thus a new dynasty, that of Pahlevi, occupied the Peacock Throne and Persia entered upon a new phase of its national existence.

In Iraq the signature of the Armistice left the British Administration in Baghdad with three potentially serious problems arising respectively from the uncertain political future of the country, from the uncertainty of its northern and western boundaries, and from the presence of two important racial and religious minorities—the Kurds in the north and the Shias in the Middle Euphrates. With regard to the country's political future. Under the secret Sykes-Picot Agreement arrived at between Great Britain, France and Russia in 1916, and made public by the Bolshevists after the Revolution, the British were to 'be allowed to establish such direct or indirect administration or control as they desire' over the Vilayets of Basra and Baghdad, while the Vilayet of Mosul, virtually all of which had been occupied by the M.E.F. before or as an immediate result of the Armistice, under the same Agreement, had been allotted to France as part of a French-protected Arab State or Confederation of States (although the Vilayet of Mosul was by no means purely Arab). In a proclamation made by General Maude, with the authority of and in fact drafted by the British Government, after the capture of Baghdad in March 1917, the desire and hope was expressed that the Arabs might 'rise once more to greatness and renown among the peoples of the earth and that they should bind themselves to this end in unity and concord'. Although vague in its wording, this proclamation could reasonably have been taken as a promise of independence for Iraq. A much more specific pledge was made to the people of Iraq in the Anglo-French Declaration issued on 7 November 1918, which read as follows:

'The object aimed at by France and Great Britain in prosecuting the war in the east is the complete and definite emancipation of the peoples so long oppressed by the Turks, and the establishment of national governments and administrations deriving their authority from the initiative and free choice of the indigenous populations. In order to carry out their intention France and Great Britain are at one in encouraging and assisting the establishment of indigenous governments and administrations in Syria and Mesopotamia now liberated by the Allies. Far from wishing to impose on the populations of these regions any particular institutions, they are only concerned to ensure by their support and by adequate assistance the regular working of governments and administrations freely chosen by the peoples themselves.'[6]

The long delay, mainly due to inter-allied dissensions, attending the implementation, or even the beginnings of the implementation, of this pledge, naturally led to a great deal of nationalist unrest, which was by no means appeased by the announcement, after the San Remo Conference in April 1920, that Iraq (with boundaries undefined) had been awarded to Great Britain as a 'Mandate'[7] as part of what looked like (and indeed was) a partition of the northern part of the Arab world between Great Britain and France without any reference to the possibility of independence or even self-governing status. Rebellion, assisted by the considerable reduction of British forces in Iraq since the Armistice, broke out in the summer of 1920 and was only suppressed after the arrival of British military reinforcements from India. Contemporaneously with this rebellion in Iraq, the Sherifian Government in Damascus came to an end and Feisal, who had been made 'king' of Syria by the Syrian Congress, was expelled from Damascus by the French in June 1920. The fortunes of the Sherifian Government had been followed with close attention in Iraq, partly because the majority of Feisal's officers in the Arab Rebellion had been Iraqis and partly because the fate of the Sherifian Government was regarded as a test of the honesty of Allied intentions regarding their promises of independence for the Arabs.

In October 1920 Sir Percy Cox, who had been doing a tour of duty as British Minister in Tehran, returned to Baghdad as Civil Commissioner. (His deputy, Sir Arnold Wilson, had been acting for him during his long absence.) Immediately before his return he had been in London in consultation with the British Government about the future of Iraq. By this time a reaction had set in from the imperialism championed by Lord Curzon and typified by the attempt at an Anglo-Persian Treaty which has already been described, and there was a strong body of opinion in favour of evacuation from Iraq. In the light of the Turkish renascence, now becoming apparent under the

63

leadership of Mustafa Kemal, this would, in all probability, have meant a Turkish reoccupation of Iraq and a considerable breach of faith towards the Arabs of Iraq whom the British professed to have 'liberated'. Cox, on his return, was authorized by the British Government to direct his policy towards the only practicable alternative to evacuation—the formation of a national Iraqi Government within the framework of the British Mandate. The fear of a Turkish reoccupation, arising from well-founded suspicions in Iraq of Great Britain's growing inclination towards the abandonment of the Mandate and the evacuation of Iraq, had caused a certain revulsion of feeling in favour of Great Britain and a certain tendency to accept temporary British protection as the least of a great many possible evils. Assisted, perhaps, by this fear of the Turks, and by the removal of the previous suspicions about a possible British withdrawal, Sir Percy succeeded, within a few weeks, in setting up a Provisional Council of State under the Presidency of the venerable Neqib of Baghdad. The next thing to be decided was the form of the new State. Was it to be a monarchy or a republic? Moslem sentiment was on the whole in favour of a constitutional monarchy, but there was no general agreement about a suitable candidate for the throne. Many names were canvassed, including those of Sheikh Khazaal of Mohammerah, Great Britain's old ally, and Sayyid Talib Pasha, a magnate from Basra who had been expelled by the British authorities during the war, but who enjoyed considerable authority in Iraq, and who was Minister of the Interior in the Provisional Council. A third candidate was Feisal, who had recently been expelled from his 'kingship' in Damascus, and towards whom the British Government had an obligation of honour as a result of his leadership of the Arab Rebellion.

At the beginning of 1921 the affairs of Iraq, which previously had been administered by the India Office, and supervised by the wartime Eastern Committee of the Cabinet, presided over by the Foreign Secretary, came under the direct control of the Colonial Office with Winston Churchill as Secretary of State. One of Churchill's first acts in his new post was to convene a conference of Middle East experts and administrators in Cairo. As one result of this Conference it was agreed that the British Government should discreetly sponsor the candidature of

Feisal for the throne of Iraq. In the following June Feisal visited
Iraq and was chosen by the Provisional Council. This choice was
subsequently ratified by a referendum, of which it may be said
that the known wishes of the High Commissioner (the title
assumed by Sir Percy Cox after his return in October 1920) and
the Provisional Council were decisive factors in securing an
overwhelmingly favourable vote. After that, events moved
rapidly and, for Feisal and the British, favourably, in spite of
recurrent distractions, which will be described later, over the
northern and western boundaries of Iraq. In August 1920 Feisal
was formally proclaimed King and recognized as such by the
British Government. The first act of Feisal and his Government
was to negotiate a Treaty between the new State and Great
Britain. There was some difficulty over this, both because the
disposal of Mosul had not yet been agreed between Great
Britain and Turkey, and because there was a strong body of
opinion in Iraq which believed that the Treaty should replace,
instead of coming within the framework of, the Mandatory
relationship with Great Britain. It was not until October 1922
that a Treaty was signed for a duration of twenty years (later
reduced to four years by a Protocol dated April 1923). The
Treaty, which left the question of Mosul open pending the conclusion of negotiations between Great Britain and Turkey, provided, *inter alia*, for the maintenance of British forces in Iraq, for
the appointment of British Advisers to Iraqi Ministries, and for a
British pledge to sponsor, before the end of the Treaty's validity,
Iraqi's request for membership of the League of Nations which,
when granted, would automatically put an end to the Mandate.
The signature of the Protocol to the Treaty was the last official
act of Sir Percy Cox as High Commissioner. He was succeeded
in May 1923 by Sir Henry Dobbs, a member of the Indian
Civil Service, who had, for a short time during the war years,
served in Iraq as Revenue Commissioner in the Civil Administration under Cox.

Cox's departure on retirement ended the career of Great
Britain's most distinguished administrator in the Persian Gulf.
Originally an officer in the Indian Army, Cox became an
Assistant Political Resident in British Somaliland, then under
the control of the Government of India, in 1892 at the age of 27.
In 1901 he was transferred to Musqat as Consul, and from then

on the whole of his service was spent in and around the Gulf. In 1904 he was promoted to be Chief Political Resident Persian Gulf with his headquarters at Bushire (a post which was combined with that of Consul General for Fars and Khuzistan). On the outbreak of war in 1914, while still retaining his post as Chief Political Resident, he was appointed as Chief Political Officer to the Indian Expeditionary Force and in 1917, after the capture of Baghdad, became Civil Commissioner for Iraq. In the autumn of 1918 he was seconded as British Minister to Tehran, where he remained until October 1920, when he became the first British High Commissioner in Iraq. Apart from his influence, both with the British Government and with the Iraqis, which was decisive in bringing Iraq along a relatively peaceful path to statehood under British protection, Cox, in his capacity as Chief Political Resident, was primarily responsible for the initiation and later consolidation of British relationships with ibn Saud in the delicate situation created by the British alliance with his rival and enemy, the Sherif of Makka. This process of consolidation, which was a vital factor in ensuring the effectiveness of the British protectorate treaties with the Persian Gulf Sheikhdoms, will be described later. It is remarkable that Cox's outstanding achievements in diplomacy and administration should have received such comparatively little recognition in his lifetime, and should have been almost forgotten by a later generation, to whom Cromer and Lawrence are almost household words but who, seemingly, have never heard of Sir Percy Cox, perhaps because he possessed neither the Roman gravitas of the one nor the Renaissance flamboyance of the other.

A Constituent Assembly was elected in Iraq in March 1924 and proceeded immediately to a discussion of the Treaty, which was submitted to it for ratification. After some discussion about the share of the Ottoman Debt to be assumed by Iraq under the Treaty, which H.M.G. agreed to reconsider after ratification, the Treaty was duly ratified[8] in June 1924, approved by the Council of the League of Nations (a necessary formality owing to Iraq's Mandatory status) in September and ratified by the British Parliament in November.

The question of Iraq's northern boundary was left undetermined by the Treaty of Lausanne between Great Britain and

Turkey and, in accordance with the terms of that Treaty (which defined the post-war settlement between Great Britain and Turkey), had been relegated to the decision of a League of Nations Boundary Commission. In order to understand the Mosul question it is necessary to go back to the years before the war. As will be explained in greater detail in the next chapter, a Company called the Turkish Petroleum Company, in which the Anglo-Persian Oil Company and Royal Dutch-Shell and the Deutsche Bank were the principal shareholders, had been formed to exploit a concession given by the Ottoman Government to search for oil in the Vilayets of Baghdad and Mosul. This interest in Mosul had apparently been overlooked by the British negotiators of the Sykes-Picot Agreement, which allotted Mosul to France, but this British interest was well appreciated at the time of the Armistice when extraordinary efforts were made to ensure that British troops were in occupation of the whole of the Vilayet of Mosul. The town of Mosul and part of the Vilayet were actually occupied after the Armistice 'in spite of rather than by reason of the terms of the Armistice'.[9] Before the end of November 1918 Lloyd George had made it clear to Clemenceau that the British Government would insist on varying the terms of the Sykes-Picot Agreement by adding Mosul to the Vilayets of Basra and Baghdad as being areas in which Great Britain would be free to 'establish such direct or indirect control as they desire'. After the Armistice the Vilayet of Mosul was administered by the British from Baghdad as part of Iraq. This added to the complications and difficulties of administration in that the population of the Vilayet was largely Kurdish and as such antipathetic to the prospect of Arab rule. There was also a minority of Assyrian Christians who looked to the British for protection against any form of Moslem rule, whether Arab, Kurdish or Turkish. Meanwhile the Iraqi Arabs, suspecting the oil riches of the Vilayet, and realizing the potential effect of such riches on the economy of the Iraqi State, became increasingly insistent on the inclusion of Mosul within the Iraqi State and made it increasingly clear that their peaceful acceptance of the British Mandate was dependent on the success of British efforts to secure ·the inclusion of Mosul within Iraq. Most of the inhabitants of the Vilayet showed a marked reluctance to incorporation into Iraq, in which reluctance they were not

unnaturally encouraged by the Turks. The district of Suleimanya abstained from voting in the referendum which confirmed Feisal as King of Iraq, and the districts of Suleimanya
and Kirkuk refused to send representatives to attend the
Proclamation of Feisal as King. At the Lausanne Conference the
Turks refused to relinquish their claim to Mosul, but eventually
agreed to abide by the decision of a League of Nations Boundary
Commission, provided that no agreement had been achieved
between the parties within nine months of the signature of the
Treaty of Lausanne. Eventually, at the end of 1925, the recommendations of the Boundary Commission, which awarded
virtually the whole of the Vilayet to Iraq, were approved by the
Council of the League on condition that the Anglo-Iraqi Treaty
was extended to a period of twenty-five years, or until the
admission of Iraq to the League, if this should take place before
that time. It is quite clear that the recommendations of the
Boundary Commission, and the decision of the League Council,
were motivated by a desire to secure British protection for the
Assyrian minority in the Vilayet from Moslem aggression,
whether proceeding from Turks, Kurds or Arabs. In the event
this British protection was removed as a result of the Anglo-
Iraqi Treaty of 1930 and the admission of Iraq to the League in
1932, whereupon most of the wretched Assyrians, who had won
considerable local unpopularity as a result of many of them
having been recruited into the British-controlled Iraq Levies—
one of whose main duties was to keep the Kurds in order—
were promptly massacred by these same Kurds. The required
revision of the Anglo-Iraqi Treaty was agreed to by the first
Iraqi Parliament (which had been elected a few months before)
in January 1926. The Turks did not at first accept the League's
award and Turkish-inspired disturbances still continued in the
Vilayet. But in June 1926 a Tripartite Treaty of Friendship
under the terms of which Turkey recognized the League's
award, was signed at Ankara, the new Turkish capital, between
Great Britain, Iraq and Turkey. This Treaty was immediately
ratified by the Iraqi Parliament. Thereafter, relations between
Iraq and Turkey were almost continuously amicable, which was
a fortunate circumstance for the new State, since Mosul might
easily have become a Middle Eastern Alsace-Lorraine.

The Turkish frontier was not the only boundary problem

which complicated the early years of the Iraqi State. The north-west frontier, in the Upper Euphrates Valley, which had been a source of trouble during the days of the Sherifian Government, had been amicably settled between the British and French after the latter had established effective control of Syria during the second half of 1920. But the south-west frontier, running through the middle of the grazing grounds of the Aneiza group of tribes, was disturbed as a result of the shifting balance of power in the north of the Arabian Peninsula, where the long-drawn-out struggle between ibn Saud and the Shammar had ended with the capture of Hail, ibn Rashid's capital, by ibn Saud in 1921.

In the last chapter it has been related how, in December 1915, a Treaty had been concluded between the British and ibn Saud and how, in September 1916, ibn Saud had been granted a British subsidy and a small supply of arms for his war against ibn Rashid. By the middle of 1917 the British were beginning to feel some anxiety at the prospect of friction developing between ibn Saud and the Sherifian forces who, in June 1917, had captured Aqaba and whose increasing pretensions could not but be unwelcome to ibn Saud. It was desirable to keep the peace between ibn Saud and the Sherifians because the friendship of ibn Saud was almost as necessary to British political interests in Iraq as the friendship of Husain was necessary to British military interests on the Palestine front. More or less amicable liaison had by this time been established between the British Arab Bureau in Cairo, who were responsible for political relations with the Sherifians, and the Civil Commissioner in Baghdad who, in his capacity of Chief Political Resident Persian Gulf, was responsible for political relations between Great Britain and ibn Saud. Although each party thought that its own particular protégé was being underrated by the other, they both saw the desirability of keeping the peace between the two, at all events until the end of the war. In July 1917 it was arranged that a joint delegation, consisting of Storrs, of the British Residency in Cairo and mainspring of the Arab Bureau, and Hamilton, the Political Agent in Kuwait, should go to Riadh in an endeavour to regulate relations between the two desert potentates. But Storrs fell ill and Hamilton went alone, later, in October, to be replaced by H. St. John Philby, then on the Civil Commissioner's staff in Baghdad. It was in this way that Philby started on his long career as a traveller in Central Arabia and unofficial adviser to ibn Saud. The object of Philby's first mission to ibn Saud was to provide him with sufficient money and arms to enable him to resume successful hostilities against the Shammar, as a means both of containing the activities of a pro-Turkish ruler and of diverting against the Shammar ibn Saud's crescent hostility towards the Sherif of Makka.

In the event ibn Saud did not resume hostilities against the Shammar until the war with Turkey was over, and his subsequent victory over the Shammar, culminating in the capture of Hail in 1921, was a source of embarrassment to the British in Iraq and Transjordan, since it brought ibn Saud's dominions up to the borders of two British-protected States which, as a result of the decisions of the Colonial Office Conference in 1921, were ruled over by Feisal and Abdullah respectively, the sons of ibn Saud's only serious remaining rival in the Peninsula—the Sherif of Makka. By this time ibn Saud's enmity towards Husain had been increased by a serious quarrel which took place in 1919 over the ownership of the oasis of Khurma, on the borderland between Nejd and the Hijaz. Towards the end of 1919 Husain was authorized by H.M.G. to occupy the oasis, ownership of which was claimed both by ibn Saud and by Husain, and ibn Saud was warned by H.M.G. to withdraw from it on pain of British displeasure. Ibn Saud, disregarding British wishes, repelled Husain's attempt to occupy the oasis and invaded the Hijaz, from which, however, he withdrew, after a marauding expedition, in belated deference to British demands.

In view of all this, relations between ibn Saud and the British-protected States of Iraq and Transjordan were not particularly cordial by the time that ibn Saud, by his conquest of the Shammar, had consolidated his hegemony over Central Arabia and found his dominions to the north, east and west marching with the territories of three Sherifian rulers. As always along desert frontiers there were fruitful causes of dissension arising from the allegiance of tribes, whose seasonal peregrinations took them on each side of the frontier, and on the use by these tribes of grazing grounds and water holes on each side of the frontier. In the case of the Iraqi-Saudi frontier, the bone of contention was provided by the great Aneiza group of tribes, part of which had owed traditional allegiance to ibn Rashid. After the final defeat of ibn Rashid and the annexation of his territory, this part of the Aneiza crossed over into Iraq to avoid submission to ibn Saud. Ibn Saud's forces pursued them and, in March 1922, there was fighting between Iraqi and Saudi forces during the course of which the Saudis were bombed by planes of the British R.A.F. The situation was resolved peacefully, mainly as a result of the great personal influence possessed by Sir Percy Cox both with ibn Saud and with the Iraqi Government. A Treaty was signed at Mohammerah between ibn Saud and the Iraqi Government in June 1922 by the terms of which the allegiances of the various tribes on Iraq's south-west border were agreed and their respective wells and grazing grounds defined. It was also provided that the Treaty should become null and void in the event of either party's existing relationships with Great Britain coming to an end. In other words Great Britain was regarded as being the guarantor of the *status quo* arrived at between the two States. In the event ibn Saud refused to ratify the Treaty of Mohammerah as the result of a further dispute about the boundaries between Nejd, Iraq and Kuwait. Consequently a further meeting was held at Uqair in December 1922 at which the boundaries between the three States were defined and agreed. The agreement come to at Uqair also provided for the demarcation of 'neutral zones' between Kuwait and Nejd and between Nejd and Iraq. (The Uqair meeting was also important in that it was attended, *inter alia*, by a Major Frank Holmes of the Eastern and General Syndicate who, during the course of the meeting, obtained from ibn Saud a four-year concession on behalf of his Syndicate for oil exploration in the province of al-Hasa. This will be referred to in more detail in the next chapter.) The Uqair meeting did not put an end to frontier difficulties between Nejd and Iraq. Such difficulties are in fact endemic along desert frontiers. In December 1923 a conference met at Kuwait, under British auspices, to discuss frontier problems which had arisen between Nejd and Iraq and between Nejd and Transjordan. This conference was terminated abruptly as a result of Iraqi anger at a serious Nejdi raid into Iraq which took place while the conference was being held.

It is convenient at this point briefly to follow the fortunes of ibn Saud (at this time known as the Amir of Nejd) up to the time when he became undisputed master of the Arabian Peninsula. In the course of his progress it is to be noted that at no time did he offer any serious opposition to the British. Right up to the end of the second world war and indeed almost up to the time of his death in 1953, while remaining entirely independent of Great Britain in his domestic affairs, and in his dealings with those of his neighbours who were not under British protection, he was content to keep his expansionist designs within the framework of British hegemony in the Middle East, so long as that hegemony lasted. We have already seen how his frontier disputes with Iraq and Kuwait were settled as a result of British mediation. He made no attempts to encroach on the British-protected independence of Bahrain, or Qatar or the Trucial Sheikhdoms. It was not until the closing years of his life, when British influence was declining, that the Imam of Oman obtained Saudi support for his claim against the Sultan of Musqat and that Saudi claims were put forward to the oasis of Buraimi. Along his desert boundary with Transjordan, the usual frontier difficulties, aggravated by the Saudi-Sherifian feud, produced the same difficulties as along the Iraqi border. As in Iraq, Saudi incursions into Transjordan were met by bombing attacks from the R.A.F. One serious raid, towards the end of 1922 and just before the Uqair meeting, was followed by massive R.A.F. retaliation on the retreating raiders, which caused hundreds of Saudi casualties. After that there was no more serious raiding.

In the Hijaz the case was different. At the end of March 1924, H.M.G., exasperated by Husain's obstinacy, misgovernment and ceaseless reproaches and exigencies, and considering no doubt that their obligations towards the Sherifian family had been amply discharged by the provision of thrones for two of Husain's sons, withdrew their mantle of protection from the ageing Sherif and discontinued the subsidy which they had been paying to him. (The subsidy of £5,000 per month which H.M.G. had been paying to ibn Saud was discontinued at the same time.) In the autumn of 1924 Saudi forces invaded the Hijaz and within a few weeks had overrun the whole country, with the exception of Medina and Jidda which were being beseiged. King Husain abdicated in favour of his son Ali and was transported by a British cruiser to Cyprus, there to spend the short remainder of his days in exile. Medina surrendered on 5 December 1925 after a year's desultory siege. On 23 December Ali, disappointed of the hope of British intervention, without money and with only a rabble for an army, negotiated the surrender of Jidda through the intermediary of the British Consulate. It was provided that Ali and his Court should be allowed to leave in peace and that ibn Saud's fanatical Ikhwan should not be allowed into the town. Thus ibn Saud became Lord of the Holy Places and King of the Hijaz as well as Sultan of Nejd. (His dominions did not become known as Saudi Arabia until 1932.) He continued to maintain his capital at Riadh in Nejd and appointed a Viceroy in the Hijaz.

During the course of the war British forces from Transjordan had occupied the districts of Maan, Aqaba, Shobek and Petra, which were claimed both by Transjordan and the Hijaz. This occupation, the increased status conferred on ibn Saud by his annexation of the Hijaz, the endemic border troubles, and the future of the pilgrim traffic, in which Great Britain, as a Moslem Power, was interested, all made it desirable to bring up to date those relations between H.M.G. and ibn Saud which were still formally regulated by the 1915 Treaty, negotiated at a time when ibn Saud was a mere desert chieftain. This Treaty placed ibn Saud in much the same protectorate relationship with Britain as the other Sheikhs of the Persian Gulf. Such a relationship was clearly inappropriate to ibn Saud's new status and, moreover, did not provide for the solution of the various problems which had arisen between H.M.G. and ibn Saud as a result of the latter's occupation of the Hijaz. On 1 January 1926 ibn Saud was proclaimed King of the Hijaz and a few months later recognized as such by H.M.G. In 1927 a British Delegation, headed by Sir Gilbert Clayton, who had been Head of the Arab Bureau during the war years, arrived at Jidda to negotiate a new Treaty. (Two Treaties, known as the Treaties of Bahra and Hadda, had in fact been concluded between H.M.G. and ibn Saud during the course of the Hijaz war providing for the regulation of frontier disputes between Nejd and Iraq and Nejd and Transjordan respectively; these Treaties were incorporated into and superseded by the Treaty about to be negotiated.) The Treaty of Jidda, signed later in the year, recognized the full

D*

sovereign status of ibn Saud and his descendants, provided for the exchange of diplomatic representatives between the two countries, and left the possession of Aqaba-Maan-Shobek-Petra in abeyance—ibn Saud refusing to relinquish his claim but agreeing to the continued occupation and administration of these districts by Transjordan. (The importance of these districts to Great Britain lay in the fact that possession of these districts provided an alternative route to Amman, Jerusalem and points northward from the east in the event of the Suez Canal becoming unavailable.) The Treaty of Jidda automatically superseded the 1915 Treaty and from henceforward relations between Great Britain and Nejd were those between sovereign States instead of those between protector and client.[10]

Throughout all the tumult of war and its troubled aftermath the other Arab States and Sheikhdoms of the Persian Gulf had pursued relatively peaceful and uneventful courses behind the shield of the British connexion which protected them from the ambitions of ibn Saud by land and from the depredations of German cruisers by sea. (None of the German raiders, which had such a spectacular career in the Indian Ocean during the early months of the war, penetrated into the Persian Gulf.)

At the beginning of the 1914–18 war Sheikh Mubarak as Subah of Kuwait mobilized his Bedouin against a possible Turkish invasion of his territory and, although he engaged in no active operations, the diversionary effect of his troops was of some importance to the I.E.F. in the early stages of the Mesopotamian campaign. In return for his assistance H.M.G. promised that, in the event of their winning the war, he and his heirs would be guaranteed in their possession of Kuwait. H.M.G. also promised to safeguard his private estates on the Shatt-al-Arab in Turkish territory. (This latter promise was not fulfilled as a result of later action by the independent government of Iraq.) So long as he lived Sheikh Mubarak was on the best of terms with ibn Saud who regarded his previous protector with respect and veneration. In the autumn of 1915 he assisted ibn Saud to put down a rebellion of the Akman tribe in al-Hasa, sending his second son Salim as leader of a military force.[11] In the middle of this campaign Sheikh Mubarak died, after a reign of some eighteen years, and was succeeded by his eldest son Jabir. Jabir only lived for just over a year after his accession and was succeeded by his younger brother Salim, a stern, reactionary Moslem who was not particularly enthusiastic about the close connexions with the British which had been initiated by his father and carried on by his brother. By the beginning of 1918 the British Navy was blockading Kuwait as a result of Salim allowing his port to be used for the smuggling of arms to the Turks in Syria via the desert. This British hostility towards Salim was used by ibn Saud as an opportunity to pursue his own ambitions against Kuwait and his own rancours against the Sheikh.[12] There was continual Saudi raiding into Kuwait until February 1921, when Salim died. Kuwaiti relations with Nejd improved as a result of the accession of Sheikh Ahmed, son of Sheikh Jabir and nephew of Salim, but the usual endemic frontier troubles continued, and were accentuated, as they were on the Iraq and Transjordan frontiers, by the fanatical and irresponsible behaviour of ibn Saud's Ikhwan, whose fanaticism was largely responsible for ibn Saud's rise to power and whose irresponsibility made it necessary for him to suppress them after he had attained power. (The story of the revolt of the Ikhwan will be told more fully in a later chapter.) At the Treaty of Uqair, to which reference has already been made, and which was in the nature of a *diktat* imposed on Nejd, Kuwait and Iraq by Sir Percy Cox on behalf of H.M.G., the frontier was settled between Kuwait and Iraq and between Kuwait and Nejd. The agreed frontiers, which involved the creation of neutral zones between Kuwait and Nejd and between Nejd and Iraq, also involved the cession by Kuwait to Nejd of much desert territory and the allegiance of several tribes. Some years later, Sheikh Ahmed, who ruled Kuwait until his death in 1950, had an opportunity to renew the quarrel with ibn Saud by siding with the Ikhwan when they revolted against their Ruler. But, under strong British pressure, he refrained from embarrassing ibn Saud by allowing his Sheikhdom to be used as a supply base and refuge for the rebels. By so doing he assisted himself towards an ultimate understanding with ibn Saud which resulted, in 1937, in ibn Saud putting an end to a boycott of Kuwait, which he instituted after the Uqair Agreement and which involved a prohibition of imports into Nejd via the port of Kuwait.

In Bahrain, the pearling industry, which had long made of Bahrain easily the most prosperous Sheikhdom in the Gulf,

75

suffered an inevitable decline during the war, but soon recovered afterwards and continued to ensure Bahrain's relative prosperity until, by the late twenties, competition from Japanese cultured pearls combined with the beginning of the slump in U.S.A. and Western Europe to give this industry what proved to be its death blow. Fortunately for Bahrain it was, by then, on the threshold of its Oil Age. Bahrain, as a result of British protection, and as a result of its having no land frontiers, remained unaffected by the Saudi expansion on the mainland as it had remained unaffected (except for the reduction in its pearling income) by the greater events of the European war.

The Trucial States were similarly unaffected. In Qatar, the ruling Sheikh, as was related in Chapter Two, signed, in 1916, a Treaty with H.M.G. similar to those already in existence with the Trucial Sheikhdoms, which made of Qatar, to all intents and purposes, a British Protectorate. In Musqat war conditions, possibly assisted by German agents, caused a renewal of attacks on Musqat by the Imam of Oman, and the Sultan required the assistance of a small British force to save his capital from capture by these invaders. The election of a new Imam in 1920 provided the opportunity for a truce (the Treaty of Sib) which succeeded in keeping the peace between Musqat and Oman for over thirty years.[13]

By the mid nineteen-twenties the affairs of the Persian Gulf seemed to have achieved relative stability, after the changes and chances of a European war and its aftermath, which had removed the Empires of Ottoman and Romanoff from the scene, which had put an end to the Qajar dynasty, and which had seen the consolidation of Central Arabia into an independent kingdom. British influence, powerful before the war, now seemed supreme. Russia, for the time being, was no longer a Great Power. Germany, likewise, and also for the time being, had been eliminated. Mesopotamia, before the war part of the Ottoman Empire, was now the Kingdom of Iraq under a British Mandate. The Arab Sheikhdoms were secured by British protection from the expanding empire of ibn Saud, whose ambitions were presciently limited by his realization of the fact of British paramountcy. Persia, after a decade of foreign invasion, civil disturbance and general chaos, seemed to have achieved political stability and the possibility of good administration under a reasonably benevolent despot who, by his ability to repel Russian, had found it possible to avoid British, encroachments on his country's independence.

The age of aircraft was beginning to give the Persian Gulf a new importance as providing staging posts for civil and military flights between Europe and India, the Far East and Australasia. The strategic importance of the Gulf, as covering the western approaches to the British Indian Empire, was as yet undiminished. And its economic importance, as providing Western Europe with a vital fuel, was just beginning to dawn.

CHAPTER FIVE

Oil, 1900–1939

SINCE THE BEGINNING of historical time, surface seepages of oil had been known about and utilized in various parts of the Persian Gulf area. For centuries bitumen derived from such seepages had been used in Persia and in Iraq as mortar by the builder and as caulking material by the shipbuilder. The gas flares of Khuzistan were used by the Zoroastrian fire-worshippers in their religious rites. The 'Greek fire', with which the ancients tipped their arrows in war, was almost certainly crude petroleum. Lamp oil, derived from some primitive process of distilling crude petroleum, seems to have been used from the earliest times. But little importance was attached to these seepages, and no attempt was made to investigate their subterranean origins, until the second half of the nineteenth century. The modern oil industry had its origin in U.S.A. and is usually taken to have started with the sinking of 'Drake's Well' in Pennsylvania in 1859. The Americans began by manufacturing lamp oil, distilled from crude petroleum, brought to the surface from deep underground deposits by mechanical drilling. By the 1880's they had demonstrated the extent of the market that existed and the size of the fortunes that could be made from the manufacture and marketing of petroleum derivatives.

American experience had made it clear that both financial capital and geological and engineering experience were necessary in order successfully to locate and commercially to exploit worth-while oil deposits, and that surface seepages were not necessarily a reliable indication of the presence of commercial quantities underneath. Neither capital nor geological and engineering experience were indigenously available in the Middle East and the Persian Gulf was neither climatically, geographically nor politically well placed to attract the European investor into what was necessarily a highly speculative enterprise. Nevertheless, some interest was taken. The comprehensive concession given by the Shah of Persia to Baron Julius de Reuter in 1872 (see Chapter Two) included a concession for the exploitation throughout Persia of all minerals, including petroleum. This concession was soon cancelled. In 1884 a small German firm, Hotz & Co., was given a concession to drill for oil in the province of Fars in Persia. Nothing came of this, but a new concession given to de Reuter in 1889 for the establishment of a Bank in Persia provided also for the right to explore for minerals, including oil, in return for the Persian Government receiving a 16 per cent share of the net profits of any successful exploitation. The Persian Bank Mining Rights Corporation, formed to explore for oil under this concession, drilled three dry wells in south Persia before abandoning their efforts.

Meanwhile, in the Ottoman Empire, interest was being taken by various parties in the possibilities of oil existing in commercial quantities in the Vilayets of Baghdad and Mosul. German experts visiting these Vilayets as early as 1871 had produced optimistic reports and the first concession obtained by the German-owned Ottoman Railway Company of Anatolia (which was financially controlled by the Deutsche Bank) in 1888 for the prolongation of the railway line through Anatolia into Iraq gave to the Company priority rights on the exploitation of minerals, including oil, along the line of the projected railway. Another interested party, acting variously on behalf of British and Russian interests, was a young, western-educated Armenian, Calouste Sarkis Gulbenkian, who, early in the nineties, made a report to the Ottoman Ministry of Mines on the possibilities of oil exploitation in the Ottoman dominions which so interested the Sultan that he took steps, by the issue of two Firmans in 1890 and 1899 respectively, to provide that any future revenues derived from oil should be paid to his Privy Purse instead of to the Ottoman Treasury.

IRAN

The first concession destined to result in the commercial exploitation of oil was that granted by the Shah of Persia on 28 May 1901 to William Knox d'Arcy, an Australian financier who had already made a fortune out of gold mining in his own country. D'Arcy had been attracted to the prospects of Persian oil by a report published in 1892 by a French archaeologist named de Morgan. Encouraged, so it is said, by the coincidence that the mining engineer who had first struck oil for him in Australia was also named Morgan, d'Arcy formed a small Syndicate which, in 1900, proceeded to Tehran to negotiate for a concession. (D'Arcy himself never set foot in Persia.) The concession obtained was for a period of sixty years and conferred on d'Arcy's Syndicate the right to find, exploit and export petroleum anywhere in Persia, except for the five northern provinces (which were excluded as a result of Russian influence). It included the exclusive right to construct and operate pipelines from the interior of Persia to the Persian Gulf. It stipulated the formation within two years of a Company or Companies to exploit the concession, the payment to the Persian Government of £20,000 in cash and a further £20,000 in paid up shares in the Company or Companies to be formed, and a royalty of 16 per cent on the annual net profits. In return for these payments the concessionaires were granted exemption from payment of taxation or Customs duties in connexion with their operations. The First Exploration Company was registered at the beginning of 1903 with a capital of £400,000 and work was started almost immediately, first at Qasr-e-Shirin on the Persian-Turkish border in Luristan, and later in the foothills of the Zagros Mountains in Khuzistan. Results were at first disappointing. By 1905 money was beginning to run short. In May of that year the Burmah Oil Company, at the request of the British Admiralty, who were already considering the possibility of using oil instead of coal on H.M. ships, came to the rescue and the Concessions Syndicate Ltd., in which Burmah Oil had a controlling interest, and of which d'Arcy was a director, was formed to take over the assets of the First Exploration Company and to provide the funds for continued exploration. At last, on 26 May 1908, when the new funds and the patience of the directors were both almost exhausted, a strong flow of oil was tapped at a depth of 1,180 feet from the first well drilled at Mesjid-e-Suleiman, on the site of an ancient fire-temple. Ten days later oil in commercial quantities was tapped at just over 1,000 feet from a second well drilled in the same locality. These finds solved the financial problem. In 1909 the Anglo-Persian

Oil Company was formed, with an initial capital of £2 million, to operate the concession. By 1912 a refinery had been constructed at Abadan, an island on the Shatt-el-Arab, and a pipeline built connecting the oilfield with the refinery. By 1914 a total of thirty wells had been drilled in the Mesjid-e-Suleiman district and refined oil was being exported from Abadan at a rate of about 250,000 tons per annum.

During the first decade of the twentieth century the actual and potential scope of the uses of petroleum products had expanded in a revolutionary way. At the end of the nineteenth century the principal use of petroleum was still seen mainly in terms of lamp oil. Ten years later the development of the internal combustion engine for automobiles and aircraft, the development of the compression ignition engine for stationary and locomotive machinery, and the possibilities of using fuel oil instead of coal for the firing of ships' boilers, together with ancillary requirements, such as lubricating oil and bitumen (for road making) arising from these major developments, all combined to make of petroleum a vital raw material socially, industrially and strategically, for any modern State. The particular importance of the Persian oil deposits in the eyes of the British Government lay in the fact that there were no indigenous oil deposits in the United Kingdom, nor, so far as was then known, in any part of the British Empire. This general consideration, and the particular consideration that it had already been decided that oil instead of coal should be the fuel of the future for the British fleet, caused the British Government to attach very great importance to the British-controlled oil enterprise in south-west Persia. In July 1914, six days before the outbreak of war, the Royal Assent was given to an Act of Parliament providing for an increase in the capital of the Anglo-Persian Oil Company from £2 million to £4 million, and for the acquisition by H.M.G. of a shareholding of £2·2 million, giving them a controlling interest.[1]

We have already seen (in Chapter Three) how the course of the campaign in Mesopotamia was conditioned by the necessity for protecting the Anglo-Persian Oil Company's installations in south-west Persia from Turkish invasion. We have also seen how these installations were the principal target of the wartime guerilla activities in south-west Persia inspired by Wassmuss and other German agents. But neither Germans nor Turks were able seriously to affect the steady increase in the production, refining and export of petroleum products, which were becoming more and more vital as a sinew of war. In 1918 the export of oil products from Persia amounted to 897,000 tons as compared with 273,000 tons in 1914 and 80,000 tons in 1913. In 1919 exports increased to 1·1 million tons and in 1923 they amounted to 2·3 million tons.

Up to the time of the accession of Reza Shah in 1925 the Company's relations with the Persian Government had, on the whole, been good. There had, however, been various incidents and various circumstances which were to lead to trouble under the new régime.

(1) At the end of the war, when the British Government were in process of negotiating a Treaty with Persia which would, had it been ratified, have reduced that country virtually to the status of a British Protectorate, the Company presented claims to the Persian Government amounting to £600,000 in respect of wartime damage to its installations for which, it alleged, the Persian Government was liable. The Persian Government put forward a counter-claim in which they maintained that the royalty due to them under the terms of the d'Arcy concession, representing 16 per cent of the net profits of the operations, should be calculated on the total profit made by the Company at all stages and not simply on the book profit made by the sale of the crude oil to the British Tanker Company (which was a 100 per cent owned Anglo-Persian affiliate). This claim and counter-claim, together with some other minor matters in dispute, were submitted, with the agreement of both parties, to the arbitration of Mr. Armitage Smith, a British Treasury official who, in anticipation of the ratification of the Anglo-Persian Treaty, had been appointed as Financial Adviser to the Persian Government. Under the terms of the Armitage Smith award, which was accepted by both parties and incorporated into an Agreement between the Company and the Persian Government signed in December 1920,[2] the basis on which future royalties were to be paid was set out in considerable detail, it being provided that the royalty was to be calculated on the basis of 16 per cent of the profits on the totality of the Company's operations in which Persian oil was used, including production, refining,

transport and marketing.[3] It was also provided that the Company should pay to the Persian Government a sum of £1 million representing a settlement on account of past royalties re-calculated on the new basis. This award, which regulated financial transactions between the Persian Government and the Company for the next twelve years, was subsequently criticized in Persia as having been imposed on the Persian Government by a British Adviser in the interest of the British-owned Company; but, in fact, the award upheld the principal claim of the Persian Government against the Company. Under the terms of the award the royalty to the Persian Government which, in 1919, amounted to £469,000 on a production of just over 1 million tons and compared with the Company's net profit of just over £2 million, had, by 1929, increased to £1,288,000 on a production of 5,460,000 tons and compared with the Company's net profit of £5,206,000.[4]

(2) It will be recalled that the d'Arcy concession covered the whole of Persia except for the five northern provinces of Azerbaijan, Gilan, Mazanderan, Astrabad and Khorassan. In 1916 a concession for the exploitation of oil in these five provinces was given by the Persian Government to a Russian subject named Khoshtaria. As a result of the war, this concession was not immediately exploited; by the end of the war it became apparent that any holder of a concession in the north could only convey any oil discovered to the Persian Gulf by favour of the Anglo-Persian Oil Company who, under the terms of the d'Arcy concession, had a monopoly for the construction of pipelines to the Persian Gulf. Largely as a result of this consideration, the Company, was able, in 1920, to purchase Khoshtaria's concession from him for £200,000, much to the annoyance of both the Persian and Soviet Governments. In 1921 the Soviet-Persian Treaty was signed providing for Soviet renunciation of any previous Russian concessions in Persia. On this ground, and on the ground that the original Khoshtaria concession was based on an invalid grant made by Shah Muzaffar-ed-Din in 1896, the Persian Government refused to recognize the validity of the concession purchased by the Company, in spite of the Company's somewhat legalistic assertion that Khoshtaria was, not a Russian, but a Georgian subject. (An argument which the Soviet Government was fond of using when it suited their

convenience.) Subsequent efforts by the Persian Government to conclude agreements with two American Companies—Standard of New Jersey and Sinclair—for the exploitation of the northern provinces were frustrated principally by the Anglo-Persian Oil Company's monopoly of exports via the Persian Gulf conferred by the pipeline monopoly under the d'Arcy concession.[5] This apparent attempt by the Anglo-Persian Oil Company to secure and enforce a monopoly of all oil operations in Persia provoked resentment and was one of the principal causes of the cancellation of the concession in 1932.

(3) Another matter of dispute, which developed between the Company and the new régime after 1925, arose from the relations maintained by the Company with local magnates in the South, and particularly with Sheikh Khazaal of Mohammerah and with the chiefs of the powerful Bakhtiari tribe. Owing to the fact that these magnates, and not the central Government, were, before the advent of Reza Shah, in effective control of the areas covered by the oil operation, the Company's negotiations regarding the leasing of land, the protection of their installations, the procurement and control of labour and so on, were conducted with these magnates rather than with the representatives of the central Government. Consequently, when Reza Shah started to break the power of these magnates and to bring them under the effective control of the central Government (which he soon succeeded in doing) it was possible to represent the Company as having encouraged, and even subsidized, these magnates in their previous defiance of the central Government, and as having, in effect, attempted to use these magnates as a means of setting up the Company as an *imperium in imperio* in Southern Persia.

All these accumulated resentments and rancours boiled over in 1932. The precipitating factor was the decline in the royalties payable to the Persian Government, as a result of the world-wide slump and the consequent reduction in the Company's net profits. In June 1932, as a result of the reduction in the Company's net profits during 1931, it was announced by the Company that Persia's royalty for 1931 amounted to only £306,872 compared with £1,288,312 for the year 1930.[6] Ever since 1926 the Persian Government had been carrying on rather desultory negotiations with the Company for an improvement in the terms of the concession, maintaining that the existing basis, as regulated by the Armitage Smith award, was invalid in that Armitage Smith had no proper authority to come to an agreement with the Company on behalf of the Persian Government. In November 1932 the Persian Government formally notified the Company of the cancellation of the concession on the ground that they could not be bound by the terms of a concession granted prior to the constitutional régime. At the same time the Persian Government notified its willingness to negotiate a new concession. There followed a course of recrimination between the Persian Government on the one side and the Company and the British Government on the other. Both Governments brought the dispute before the Council of the League of Nations in January 1933. After the presentation of arguments on both sides it was agreed to resume direct negotiations between the Persian Government and the Company under the auspices of a Rapporteur appointed by the League. In April 1933 a new concession was agreed upon and signed by the two parties. In this new concession[7] the most important provisions were as follows:

(*a*) The concessionary area was reduced to 100,000 square miles, to be selected by the Company from the area covered by the original concession (Article 2).

(*b*) The basis of payment was revised to provide for a royalty of four shillings a ton on all oil produced plus a sum equal to 20 per cent of any annual distribution to the Ordinary stockholders of the Company in excess of £671,250, with a guaranteed minimum of £750,000 in respect of the sum of these two amounts (Article 10).

(*c*) On the expiry or surrender of the concession the Company was to pay to the Persian Government a sum equal to 20 per cent of the increase in the sum of the Company's General Reserve and cash balance accrued between 31 December 1932 and the date of the expiry or surrender of the concession.

(*d*) The period of the new concession was to be for sixty years i.e. until 1992. (The original concession would have expired in 1961.)

(*e*) Royalties for 1931 and 1932 were to be calculated on the basis of the new concession and the Company, in addition, were to pay £1 million to the Persian Government in full settlement of all outstanding claims on the Company by the Government.

85

(*f*) Arrangements were made for payments in lieu of taxation amounting to a minimum of £300,000 per annum.

(*g*) Article 21 of the new concession provided that 'This concession shall not be annulled by the Government and the terms therein contained shall not be altered either by general or by special legislation in the future, or by administrative measures or by any other acts whatever of the executive Authorities'.

As a result of the new Agreement the royalty payable to the Persian Government for 1931 was increased by £1,219,011 from £306,872 to £1,525,883. The payment of a flat rate royalty instead of a share in the Company's net profits continued to be advantageous to the Persian Government in subsequent years as will be seen from the following figures:[8]

Year	Company's Net Profit	Production in Tons	Royalty
1933	£2,653,978	7,086,706	£2,189,853
1936	£6,123,469	8,198,199	£3,545,313
1938	£6,109,477	10,195,371	£4,270,814

For the time being the Persian Government and Persian public opinion remained satisfied with the terms of the new concession and, with the steadily increasing income derived from the new concession, relations between the Company and the Persian Government were, for the next few years, peaceful and uneventful.

IRAQ

It will be recollected that, during the last decades of the nineteenth century, both the Deutsche Bank, the financial backers of the Anatolian Railway, and Calouste Gulbenkian, acting on behalf of various British and Russian interests, were pursuing the possibilities of oil in the Mosul and Baghdad Vilayets. The Anatolian Railway which had, in 1888, been given prior rights on the exploitation of mineral resources along the line of the proposed extension of this railway through Iraq to the Persian Gulf, obtained, as part of the Baghdad Railway Convention signed in 1903, the right to explore for oil along a 20-kilometre strip on each side of the projected railway line. In 1904 this right was converted into a specific concession, initially for one year, to search for oil in the Baghdad and Mosul Vilayets on the understanding that a forty-year exploitation concession would be granted to them if oil were found in commercial quantities. This exploration concession was renewed annually until 1907, without any oil being found, after which the concession lapsed. There were several powerful competitors ready and anxious to replace the Deutsche Bank, including d'Arcy who was already exploring for oil in Persia, an American Syndicate represented by Rear-Admiral Chester, and the Royal Dutch-Shell Group (Shell and Royal Dutch were amalgamated in 1907), now represented by Gulbenkian. But in 1908 the Young Turk revolution put an end to concession hunting until 1910.[9] By this time the Anglo-Persian Oil Company had been formed and were actively interested, and the Deutsche Bank were back in the field, hoping to get their old concession renewed by the new régime. The British Government were interested at that time in trying to come to an agreement with Germany over the question of the Berlin–Baghdad Railway and, with the assistance of Sir Ernest Cassel, a German-born British banker, and C. S. Gulbenkian, were instrumental in forming, in 1911, a Company registered in London and called the African & Eastern Concessions Ltd. for the purpose of oil operations throughout the Ottoman Empire. This Company was formed with a capital of £80,000 in £1 shares. The Deutsche Bank was allotted 20,000 shares in return for its more or less worthless expired concession, the National Bank of Turkey, a British-owned Bank founded in Turkey two years before, received and paid for 28,000 shares, C. S. Gulbenkian 12,000, and Royal Dutch-Shell, through Gulbenkian, 20,000. In 1912 the name of the Company was changed to the Turkish Petroleum Company. The Company proceeded to apply for licences and concessions for oil exploration in various parts of Turkey. At the same time the various groups of shareholders in the Company agreed with each other not to seek for oil concessions in the Ottoman Empire outside the framework of the Turkish Petroleum Company.

In 1913 the British Government, which had been instrumental in bringing about the reconciliation of British and German interests represented in the Turkish Petroleum Company, and which was in negotiation to secure a controlling interest in the Anglo-Persian Oil Company (then seeking concessions in the

Ottoman Empire in competition with the Turkish Petroleum Company) intervened to bring about a coalescence of interests between the Anglo-Persian Oil Company and the Turkish Petroleum Company. As a result of this intervention, an agreement was arrived at in March 1914 by which the capital of the Turkish Petroleum Company was doubled, from £80,000 to £160,000, and completely reallocated. Anglo-Persian took up £80,000 and the Deutsche Bank and Royal Dutch-Shell £40,000 each. A 5 per cent interest for Gulbenkian was provided in equal parts from the Anglo-Persian and Royal Dutch-Shell shares. The National Bank disappeared from the picture and the new shareholders reaffirmed the pledge not to seek concessions in the Ottoman Empire independently of each other. The British Government's successive interventions had secured that the most powerful group in the oil concession field in the Ottoman Empire was firmly under British majority control. (Royal Dutch-Shell was 40 per cent British, representing the Shell share in the Group; this, added to the Anglo-Persian 50 per cent share, provided for a total British interest of 60 per cent.) Also, it appeared that a useful political purpose had been served by providing for Anglo-German co-operation in an area where Anglo-German rivalry was one of the factors which seemed to be leading inexorably towards a European war. In retrospect, it is interesting to note that in June 1914, within two months of the outbreak of war between Great Britain and Germany, joint representations in Constantinople by the British and German Ambassadors led to the issue of a letter by the Turkish Grand Vizier agreeing to lease the petroleum deposits 'discovered or to be discovered' in the Vilayets of Mosul and Baghdad to the Turkish Petroleum Company.[10] Negotiations for the grant of a concession in accordance with the terms of this letter were overtaken by the outbreak of war.

This brief account of events will explain the British anxiety to occupy the whole of the Vilayets of Baghdad and Mosul by the time of the Armistice; it will also explain Lloyd George's intimation to Clemenceau, just after the Armistice, that the British Government wished to vary the terms of the Sykes-Picot Agreement by claiming for themselves the Vilayet of Mosul, which had been allocated to France under the Sykes-Picot Agreement. Clemenceau was, of course, well aware of the nature of the

British interest in Mosul, and there followed a long and some-times acrimonious course of negotiations between Great Britain and France (known as the Long-Berenger negotiations),[11] which issued in an Agreement under which the French, in return for relinquishing the territorial 'rights' on Mosul pro-vided for in the Sykes-Picot Agreement, should receive the 25 per cent ex-German interest in the Turkish Petroleum Com-pany.[12] At this point the Americans who, it will be remembered, had been interested in but unsuccessful in obtaining Ottoman oil concessions before the war, advanced the 'Open Door' principle[13] and demanded a substantial share in the Turkish Petroleum Company (although the United States had not been at war with Turkey). Since the success of the delicate peace negotiations with Turkey (which were prolonged until 1924 as a result of the Kemalist revolution in Turkey) were to some extent dependent on American goodwill, and since Great Britain and France were heavily in debt to the U.S.A., it was necessary to take this claim seriously. Eventually, in 1923, it was agreed, after long and wearisome negotiations, that the group of seven American oil companies which had been formed to negotiate for a share in the Turkish Petroleum Company would receive a 25 per cent share to be provided out of the Anglo-Persian share (the Anglo-Persian was to receive in compensation 10 per cent of all oil produced by the Turkish Petroleum Company) in return for an undertaking by the State Department not to organize any opposition to the validity of the Turkish Petroleum Company 'concession'—represented by the June 1914 letter by the Grand Vizier to the British and German Ambassadors. This, however, was not the end of the affair. The long-drawn-out Lausanne Conference, ending with the signature of the Treaty of Lausanne in July 1923, did not succeed in agreeing the frontier between Turkey and Iraq and consequently did not settle the future destination of Mosul. Direct negotiations between Great Britain and Turkey having failed, the question was, as provided for in the Treaty of Lausanne, referred to the League of Nations which, in December 1925, awarded the whole of Mosul Vilayet to Iraq. This award was accepted by Turkey and, on 6 June 1926, a tripartite Treaty was concluded between Great Britain, Turkey and Iraq which defined the frontier substantially in accordance with the terms of the League of Nations award and provided that Iraq should pay to Turkey 10 per cent of any profits derived from oil production in Mosul Vilayet for a period of twenty-five years.

It was then necessary to square Mr. Gulbenkian who, it will be remembered, had, under the 1914 Agreement, a 5 per cent share in the Turkish Petroleum Company derived in two equal parts from the Anglo-Persian and Shell holdings, and who had not been a party to the agreement with the Americans. After more negotiations it was provided that Anglo-Persian, Royal Dutch-Shell, the American group and the French group (Compagnie Française des Pétroles) should each have a 25 per cent share and that each of these four groups should contribute $1\frac{1}{4}$ per cent of their 25 per cent share so as to provide a 5 per cent interest for Gulbenkian. The final shareholding was therefore as follows: Anglo-Persian $23\frac{3}{4}$ per cent; Royal Dutch-Shell $23\frac{3}{4}$ per cent; Compagnie Française des Pétroles $23\frac{3}{4}$ per cent; the American group (later to be called the Near East Development Corporation) $23\frac{3}{4}$ per cent; Mr. C. S. Gulbenkian 5 per cent.

While these negotiations were in progress the Turkish Petroleum Company obtained from the Iraqi Government on 24 March 1925 a seventy-five-year concession giving them exclusive rights for the exploration and exploitation of petroleum resources in Iraq, except for the Province of Basra, in return for a royalty of four shillings (gold) per ton on all oil produced. It was provided that the Company should be registered in U.K. and that it should remain British-controlled. In deference to the American 'Open Door' principle, and to provide for possible future pickings for oil companies not included in the Turkish Petroleum Company, it was stipulated that within four years of the grant of the concession the Company should select, at their option, certain areas for exploitation within the area of the concession and that the Iraqi Government should offer areas of a similar size, outside those chosen for exploitation by the Company, for competitive bidding by outsiders.

One of the conditions which the British shareholders in the Turkish Petroleum Company wished to impose on the American shareholders was agreement to the self-denying ordinance previously entered into by the British and German shareholders (and which had been agreed to by the French shareholders) providing that the partners in the Turkish Petroleum Company would not seek other oil concessions in what had previously been the Ottoman Empire except through the Turkish Petroleum Company. This was held by the State Department to be in opposition to the Open Door principle, in that it appeared to limit the prospects of American participation in the search for oil in the Middle East. This difficulty, however, was overcome and, on 31 July 1928, after the American group, now reduced to five Companies[14] had formed the Near East Development Corporation for the purpose of participating in the Turkish Petroleum Company, the so-called Red Line Agreement was signed in which the various Turkish Petroleum Company interests bound themselves not to seek any independent concessions within an area which included the whole of Iraq and the Arabian shore of the Persian Gulf excluding Kuwait and which was defined by a red line on a map annexed to the Agreement. This Agreement was, during the thirties, destined to introduce some complications into the hunt for concessions along the western shores of the Persian Gulf. Later, after World War Two, the Red Line Agreement was abandoned as a result of State Department pressure alleging that the Agreement was in contravention of Anti-Trust legislation.

In March 1931 a new concession, superseding the 1925 concession, was obtained from the Iraqi Government under the terms of which the original provision for the plots to be selected and competed for by outsiders was replaced by a provision in which the Turkish Petroleum Company (renamed the Iraq Petroleum Company at the time of the new concession) was given rights of exploitation east of the Tigris while that part of the Provinces of Baghdad and Mosul lying west of the Tigris was relinquished. (The relinquished part of the concession was put out to competitive tender by the Iraqi Government and awarded to British Oil Developments Ltd. on a seventy-five-year concession. Subsequently the British Oil Developments concession was purchased by the Iraq Petroleum Company, which formed a subsidiary Company, the Mosul Petroleum Company, to exploit it.) Other provisions of the new concession were: (*a*) the four shillings (gold) royalty stipulated in the 1925 concession was made subject to a minimum payment of £400,000 per annum; (*b*) certain annual payments to the Iraqi

Government were stipulated pending the discovery and export of commercial oil; (c) the Company undertook to construct a pipeline to the Mediterranean for the export of oil when found.

Since the principal demand for Iraqi oil would be in the markets of the West it had long been apparent that the most economical method of export would be by way of a pipeline to the Mediterranean and not to the Persian Gulf. Such a pipeline could be constructed either across French Mandated territory to a Syrian or Lebanese port or across British Mandated territory to the port of Haifa. In point of distance the nearest Mediterranean port was the Lebanese port of Tripoli. In the event two pipelines were constructed, one passing through French Mandated territory to Tripoli and the other through British Mandated territory to Haifa, both lines being completed in 1934. In 1937 a refinery was opened at the terminal of the Haifa line.

Although commercial oil was first struck in 1927[15] intensive production had to await the completion of the pipelines. Thus production, which in 1933 only attained 123,000 tons, just exceeded 1 million tons in 1934 and by 1938 had increased to 4,298,000 tons, with royalty income to the Iraqi Government of just under £2 million, or some 25 per cent of the Government's total revenue.[16]

The exploitation of oil in the Province of Basra, which had been excluded both from the 1925 and 1931 concessions, was the subject of a new concession granted by the Iraqi Government to the Iraq Petroleum Company in July 1938 under the terms of which the I.P.C. were given a seventy-five-year concession for the exploration and exploitation of petroleum resources in the Province of Basra under substantially the same conditions as had been agreed for the rest of Iraq under the 1931 concession and under the Mosul concession awarded to British Oil Developments and subsequently taken over by I.P.C. The I.P.C. formed a subsidiary Company, the Basra Petroleum Company, to exploit the new concession, but no commercial oil had been produced up to the time of the outbreak of World War Two.

THE ARABIAN SHORE

The self-denying ordinance entered into by the Turkish Petroleum Company shareholders, and the Treaties entered into by the various Sheikhdoms which debarred them from giving any concessions to non-British foreigners without the consent of the British Government, combined to delay the post-war hunt for oil concessions along the Arabian shore of the Persian Gulf. First in the field was the Eastern and General Syndicate Ltd., a British company registered in London in 1920 and represented in the Middle East by a Major Frank Holmes. The Eastern and General Syndicate was not an oil company and the avowed object of its concession-hunting was to obtain concessions with a view to selling them to an oil company. The Syndicate's first venture was in al-Hasa which was included within the expanding dominions of Abdul Aziz ibn Saud Sultan of Nejd. Major Holmes met ibn Saud at Uqair in November 1922 during the course of the meeting, presided over by Sir Percy Cox, to settle boundary disputes between Nejd, Kuwait and Iraq. In spite of competition from the Anglo-Persian Oil Company, whose representative, Sir Arnold Wilson (previously Deputy Civil Commissioner in Iraq) who was also present at the meeting, and, it appears,[17] in spite of advice given by Cox to ibn Saud against having anything to do with the Syndicate, Holmes succeeded in obtaining from ibn Saud an exploratory concession covering the province of al-Hasa against an annual rental of £2,000. The concession came into force in August 1923; the rent was paid for two years and a certain amount of geological exploration done by the Syndicate. After that they appear to have lost interest. They defaulted on the rental payments and, in 1928, ibn Saud cancelled the concession.

In the meantime, in December 1925, Holmes obtained, on behalf of the Syndicate, an exploratory concession from the Sheikh of Bahrain, valid for two years. In 1927 Holmes sold this concession, and the accompanying option, to the Gulf Oil Corporation. Gulf, however, which was still a member of the American shareholding group in the Turkish Petroleum Company (they subsequently sold their interest to Standard of New Jersey) were unable to use their option as a result of the Red Line Agreement then being negotiated and, after having offered it to T.P.C., who refused it, sold it in December 1928 to Standard of California, which was not a shareholder in T.P.C. and therefore not bound by the Red Line Agreement.[18] After an agreement with the British Government, whose consent was necessary in view of Bahrain's Treaty relationship with Great Britain an arrangement was made by which the Bahrain Petroleum Company (B.A.P.C.O.), registered in Canada, was formed to exploit the option, which was in fact a renewal of the exploration concession originally obtained by Holmes. Drilling started and commercial oil was struck in May 1932. In 1934 an exploitation agreement was signed between the Sheikh of Bahrain and B.A.P.C.O. by which Bahrain was to receive a royalty of Rs. 3 as. 8 per ton of oil produced with a minimum annual payment of Rs. 75,000, later raised to Rs. 150,000. Exports started in 1935, in which year Standard of California sold a half share in B.A.P.C.O. to the Texas Oil Company. By 1938 a refinery had been built and exports of crude and refined oil from Bahrain exceeded 1 million tons per annum.

The discovery of oil in Bahrain naturally stimulated the efforts of concession-hunters as well as the interest of Rulers in adjacent territories. In Saudi Arabia particularly, ibn Saud, badly in need of money as a result of a drop in revenue from the pilgrimage, was anxious to sell oil exploration rights in his territory for as much as they would fetch. In May 1933, Standard of California, in face of competition from Major Holmes (who was rapidly eliminated as a result of his non-payment of rental in respect of his previous concession) and Iraq Petroleum Company (who for some reason do not appear to have been particularly enthusiastic, only being prepared to offer a down payment of £10,000 on account of future royalties against the £100,000 demanded by ibn Saud),[19] obtained, against a down payment of £100,000, a sixty-year concession giving the Company exclusive rights to explore for and to produce oil in an area in the east of Saudi Arabia covering 360,000 square miles. Royalty payments were fixed at four shillings (gold), or, at the Company's option one dollar plus the difference in market value between one dollar and four shillings (gold) less 10 cents, per ton of oil produced. The Californian-Arabian Standard Oil Company (C.A.S.O.C.) was formed to exploit the concession. Exploration work was started immediately and, in 1936, Standard of California, in the same way as had happened over their Bahrain concession, sold a half share in C.A.S.O.C. to the Texas Oil Company.[20] Commercial oil was struck at Damman, near the coast of the Persian Gulf in al-Hasa province, in March

1938, and exports started in May 1959 through a thirty-nine-mile pipeline constructed from Damman to the coast at Ras Tanura. In the same month the area covered by the concession was increased by 80,000 square miles to a total of 440,000 square miles against a lump sum payment of £140,000 in gold and the promise of additional sums when commercial oil was struck in the supplemental area.[21]

In the course of his concession-hunting during the early twenties, Holmes had obtained an option on a concession from the Sheikh of Kuwait. (Kuwait was excluded from the area subsequently covered by the Red Line Agreement.) Eventually, after considerable negotiation between the State Department and the British Government, whose permission had to be obtained for the grant of any concession by the Sheikh of Kuwait to non-British foreign national, the Holmes option was acquired jointly by the Anglo-Persian Oil Company and the American Gulf Oil Corp. In February 1934 these two Companies formed the Kuwait Oil Company, in which A.P.O.C. and Gulf each had a 50 per cent interest, to negotiate with the Sheikh for a concession on the basis of the option which had been acquired from Holmes. In December 1934 a seventy-five-year concession was acquired by the Kuwait Oil Company covering an area of 6,000 square miles in the Sheikhdom of Kuwait against a down payment of Rs. 470,000, an annual dead rent of Rs. 95,000 and a royalty payment of Rs. 3 per ton on all oil produced with a minimum of Rs. 250,000 per annum. Taxation was commuted against an additional payment of As. 4 per ton. Exploration started immediately and the first well was drilled in May 1936. Commercial oil was struck in April 1938, but the outbreak of war put a stop to further development and no oil was to be exported until 1946.

In 1935 the Anglo-Persian Oil Company, acting on behalf of the I.P.C., to whom the concession was afterwards transferred, obtained from the Sheikh of Qatar a seventy-five-year concession conferring exclusive rights of oil exploration and exploitation over an area of 4,000 square miles in the Sheikhdom of Qatar against a down payment of Rs. 400,000, an annual dead rent of Rs. 150,000 (to be increased to Rs. 300,000 after five years), and a royalty of Rs. 3 per ton on all oil produced. After preliminary exploration, drilling started in October 1938 but no commercial oil had been found by the time of the outbreak of war, when operations were suspended for the duration.

In addition the I.P.C., having been offered and having refused participation in the Bahrain concession when it had been offered to them by Gulf (while Gulf was still a member of the American shareholding group in I.P.C.), having failed in their rather half-hearted attempt to obtain the Saudi Arabian concession, and having seen both these concessions awarded to 100 per cent American companies, made a determined attempt to obtain concessions covering all areas within the Red Line Agreement area for which concessions had not yet been awarded. In 1933 they formed a wholly owned subsidiary Company, Petroleum Concessions Ltd., which, during the next six years, obtained exploration concessions from the various Sheikhs of the Trucial Coast and from the Sultan of Musqat and Oman. No drilling had taken place and no oil had been produced in any of these areas by the time of the outbreak of World War Two.

Such, briefly described, were the negotiations and concessions which led, at varying intervals, to the production of commercial quantities of oil in the Persian Gulf area and, in varying degrees, to a revolution in the habits and standards of living of the inhabitants of the Persian Gulf area. By the beginning of World War Two in the autumn of 1939 Iran was already a big producer, exporting at a rate of over 10 million tons per annum and receiving a royalty income of nearly £5 million per annum. By the same date Iraq was exporting some 4 million tons per annum and receiving royalty income of about £2 million per annum. On the Arabian shore Bahrain was exporting some 1 million tons per annum and receiving royalty income of some £½ million per annum. There was only a small export from Saudi Arabia and none at all from Kuwait and Qatar. The Middle East contribution to world oil supplies was as yet inconsiderable (about 8 per cent in 1938) and the contribution made by oil revenues to the budgets of the producing States, although useful, was relatively unimportant (except in the case of Iraq where oil revenue amounted to about one-quarter of the whole). But something of the size of the oil reserves in the Persian Gulf was already known and the new strategic and industrial importance of the Persian Gulf, as conferred by these oil reserves, was already apparent.

One of the most important aspects of the oil discoveries was the appearance of U.S.A. as a Great Power which had acquired a major commercial interest in the Persian Gulf. Apart from the State Department's invocation of the Open Door principle to secure for American oil companies a 23¾ per cent share in the I.P.C., American companies had obtained, by their own efforts, a 100 per cent share in the exploitation of the oil resources of Bahrain and Saudi Arabia and a 50 per cent share in the exploitation of the oil resources of Kuwait. Although the actual production accruing to U.S. interests from these concessions was insignificant compared with the vast U.S. domestic production, it was apparent that U.S.A. was keenly and increasingly interested in obtaining and developing as large a share as possible of the oil resources of the Persian Gulf area in order to offset the diminishing oil reserves within U.S.A. and in order to prevent majority control over the world's future oil resources from getting into British hands as a result of Great Britain's political predominance in the Gulf—a predominance which World War One seemed to have consolidated. In retrospect it seems surprising that this political predominance was not used to secure a virtual British monopoly of the oil resources of the Gulf (apart from Iraq where the delicate political considerations which have been described dictated some form of internationalism). But, in the event, American concession-hunting activity between the two wars was to result (by 1960) in something like a 60 per cent U.S. share in the oil production of the Persian Gulf area.

CHAPTER SIX

Despotism and Democracy

THE CAPITAL WHICH was attracted to the Persian Gulf
during the nineteen-thirties by the promise of oil wealth
was only forthcoming as a result of the political stability
which appeared to be assured in that region. This was due partly
to the disappearance of the Ottoman Empire and the consequent disappearance of the rivalries engendered by its latter-
day decrepitude, partly to the temporary eclipse of Russia as an
aggressive Great Power, and partly to the *pax britannica* which
the First World War had confirmed over the waters and coasts
of the Persian Gulf and established over Mesopotamia. But it was
also due to the emergence, in the land masses of each side of the
Persian Gulf—in Persia on the east and in the Arabian Peninsula on the west—of two great rulers, who established over their
respective dominions the authority of a strong central government, capable of collecting taxes, of maintaining security and
repelling invaders, and of subduing and keeping under control
the local magnates and tribal chiefs who previously had disputed among themselves such precarious authority as was to be
found at all in these regions.

By the end of the First World War the power of the central
government in Persia had been reduced almost to zero. During
the course of hostilities the country's proclaimed neutrality had
been violated simultaneously and with impunity by British,
Turks and Russians. The Turks had laid waste much of the
north-west of the country. A large area between Qazvin and
Hamadan had, since 1915, been in the hands of the Jangali
rebels under Kuchik Khan, who had rebelled successfully
against and had established an independent rule in defiance of
the central government. Within a few months of the armistice
Kurdistan was also in successful and virtually unresisted
rebellion. In the south the powerful tribal leaders of the Lurs,

the Bakhtiari and the Qashgai were kept in temporary and precarious subjection by a British-raised and British-officered force—the South Persia Rifles. The only other effective military force under the nominal control of the central government was the Cossack Brigade, officered by White Russians, who were more interested in the prospects of a counter-revolution in Russia than in serving the interests of their nominal Persian masters. The Treasury was empty. A large part of the population was starving. Lack of roads and railways, and endemic banditry, prevented regular communications between capital and provinces. The Bolsheviks, busy putting down rebellion and establishing their authority over the Russian provinces in Trans-caucasia and Transcaspia, were a potential menace to what remained of Persian independence from the north. The British, with their troops in Iraq, with their command of the Persian Gulf, and their lines of communication from Kermanshah to the Caspian (which they operated in unofficial treaty relationship with the rebel Kuchik Khan and without more than formal reference to the central government), were an immediate menace to this independence from the south. For a time it seemed as if the central government, *faute de mieux*, were prepared to accept British protection as a means of attaining some sort of financial solvency and some sort of political authority. But divided counsels in Great Britain led to a steady evacuation of British troops from Persia simultaneously with the attempted negotiation with Persia of a Treaty, whose principal merit in the eyes of the Persian Government, was the protection which such a Treaty would afford from foreign invaders and domestic rebels. In the spring of 1920 the failure of the remaining British troops to prevent the landing of Bolshevist troops at Enzeli and the establishment of a Soviet Socialist Republic in Gilan, in alliance with Kuchik Khan, killed such prospects as by that time remained for the ratification of the Anglo-Persian Treaty, which had been signed the previous autumn, but which was never ratified and which was, early in 1921, formally denounced by the Persian Government. Meanwhile, in spite of the existence of a S.S.R. in Gilan, and in spite of Bolshevist-inspired rebellion and separatist propaganda in Azerbaijan, Mazanderan and Khorassan, the Persian Government, either rejecting the prospect or despairing the efficacy of British protection, opened negotiations with Moscow. As early as January 1918 the Soviet Government had addressed a Note to Persia in which they repudiated all Tsarist privileges which were incompatible with the independence of Persia and offered assistance to Persia in expelling all British and Turkish troops from the country. The Brest-Litovsk Armistice in December 1917 had provided for the evacuation of all Russian troops from Persia, and in the Brest-Litovsk Treaty of March 1918 the Soviet Government bound themselves to respect the independence and territorial integrity of Persia and Afghanistan. In June 1919, when the Bolsheviks had already an unofficial representative (Kolomyitsev) in Tehran, they presented a Note to Persia which offered (a) to annul all Persian debts owed to Tsarist Russia; (b) to abolish all privileges previously exercised by Tsarist Russia in Persia, including capitulatory rights for Russian subjects,[1] and to abandon all property rights in Persia previously owned by Tsarist Russian citizens. Since, at that time, the Bolshevist Government had not yet succeeded in establishing their authority over Transcaucasia and Transcaspia, these overtures, which amounted to a renunciation of rights which were no longer operative and which the Bolshevist Government were not in a position to enforce, had little effect on Persian opinion and did not prevent the Persian Government from advancing large claims on Russian territory through the unofficial Persian delegation to the Peace Conference. But a year later the case was altered. Vossuq ed Dowleh, the architect of the abortive Anglo-Persian Treaty, was out of office and the Treaty to all intents and purposes dead. The counter-revolutionary movements in Transcaucasia and Transcaspia, deprived of effective British support, had been all but broken and the Bolsheviks were not only establishing themselves along the pre-war Russian frontiers but also spreading their tentacles and subversive propaganda beyond these frontiers and into the northern provinces of Persia. An agreement with Russia was desirable which would, if possible, limit this subversive activity and confirm the concessions which Russia had offered a year before. Consequently, in November 1920, diplomatic relations were established between Persia and the Soviet Union and a Treaty negotiated, which was signed in February 1921. This Treaty confirmed the previous Russian undertakings given about Tsarist rights in Persia and confirmed the existing frontiers between the two countries. In return for the Russian concessions, Persia agreed not to cede any of the abandoned Russian rights or properties to any other foreign power or to the nationals of any other foreign power and, more importantly, agreed to allow Russia to send troops into Persia in the event of Persia becoming a base for any third party intending to launch an attack on Persia.

In February 1921, after this Treaty had been negotiated, but before it had been signed, there was a bloodless *coup d'etat* in Persia led by two men. One, who became Prime Minister following the coup, was Sayyid Zia-ed-Din, a young reformist politician. The other, who became Commander-in-Chief of the Army after the coup was a soldier, Reza Khan, commanding the Cossack Division (it had previously been raised in strength from a Brigade to a Division and its White Russian had been replaced by Persian officers. This had been done under the transient British influence which had existed in Persia during 1919). The first acts of the new Government were to sign the Russian Treaty and to denounce the Anglo-Persian Treaty. At the same time, however, Zia-ed-Din refused to admit into Persia the Soviet Ambassador, who had been appointed on the resumption of diplomatic relations in November, until Bolshevist troops had been withdrawn from Gilan. He also requested the British to delay the final evacuation of their troops from Persia. He, thus, in some sort, demonstrated the new Government's impartiality as between Persia's two powerful would-be protectors.

Zia-ed-Din's period of authority was short-lived. He soon quarrelled with Reza Khan and, in May 1921, fled the country, of which Reza Khan was now the real master. Reza Khan, however, before assuming the appearance as well as the reality of supreme power, was determined to restore authority and independence to the central government. As Commander-in-Chief and as Minister of War in the new Government, he had complete control of the Army and of the Government. During the next four years he extended the effective authority of that Government throughout Persia. In September 1921 Soviet troops, after repeated Persian protests, were withdrawn from Gilan, which was then rapidly and effectively occupied by Reza Khan. He then proceeded to deal with the rebel Kuchik Khan who, in October 1921, was captured and executed. During 1922 armed revolts in Kurdistan, Azerbaijan and Khorassan were put down and the ringleaders executed. Then came the turn of the southern tribal magnates, who were successively brought to heel, their private armies disbanded, their local influence destroyed, and much of their private property confiscated. The British protégé, Sheikh Khazaal of Mohammerah, was dispossessed and imprisoned and, for the first time, the Anglo-Persian Oil Company found themselves, in their day-to-day relationships, dealing direct with a nationalist Persian Government instead of with a local tribal Sheikh.[2] Similarly, all foreign individuals and organizations in Persia, as a result of the abolition of Capitulations[3] became, for the first time, effectively subject to the Persian Government instead of enjoying a large measure of territorial rights.

Not until the work of pacification and repression had been completed did Reza Khan, who had become Prime Minister in 1923, have the *fainéant* Ahmed Shah, the last of the Qajars, deposed and have himself proclaimed as Reza Shah Pahlevi, the first of the Pahlevi dynasty. It is noteworthy that, in the course of his rise to power and during his eighteen-year tenure of it, Reza Shah, although in fact a dictator, never abrogated the Constitution and at all times had his acts confirmed and legalized by an obedient Majlis. This was a source of strength to him both at home and abroad in that, by reference to the Constitution, he was able to assert the legitimacy of his rule, as against that of the Qajars, whose deposition, like his own accession, had been the acts of the Majlis.

Having established the authority and independence of his Government, Reza Shah turned his attention to social and economic reform. His social reforms, which appear to have been inspired by the example of Mustafa Kemal, although very much more moderate, were designed to break the fanatical obscurantism of the Shia Mullahs who, as a result of their prescient support of the Constitutionalists in their pre-war struggles, had been able to preserve and even to increase their influence during the Constitutional régime and to a large extent to become instrumental in thwarting and perverting the original aims of the Constitutionalists. Reza Shah encouraged the wearing of European dress, introduced female education, discouraged and finally prohibited the wearing of the veil, founded a secular university in Tehran, and forbade the sartorial and other disabilities previously imposed on Christians, Zoroastrians, Bahais and other non-Moslems. All these measures, and particularly the last, infuriated the Mullahs, who attempted to rouse public opinion against the Shah. Such attempts were ruthlessly suppressed and the Mullahs eventually found it prudent either to withdraw from the country to the Shia Holy Cities of Nejaf and Kerbela in neighbouring Iraq, or else to hide their chagrin and wait for better times. The Mullahs' lack of success in rousing public opinion against the Shah was probably due to the fact that the Shah's reforms, while distressing to the fanatical and obscurantist, were not sufficiently radical seriously to disturb anybody else. In secular matters, he was content to curtail the power of the magnates politically without expropriating them economically. There was no reform in land tenure and, in general, no attempt to create any popular basis for a revolution which remained founded on force and which only lasted for as long as there was an iron will to sustain it.

Reza Shah's economic policies were comparable with those of Mohamed Ali in Egypt a century before. His administration, and particularly the army by means of which he had established his authority and the Gendarmerie by which he maintained it, required money and he was determined to preserve Persia's independence and not to resort to foreign loans. So he resorted, as Mohamed Ali had done, to State monopolies which became in effect a means of imposing heavy taxation both on the primary producer and on the consumer.[4] He could not monopolize the country's most valuable mineral asset—oil—as he realized that the oil could neither be produced, refined, nor sold without the agency of the British concessionary Company. As we have seen, he succeeded in obtaining very much more favourable terms from that Company, but its continued status in South Persia as an *imperium in imperio* continued to irk him and he was careful to employ British advisers and British contractors as little as possible either in his administration or in his various constructional schemes. Also, in 1931, he nationalized the British-owned and British-controlled Indo-European telegraph system running through Persia. The British advisers who had come to Persia in anticipation of the Anglo-Persian Treaty being ratified were gradually got rid of. In 1922 the British Financial Adviser was replaced by an American, Dr. Millspaugh, who is said to have recommended the policy of State monopolies. Under his advisorship the currency was reorganized and the National Bank founded with a Charter to issue and control currency, a right previously possessed by the British-owned Imperial Bank.[5] When Millspaugh left in 1927 he was replaced by a German.

Under the State monopoly régime a number of sugar, textile, glass and match factories were started, but Reza Shah's most ambitious industrial scheme was the construction of the Trans-Iranian Railway,[6] running from Bandar Shapur, a new harbour in the Persian Gulf created by Reza Shah, up the Karun Valley, over the mountains to Tehran and thence to another new port, Bandar Shah, on the Caspian. We have already seen how Persia missed the great railway construction boom during the second half of the nineteenth century as the result of Anglo-Russian rivalry, and this was the first railway to be built in Iran.[7] It was completed from coast to coast in 1938. The railway was built out of taxation derived from monopolies on tea and sugar and owed nothing to foreign loans. The contractors were drawn from a variety of mostly small countries and the route of the railway was deliberately chosen so as not to link up either with the British railway system in India or with the Russian railway systems in Transcaucasia or Transcaspia. Ironically, the existence of this line was a major factor in the British choice of Persia as a channel for sending munitions of war to Russia in 1941, a choice which involved a violation of Persian neutrality and the abdication of Reza Shah.

In his relationships with foreign Powers Reza Shah was conciliatory, but showed a steady determination to avoid coming under the influence of any Great Power or group of Great Powers. As an offset to Russian and British influence he encouraged close trading relationships with Germany. Agricultural producers in the north depended, as always, largely on the Russian market, which was situated so conveniently geographically and which needed the agricultural products which Iran could supply. But, by 1938, Russia's predominant share in Iran's foreign trade had been taken over by Germany who, by that time, was taking 41·5 per cent of Iran's exports as compared with Russia which was taking 11·5 per cent.[8] Reza Shah also devoted himself to improving relationships with Turkey and Iraq to the west and with Afghanistan to the east, with the object of forming a small Power bloc strong enough to resist outside pressure from the Great Powers. In pursuance of this object the Saadabad Pact of non-aggression and consultation was signed in 1937 between Iran, Turkey, Iraq and Afghanistan. In the event this Pact had little effect in securing any unity of action between the signatory Powers, although it was a sign of the amity which Reza Shah had succeeded in establishing with Iraq and Afghanistan, with both of which countries Iran had boundary disputes which could easily have been used for picking quarrels had Reza Shah been disposed to do so.

Like many eastern dictators during the last century or so, Reza Shah was a curious mixture of the modern and the primitive. On the one hand he introduced western techniques to Iran, discouraged Moslem fanaticism and obscurantism, and made of Iran something like a reasonably efficient State on modern lines. On the other hand he was, especially towards the end of his reign, addicted to gross physical cruelty and to the cruder forms of tyrannical greed, including particularly the forcible seizure of great tracts of land for his private estates. The intensely personal nature of his rule, the fear which he inspired in his immediate entourage, and his refusal to allow any independent authority in the shadow of his throne, combined to ensure that most of the reforms which he had inaugurated should wither away after his disappearance and that most of the principles for which he stood should be forgotten when he was no longer there to enforce them. He succeeded in founding a dynasty; he failed to perpetuate a revolution.

While Reza Shah was restoring the authority of the central government in Persia, Abdul Aziz ibn Abdul Rahman ibn Saud was establishing the authority of his House and of his person over the greater part of the Arabian Peninsula. In order to understand the nature of the Saudi rule it is necessary to go back in time to the second half of the eighteenth century. Towards the end of the seventeenth century there was born in a village in Nejd, in Central Arabia, a certain Mohammed Wahhab. He was one of the great figures of Islamic history, a sort of Moslem John Knox who, basing himself on the Hanbali rite, which is

E*

the strictest of the four orthodox sects into which Sunni Islam is divided, founded, among the Bedouin of Arabia, a Moslem religious movement, analogous to the extreme Puritan sects of Protestant Christianity, which preached and practised a return to what Mohammed Abdul Wahhab regarded as the original purity of the Islamic faith. To the Bedouin of Central Arabia who had, by that time, almost entirely abandoned even the conventional practice of Islam and had, to a large extent, reverted to the primitive beliefs of pre-Islamic paganism, he denounced idolatry, even in such forms as the building of domes over the graves of holy men, as commonly practised in orthodox Islamic countries, strove to inculcate the habit of observing the five daily hours of prayer, and preached the wickedness of such acts of carnal indulgence as coffee drinking, tobacco smoking, singing and the playing of musical instruments. His object was, not merely to convert the Bedouin of Central Arabia to the practice of what came to be known as Wahhabism, but to use these Bedouin as a spearhead with which to purge the whole of Islam from what he regarded as the state of idolatrous laxity into which it had fallen. His most influential convert was Mohammed ibn Saud, the Sheikh of one of the numerous branches of the great Aneiza tribe, and the ruler of Aridh, Abdul Wahhab's birthplace. Under the fiery impulse of the reformed faith Mohammed ibn Saud rapidly established his authority over a large part of Central Arabia and, in 1745, became Amir of the whole province of Nejd with his capital at Dariyya.

Mohammed ibn Saud died in 1765 and was succeeded by his son Abdul Aziz who carried on his work of conquest, proselytization and the attempted chastisement of all non-Wahhabi Moslems, both Sunni and Shia, whom the Wahhabis openly denounced as heretics and idolaters. As we have seen earlier this involved, *inter alia*, Wahhabi raids down to the shores of the Persian Gulf, to the temporary occupation of many of the Persian Gulf Arab Sheikhdoms, and to the temporary or permanent conversion to Wahhabism of many of the inhabitants of the Sheikhdoms, who found an outlet for their fanaticism, as well as a means of livelihood, in the intensified practice of piracy, directed impartially against the Christian and Moslem shipping of the Gulf. Wahhabi raids to the north, east and west of Nejd soon brought the Amir into conflict with his Ottoman suzerain.

Abdul Aziz died in about 1800 and was succeeded by his son Saud who, in 1803, caused consternation throughout the Islamic world by the invasion of the Hijaz and the capture and sack of the Holy Cities of Makka and Medina. This was a direct challenge to the Sultan of Turkey in his capacity as Khalif-al-Islam and, in 1808, he deputed his powerful vassal Mohamed Ali, Viceroy of Egypt, to deal with the Wahhabi menace, promising him the Pashalik of the Hijaz as an incentive for doing so. Makka was reoccupied by Egyptian arms without very much resistance, but a long and troublesome series of campaigns was necessary before Wahhabi power was destroyed as a result of the capture of Dariyya in 1818. The Wahhabi Amir, Abdullah ibn Saud, who had succeeded his father in 1814, was taken prisoner and sent to Constantinople where he was executed.

Although the Banu Saud remained as Amirs of Nejd, ruling from a new capital at Riadh, Wahhabism remained in eclipse, and the Amirs of Nejd in comparative impotence, until the triumphant return of Abdul Aziz ibn Abdul Rahman ibn Saud to Riadh at the beginning of the twentieth century. The restoration of Saudi supremacy in Central Arabia, like its original establishment, was accomplished by the systematic exploitation of the qualities of fanaticism and loyalty engendered by the Wahhabi faith which ibn Saud, by practice and by precept, restored, first among his own immediate followers, and then among the surrounding tribes. This fanaticism, while it provided him with the sinews of war and ensured ultimate victory in his long-drawn-out contest for the mastery of Central Arabia with the Banu Rashid of the Jebel Shammar, began to raise serious problems for ibn Saud in his relationships with the outer world, as immediately represented by international Moslem opinion in respect of the Holy Cities of the Hijaz and by Great Britain in respect of Iraq, Transjordan and the Persian Gulf Sheikhdoms. After the capture of Hail in 1921, the fanatical clan of the Ikhwan—literally 'the Bretheren', the Ironside *corps d'élite* of dedicated Wahhabis who formed the spearhead of ibn Saud's conquering armies, led them into collision with the British as a result of raids into Iraq and Transjordan. Ibn Saud, who recognized that his position in Arabia was still entirely dependent on British goodwill, was fully aware of the necessity for bringing under control the powerful force which he had conjured into being. He was to some extent successful in doing so. Principally as a result of his success in diverting much of the fanatical Wahhabi energy into the establishment of Ikhwan agricultural settlements, such as Artawiyya and Ghat-Ghat, where agriculture and craftsmanship were practised in strict Wahhabi communities, he began gradually to wean Wahhabi tribesmen away from their traditional habits of *ghazzu* (raiding) which they were accustomed to carry on without much regard either to the existence of international frontiers or to the existence of those external standards of international morality, and external methods of enforcing them, which ibn Saud was beginning to have to take into account.

A test of the extent of ibn Saud's success in controlling the Ikhwan was provided during his invasion of the Hijaz in 1924–1925. The immediate pretext for this invasion was the action of King Husain in declaring himself Khalif-al-Islam during the course of a visit to his son Abdullah in Amman. This action was generally ill-received in the Moslem world, which was in any case dissatisfied with Husain owing to the inefficiency and corruption which accompanied the arrangements for the Pilgrimage under his rule. But there was considerable disquiet in the Moslem world at the prospect of the Holy Cities becoming once more under Wahhabi domination. In the event ibn Saud succeeded in allaying this disquiet. The iconoclasm of the Wahhabis in the Holy Cities was restrained and ibn Saud was able to prevent the Ikhwan from entering Jidda, with its large foreign population. Subsequent arrangements for the Pilgrimage were much better organized than under Husain, and orthodox Moslems were not subjected to any tiresome or humiliating restraints. The Hijaz was not absorbed into Nejd and ibn Saud's kingdom became, in effect, a dual monarchy, with ibn Saud as King of the Hijaz and Nejd and Dependencies, and with his son Feisal acting as his Viceroy in the Hijaz.

The conquest of the Hijaz marked the end of ibn Saud's status as a desert Amir in what amounted to a protectorate relationship with Great Britain. He became a fully sovereign monarch, exchanging diplomatic missions with most of the Powers. His relationship with Great Britain, regulated by the Treaty of Jidda (1927), remained close and friendly, but without any overtones of subordination to Great Britain and without any unilateral restrictions on his activities imposed by Great Britain.

Ibn Saud had a very powerful reason for conciliating the outside world over the matter of the Pilgrimage, and for ensuring that prospective pilgrims would not be frightened off by any displays of Wahhabi fanaticism. The revenues for the administration of the Hijaz were almost entirely derived from the profits made out of the Pilgrimage, and it was important to avoid any serious diminution of these revenues. When these revenues did become seriously affected, from 1929 onwards, as a result of the world slump, ibn Saud found himself in a difficult position. For he had not only to provide for the administration of the Hijaz but also to provide subventions for the Nejdi Ikhwan if they were to be deterred from their traditional habits of *ghazzu*, tolerance of which had now become incompatible with ibn Saud's sovereign status.

Some of the Ikhwan leaders were becoming increasingly restive at the restraints imposed on them, and at what they regarded as the impious toleration being shown by ibn Saud both to idolatrous Moslems and to infidel Christians. For, apart, from keeping Nejdis almost entirely away from the administration of the Hijaz, he was also employing an increasing number of Arab foreigners—Syrians, Lebanese and Iraqis principally—in the administration of Nejd itself. In addition he had begun to have contacts with western experts with a view to exploiting the natural resources and so increasing the revenues of the country. All this was gall and wormwood to the more fanatical and more ambitious of the Ikhwan.

Matters came to a head between ibn Saud and the Ikhwan during 1929–30. Some of the Ikhwan leaders began seducing the Nejdi tribes from their allegiance to ibn Saud and started to wage open rebellion against him. In a series of desert campaigns the rebels were crushed and their leaders killed or imprisoned. The Ikhwan colonies were razed to the ground and the Ikhwan movement proscribed. By the end of 1930 ibn Saud was supreme within his own dominions and no longer under the necessity of deferring to or compromising with the views of his fanatical followers who, having been instrumental in bringing him to power, had proved unable to understand the conditions necessary for retaining that power. The most immediate effect of the crushing of the Ikhwan was an improvement in ibn Saud's relations with the British. As we have seen, these relations had frequently been strained by Ikhwan-inspired raids into Iraq and Transjordan and Kuwait. During the Ikhwan rebellion the British had used their influence in these countries to prevent assistance being given to the rebellious Ikhwan, and ibn Saud's task in dealing with the rebels had been materially lightened by this British intervention.

By the time that the Ikhwan revolt had been crushed ibn Saud was in severe financial straits. His expenses were increasing. He now had to have a paid army and could no longer rely on the voluntary services of Wahhabi tribesmen. At the same time revenue from the annual Pilgrimage was decreasing. He had for some time been interested in the possibility of finding petroleum, and in the possibilities of developing other natural resources in his dominions. He was in touch with Karl Twitchell, an American engineer and Middle East representative of Charles Crane, an American millionaire philanthropist who was interested in the material development of Middle Eastern countries. Twitchell, on ibn Saud's behalf, had already started a rather unsuccessful gold mine near Jidda and had been prospecting for water all over Nejd. He had also been investigating the possibility of oil deposits in Nejd. As early as 1922 ibn Saud had awarded (to Major Frank Holmes) a concession, renewable yearly, to look for oil in al-Hasa. Nothing had come of this, but in 1933, as we have seen, a concession was awarded to Standard of California which, five years later, resulted in the first commercial production of oil in Saudi Arabia. During those five years of exploration considerable sums of money, in the form of rental payments, wages, etc., flowed into Saudi Arabia from the oil company. These sums, together with some revival of the Pilgrimage traffic, went far towards solving ibn Saud's immediate financial problems. More importantly the influx of American technicians, and the increasing employment of Nejdis by the oil company, went a long way towards breaking down the psychological and physical barriers which still existed between the Nejd and the outer world and did much to erode the Wahhabism whose martial force had already been broken as a result of the defeat of the Ikhwan rebellion. This Wahhabism was replaced by nothing better than an insensate covetousness, which destroyed the sincerity and tarnished the asceticism, without much affecting the outward fanaticism of the creed. But that is another story, which will be pursued later.

The effect of the oil discoveries in al-Hasa, whose potential contribution to the State revenues was far greater than that likely to be derived from the Pilgrimage, gradually swung the centre of gravity in Saudi Arabia away from the Red Sea in the west over to the Persian Gulf in the east, in much the same way as the industrial revolution in England had swung the country's centre of gravity away from the sheep-folds and wheat fields of the south towards the factories and coal mines of the north and midlands. But, before this happened, ibn Saud had taken one further step to increase and consolidate his position in the Arabian Peninsula and his influence in the Arab world. After ibn Saud had occupied the Hijaz he found himself heir to an endemic quarrel with the Imam of the Yeman over the little principality of Asir, situated between Hijaz and Yeman and ruled by the Idrisi family. In 1926 Asir, by agreement between ibn Saud and the Ruler, Sayyid Hasan al Idrisi, became a Saudi protectorate and was garrisoned by Saudi troops. This soon led to a quarrel between ibn Saud and Imam Yehia of the Yeman over the fertile Wadi Nejran, in the south of Asir and claimed by the Yeman. This quarrel led, in 1934, to a war between Saudi Arabia and the Yeman, in which Saudi forces advanced along the coast and captured Hodeida on the Red Sea, the principal port of the Yeman. A truce was arranged and peace negotiations opened in Taif. During the course of these negotiations a deputation arrived at Taif from other Moslem States pleading for peace and conciliation. Ibn Saud took the hint and made proposals for a peace based on 'Moslem friendship and Arab brotherhood'. His terms, which were accepted by the Imam, demarcated the frontier between Asir and the Yeman and left Yeman an independent State, both rulers declaring that their two people were part of one single Arab nation.

It may not be altogether fanciful to see in this Treaty the first stirrings of that Arab nationalism which, two years later, was to manifest itself over Palestine and which, ten years later, was to attain international importance through the medium of the Arab League. At all events, it enabled ibn Saud to present himself to the Arab world as a magnanimous victor paying tribute to the cause of Arab brotherhood. Two years later, in 1936, ibn Saud still further increased his reputation as a statesman and peacemaker in the Arab world by concluding the Treaty of Baghdad with Iraq, ruled over by his Sherifian rivals. In this Treaty the two parties, if not quite sincerely or quite effectively, put an end to the long-standing quarrel between Saudites and Hashemites and both parties expressed the wish to see every independent Arab State united together in Moslem friendship and Arab brotherhood. This conception of Arab brotherhood which was illustrated, *inter alia*, by the virtual cessation, since 1931, of frontier raids by the Saudis into Iraq and Transjordan, had only been made possible by the breaking up of the Ikhwan and by a tacit understanding that Wahhabism was not an article for export. This prohibition of proselytism, together with increasing prosperity due to oil revenues, really put an end to that Wahhabi revival which started with the capture of Riadh by ibn Saud at the beginning of the century. From about 1932 on, Wahhabism not only ceased to be of political importance outside the Nejd, but gradually ceased to be of very much practical importance in the Nejd itself. The increasing importance of ibn Saud in the Arab world and beyond it was due, not to any threat or promise posed by Wahhabism, but to the wise statesmanship of ibn Saud himself, which enabled him to exercise an influence, first in the Arab world and later in the world beyond, far in excess of his country's military, economic or cultural importance.

During the Palestine Arab rebellion of 1936–9 ibn Saud still further advanced his crescent reputation as an Arab statesman. Together with other Arab rulers he intervened to persuade the Palestine Arabs to call off their strike in the autumn of 1936 and later to persuade them to call off their boycott of the Peel Commission. In 1937 his advice helped to persuade the British Government to abandon the scheme of partition recommended by the Peel Commission and provisionally accepted by the British Government. And in 1938 his counsel was sought and listened to by the British Government in the framing of the policy which emerged in the 1939 White Paper and which was, ultimately, accepted by Arab opinion as a possible basis for the settlement of the Palestine question.

Ibn Saud's influence in the Fertile Crescent was not confined to Palestine. He was in close touch with the National Bloc in Syria, then alternately negotiating and struggling with the French for independence. His object was to sustain an anti-Sherifian party capable of defeating designs nourished by Abdullah for the creation of an independent Hashemite, Greater Syria, consisting of the Mandated States of Syria, Lebanon and Transjordan, which Abdullah would have liked to have seen elevated into a Kingdom with himself as King.

In Egypt too, after a period of coolness following on the annexation of the Hijaz, which resulted in a rupture of diplomatic relations for some years between the two countries, ibn Saud was making friends and influencing people. His grand design in all these matters was not so much Arab unity, as a balance of power in the Arab world which would prevent the rise of any powerful Hashemite combination in the Fertile Crescent. For he knew that such a combination would, by Arab tradition, be almost compelled to revenge itself on the man who had expelled Husain and Ali from the throne of the Hijaz.

It remained ibn Saud's fixed policy to keep on good terms with, while maintaining his entire independence of, the British. Over Palestine he was conciliatory with the British Government and his conciliatoriness probably achieved more for the Arab cause than the denunciations of others. When the Second World War broke out in the autumn of 1939 his reputation in the Arab world was such that his declared neutrality for his country, combined with a personal conviction, which he never tried to conceal, that Great Britain would win in the end, had a profound effect in the Arab world, where there existed, for the most part, a belief in, and a hope for, a German victory.

Among those who most strongly believed in, and most ardently hoped for, such a German victory were a group of soldier-politicians in Iraq known as the Golden Square. In order to trace the origin of this group it is necessary briefly to follow the course of Iraqi history from the time of the conclusion of the Treaty with Great Britain in 1922 to the outbreak of war in 1939.

Iraq started its national existence under manifold disadvantages. It was not, in the ordinary sense of the word, a nation. It was a region, the exact boundaries of which had been fixed, not on any ethnological, geographical or historical basis, but with reference to the exigencies of international politics. Its boundary with Persia was subject to dispute, with Nejd uncertain and with Turkey the result of an international arbitration which was bitterly resented by the Turks. There was no racial or religious unity to provide cement for the new State. The provinces of Baghdad and Basra were almost entirely Arab. But in the province of Mosul there was a large and turbulent Kurdish minority, a small Yezidi[9] minority, and a number of Armenian and Assyrian refugees from Turkey. Among the Arabs there was a large and powerful minority of Shia Moslems (mostly located in the middle Euphrates) who, influenced by their religious leaders in the holy cities of Nejaf and Kerbela, were only doubtfully loyal towards the Sunni Moslem dynasty. The dynasty itself, although Arab, was alien to Iraq, had no roots in the country, and had been elected under strong British pressure. King Feisal himself was regarded, with some reason, as a British puppet. The semi-nomad and semi-independent Shia tribes of the middle Euphrates were a potential menace to the authority of the central Government. The finances of the new State were precarious and were to remain so until oil revenues came to the rescue. Failing the strong and ruthless methods of a Reza Shah to establish and maintain the authority of the central Government—which methods were inhibited both by the presence of the British and by the character of the King—it was fairly obvious that the new régime would be a breeding ground for faction.

Even before the war the urban intelligentsia of Iraq had begun to attain political consciousness by way of the Arab nationalist movement, which affected Iraq only less than it affected Syria. During the war enthusiasm for Arab nationalism was sustained and fostered by the Arab Rebellion in the Hijaz. Many of Feisal's principal officers in the campaign and, subsequently, many of the members of the Arab Provisional Government in Damascus, were Iraqis. In consequence the Iraqi intelligentsia reacted in much the same way as their counterparts in Syria to the various and conflicting Allied commitments, promises and pledges affecting the Arab world, such as the Sykes-Picot Agreement, the Balfour Declaration and the Treaty of San Remo on the one hand, and the McMahon Pledge, the Fourteen Points and the Anglo-French Declaration of November

1918 on the other. The 1920 rebellion, although most of the trouble came from the tribes on the middle Euphrates, was certainly influenced by what was regarded in Iraq as a series of Allied betrayals of the Arab cause, culminating in the imposition of the Mandatory system at the Treaty of San Remo and the expulsion of Feisal from Damascus which closely followed it.

This political consciousness, and its successful assertion, dictated, according to the nationalist fashion of the time, that the régime set up under the Mandate must be a constitutional one. The British connexion made it almost inevitable that it should be a constitutional monarchy. The circumstances of the British connexion, and the unpopularity of the Mandate, made it inevitable that anti-British fervour should be an obligatory attitude for the constitutional opposition, and also made it inevitable that successive governments, within the limits imposed by the Mandatory relationship and by the assistance which they needed from Great Britain, should vie with the opposition in this anti-British fervour as being the only alternative to dictatorship as a means of keeping themselves in office.

The disguise of the Mandatory relationship provided by the 1925 Treaty was by no means satisfactory to Iraqi nationalist opinion, which only acquiesced in the Treaty because of the necessity of obtaining British support, first for the acquisition of Mosul and then for the admission of Iraq to the League of Nations and for its consequent release from Mandatory status. Patriotic competition between successive governments and successive oppositions, concentrated as it was on obtaining relief as soon as possible from the Mandatory status, led to the conclusion, in 1930, of a Treaty between Great Britain and Iraq which superseded the 1922 Treaty, which provided for the limitation of the British garrisons in Iraq to two R.A.F. bases (Habbaniya near Baghdad and Shaiba near Basra) and for a drastic reduction in British personnel in the Administration, and by which the British Government undertook to use their best efforts to secure Iraqi admission to the League of Nations within two years. This Treaty conferred the near prospect of sovereign independence on Iraq, limited only by a commitment to provide for the presence of British R.A.F. bases and by an obligation to give preference to British nationals when employing foreigners in Government service. But 'anti-imperialism' had by that time become a recognized badge of opposition and the new Treaty did little or nothing to abate the steady pressure exerted on successive Governments to achieve complete independence, i.e. the complete abrogation of any Treaty relationship with Great Britain.

A significant development over the previous ten years had been a steady increase in the influence and popularity gained by the Iraqi Army. In the early days of the Mandate successive Iraqi Governments had had to rely heavily on the British both for the protection of their frontiers and for the maintenance of internal order. A desire to escape from what was regarded as a humiliating dependence resulted in the allocation of a large share of the exiguous Budget to the building up of an Army. By 1932 external threats to Iraq had (largely as a result of British influence) disappeared, and the Iraqi Army was sufficiently strong to maintain internal order well enough to provide for the continual enhancement of its prestige. Soon after the admission of Iraq to the League of Nations in 1932, there was trouble with the Assyrian refugees, who were regarded by the Iraqis as British protégés and who were, justifiably, apprehensive about their future prospects in Iraq under an independent régime. This trouble was magnified by the Army into a serious threat to the Iraqi State and an Army-inspired massacre of Assyrians ensued. This grisly event, so far from diminishing, greatly increased the prestige enjoyed by the Army, whose leaders represented themselves as saviours of the State and the safeguarders of its independence. Soon afterwards, in August 1933, King Feisal died suddenly while on a visit to Europe, and was succeeded by his son Ghazi, a boy of 21. Feisal's death removed almost the last element of stability from the newly independent State. Although Feisal had not been a strong man, nor a particularly clever one, he had managed, by his popularity and by his diplomacy, to keep the war of factions and the disloyalty of minorities within constitutional bounds and to confine the manifestations of anti-British feeling within the requirements of Iraq's Treaty obligations. Under the new King, who was young and inexperienced and who moreover proved to have no interest in the responsibilities and no instinct for the intricacies of his office, this precarious stability came to an end and, for the next eight years, the history of Iraq was to be a turbulent one. The most immediate result of Feisal's death was a renewed rebellion among the Shia tribes on the middle Euphrates and among the Kurdish tribes in the province of Mosul. The measures necessary to put down these rebellions placed more and more power into the hands of the Army and, in October 1936, an Army General —Bekr Sidqi—executed a *coup d'état* which placed his nominee, Hikmat Suleiman, in office as Prime Minister, with himself as C.-in-C. and the real power in the land. But the Army itself was rent with faction and, after nine months of power, Bekr Sidqi was murdered and the régime he had inaugurated overthrown. From that time on domestic politics in Iraq began to resolve themselves into two increasingly definite and opposing forces. On the one side were the 'pro-Treaty' politicians, who accepted the British connexion, never with enthusiasm but with varying degrees of resignation, who supported the reigning dynasty and the existing social order generally and who, increasingly, identified themselves with the dawning concept of Arab unity, which they saw as a Hashemite-dominated confederation of the Arab lands of the Fertile Crescent. As the dominant personality in this group there gradually emerged the figure of Nuri Pasha as Said. Nuri Pasha was an ex-General, who had been, first Chief of Staff and later C.-in-C. of the Iraqi Army. He had been a member of several Cabinets since 1932 and Prime Minister of two. In December 1938, sixteen months after Bekr Sidqi's fall, he again became Prime Minister, after a long period out of office which he had used in becoming known throughout the Arab world as a foremost champion of the Arab cause in Palestine as a result of efforts (which were already beginning to bear fruit) to persuade the British Government that continued Arab co-operation with the British in the Middle East was dependent on some satisfaction being given to Palestine Arab claims on Great Britain. On the other side were the 'nationalist' politicians, who repudiated the British connexion (and in consequence, in the light of the European situation at the time, cultivated the friendship of Germany and Italy). This group enjoyed powerful support in the Army, and in particular from a group led by four senior officers—three divisional commanders and the head of the Iraqi Air Force—which became known as the Golden Square. They showed little interest in Arab unity and concentrated rather on a narrow Iraqi nationalism, expressed largely in the form of organized Youth Movements after the fashion set in Italy and Germany. Their opposition to the big landlordism characteristic of the 'pro-Treaty' group earned them the support of progressives and liberals. In a political milieu in which nationalism was a condition of political and even of physical survival, the pro-Treaty group represented the right wing, as the anti-Treaty group represented the left wing of the Iraqi nationalist movement. The right wing was prepared to collaborate with the British as a matter of expediency; the left wing felt itself compelled to oppose the British connexion as a matter of principle.

Nuri Pasha succeeded to the Premiership in December 1938 after his predecessor, Jamil Madfai, had resigned as a result of Army pressure exercised by members of the Golden Square. He was already beginning to emerge as Iraq's strong man. Four months later, in April 1939, King Ghazi was killed in a motor accident. His son, who became King as Feisal II, was a baby and the Amir Abdulillah, a grandson of Husain, Sherif of Makka, a cousin of the late King, and a brother of the Queen Mother, became Regent. The alliance between the Regent, who lent the weight of his influence to the side of the 'pro-Treaty' group, and Nuri as Said was to be a permanent feature of Iraqi politics for the next twenty years, until both men, together with their King, were to be butchered in a revolutionary night of long knives instigated by a rebellious General of the Iraqi Army who had inherited the tradition formed by Bekr Sidqi in 1936.

During all these years of endemic political turmoil and tribal revolt, accompanied by chronic financial stringency, it would have been unreasonable to expect anything very remarkable in the way of social, economic or administrative advance. Nevertheless, something was done, mostly under the impulse of the British officials, who had governed the country until 1921, and who provided nearly every Ministry with Advisers until 1930 after which the British element in the Administration was steadily cut down. Reasonably efficient administrative arrangements had been established in the principal cities and towns. A start had been made towards the reconstitution of the irrigation system which had remained derelict since it had been destroyed, some seven hundred years previously, during the Mongol invasions. A railway was constructed between Baghdad and Basra which had, by 1939, been extended northwards to Tel Kotchek on the Syrian frontier, to link up with the line to Istanbul, thus realizing the old dream of the Berlin–Baghdad Railway in an epoch when railways had lost much of their commercial and strategic importance. By 1939 oil royalties were already forming a large and increasing part of the Government's revenue and it was already clear that Iraq's future prospects of material progress were largely dependent on the development and wise use of future revenues from oil. (The fact that the realization of these revenues still at that time wholly depended on being able to export the oil by pipeline across Syria to the Mediterranean was of considerable importance in the formation of Iraq's Arab unity policy.) Socially, the basic and related problems of land reform and the dispossession of the great tribal sheikhs had hardly been touched and the discontents arising from the prevalence of absentee and irresponsible landlordism combined with endemic political faction in the towns to make permanent a state of affairs in which the only ultimate alternatives to a reform which was inhibited by the obstruction of vested interests, were repression and revolution.

During the period between the two world wars the Arab Sheikhdoms of the Persian Gulf had been shielded by their status as British allies or British Protectorates from the effects of the political developments proceeding all around them. As we have seen, the prospect of the discovery of oil on the islands of Bahrain had caused Reza Shah to assert a claim to Persian sovereignty over the archipelago. British protection prevented this claim from being effectively pursued and the Sheikh of Bahrain, with the assistance of increasing oil revenues and the counsel of a British Adviser[10] was able, during the thirties, to make of his tiny State something of an oasis of relative prosperity in the desert-ringed and poverty-stricken lands of the Middle East. His methods, and those of his British Adviser, if more enlightened, were not less autocratic than those of his sheikhly neighbours, but education was not yet sufficiently extended, nor was the appeal of Arab nationalism yet sufficiently clamant, to cause this autocracy, sweetened as it was by relative prosperity, to be actively resented.

The Sheikhdom of Kuwait, ruled over from 1921 to 1950 by Sheikh Ahmed as Subah, also owed its continued independent

119

existence to British protection. Much of the hinterland of the port of Kuwait, which was traditionally part of the Sheikhdom, had been lost to Nejd as a result of the British-sponsored frontier settlement at Uqair in 1922. But the territory left to the Sheikhdom was at least secured from Nejdi aggression by a British guarantee. In 1929–30 the Ikhwan revolt again brought trouble to Kuwait's desert borders and it was necessary for the Sheikh, with British assistance, to defend his frontiers against Ikhwan incursions in order to avoid the risk of subsequent intervention in his territories by the redoubtable ibn Saud. Later in the thirties, there was threatened trouble from Iraq, which had a shadowy claim to Kuwait based on the previous inclusion of the Sheikhdom in the Vilayet of Basra. But here again British protection, as well as British influence with the Iraqi Government, served Kuwait in good stead and the threat never materialized. It was clear, if the oil which was already being sought in Kuwait were found in large quantities, that the Sheikh would have to rely heavily on British protection to save his territory from the avarice of his two powerful neighbours. By the time of the outbreak of the Second World War there had been no commercial development of the oil deposits now known to exist in Kuwait which, unlike Bahrain, had no important alternative economic resources. And so, up to that time, life for the 200,000 odd inhabitants of Kuwait remained much as it had been for the previous hundred years, under the personal, although mainly benevolent (by Arab standards) autocracy of an hereditary Ruler who as yet had not needed either to temper this autocracy by consultation or reinforce its extraordinary measures of coercion in response to the liberal and Arab nationalist Zeitgeist which was already breaking up the old order in other and more sophisticated Arab lands. Poverty and the British-imposed protective cordon combined to keep things much as they had been for so long, thus delighting the European traditionalist as much as it scandalized the European progressive.

Similarly, the Qatar Peninsula, whose Ruler had accepted British protection in 1916, was secured by that protection from Nejdi incursions, although the Wahhabi faith of the ruling house and of most of the inhabitants, together with the traditional Qatari hostility towards Bahrain, caused ibn Saud to be regarded rather as an additional protector than as a potential conqueror. In Qatar, poverty and religious obscurantism combined to preserve a state of affairs more primitive even than that prevailing in Kuwait or in the relatively prosperous Bahrain. The ruling family of al Thani had neither the education and relative sophistication nor the comparative material wealth enjoyed by the Rulers of Bahrain and Kuwait and still lived much as tribal Sheikhs, in tents rather than in palaces, eating much the same food and having much the same habits as the humblest among their free subjects. The entire population of Qatar did not amount to more than about 30,000 people, of whom many were domestic slaves. Some of these were employed by their masters in the now declining industry of pearl fishing. For the pearl fisheries of Qatar, although very much less lucrative and important than those of Bahrain, were, until the advent of oil, the most important and indeed almost the only source of wealth in Qatar.

The Trucial Sheikhdoms were in much the same state of economic and social backwardness, and enjoyed the same measure of British protection, as the Sheikhdom of Qatar. Strife between the various Sheikhdoms was continuous, arising from frontier disputes, grazing rights, blood feuds and family quarrels. In 1932, and for some years thereafter, the Sheikhdom of Sharja assumed some importance in the system of British imperial communications as the result of an agreement arrived at between the Sheikh of Sharja and the British Government providing for the use of Sharja as a staging post for the British Imperial Airways (later B.O.A.C.) far eastern route between Basra and Karachi.[11] Most of the Trucial Sheikhdoms also, during the thirties, signed oil agreements with the I.P.C. providing for the exploration of their territories for oil against small annual rental payments which served to mitigate their perennial poverty.

The Sultan of Musqat and Oman, Taimur bin Feisal, abdicated in 1932 and was succeeded by his son, Said bin Taimur, then aged 22, who is still (1961) on the throne. The Sultanate, which is not a British Protectorate, but a sovereign State in alliance with Great Britain, was, in its trading relationships, in its general orientation, and even in its geographical position, much more closely connected with India than it was with the Persian Gulf territories. The now undisputed British naval and political supremacy in the Persian Gulf and Indian Ocean had robbed Musqat of the strategic importance it had once possessed as commanding the entrance to the Persian Gulf. The time was soon to come when the Sultanate would be sucked back into the politics of the Arab world by rumours of oil deposits and by renewed disputes with the Imams of Oman, arising out of these rumours, over the control of the interior of Oman. Relationships between the Sultan of Musqat and the tribes of the interior of Oman had, as we have seen, been an endemic source of trouble ever since Musqat had become independent of the Imamate of Oman in 1793. These tribes, who belonged to the Ibadhi sect of Islam, acknowledged a combined spiritual and temporal allegiance to an elected Imam. They never acknowledged the authority claimed by the Sultans of Musqat over the whole of Oman and, in 1913, under a newly-elected Imam, rebelled against him. The Imam was murdered in 1920 and the Sultan of Musqat, in that year, signed an Agreement, known as the Treaty of Sib, with his successor, Abdullah bin Mohammed al Khalili. By the terms of this Treaty the Imam bound himself to restrain the tribes from invading the coastal regions in return for an undertaking by the Sultan not to interfere in the internal affairs of the Imamate. The Treaty also provided for peaceful access by the tribesmen to the coastal areas and appears to have involved the acknowledgment by the Imam of the Sultan's suzerainty over the whole of Oman.[12] This suzerainty was, as we shall see, repudiated on Imam Khalili's death in 1954 by his successor Imam Ghalib bin Ali al-Hinawi.

CHAPTER SEVEN

The Second World War

THE DEPTHS TO which Great Britain's reputation in Europe had descended by the time of the outbreak of the Second World War, and the pact between Germany and Russia which immediately preceded it, were hardly reflected at all in the surface appearance of British power in the Persian Gulf. Here the British position seemed unaffected either by events in Europe, or by the Indian nationalist threat (reinforced by the potential menace of Japan) to the British position, or by lowered British prestige in the Arab world, where the concessions made to the Arabs over Palestine in the 1939 White Paper were more than offset by a general belief in the inevitability of a German victory. In the Persian Gulf, Great Britain was still a commanding presence and Germany, Italy, Japan and even Russia seemed almost infinitely remote. Among the Arab Sheikhdoms this British presence, together with ibn Saud's openly expressed confidence in a British victory, carried more weight than the doubts and dislikes covertly expressed in more sophisticated Arab quarters. In Iran, German sympathies were strong but German might was too remote to do more than confirm Reza Shah in a policy of neutrality which, at that time, there seemed no reason for any of the belligerents to violate. Even in Iraq, where pro-German and anti-British activity were seething beneath the surface, the pro-Treaty combination of Nuri as Said as Prime Minister and Abdulillah as Regent was, for the time being, precariously in control of the situation. Germany's pact with Russia seemed to have concentrated the war in Western Europe.

The collapse of France and Mussolini's irrevocable act of commitment to what he was now convinced was the winning side brought the war into the Middle East and a little nearer to the Persian Gulf. But the Battle of Britain, Wavell's victories over the Italians in the Western Desert, Turkey's determined neutrality, and the assistance coming from India for the British cause, all combined to convince the rulers in the Persian Gulf of Great Britain's undiminished power of survival. Germany was still very far away, Italy was not to be taken seriously, and Russia, in spite of her pact with Germany, was too anxious about her western frontier to be willing to risk adventures further east. But, in the spring of 1941, the German invasion, first of Crete and then of Greece, the first British reverses in the Western Desert (caused by the diversion of British forces from the desert to the defence of Greece) and the (much exaggerated) rumours of German-Italian penetration into Vichy Syria, brought the war, for the first time, right into the Persian Gulf.

In Iraq the Nuri as Said Government had resigned, on a domestic issue, in March 1940. Nuri was replaced as Prime Minister by Rashid Ali Qailani, who soon fell under the (by now) openly Germanophile influence of the Golden Square faction of the Iraqi Army. The British, out of deference to Iraqi nationalist opinion, in view of the apparent remoteness of Iraq from the war, and because of pressing military commitments elsewhere, had no troops in Iraq other than the peacetime R.A.F. garrisons at Habbaniya and Shaiba authorized under the 1930 Treaty. They could therefore only exercise a moral influence over the course of events. The strength of this moral influence waned with the tale of Axis successes. By the beginning of 1941 the Iraqi Army, now dominated by the Golden Square, were in control of the situation. In February 1941, during the course of a desperate attempt by the Regent to regain control, Rashid Ali Qailani resigned and was replaced for a few weeks as Prime Minister by Taha al Hashemi, but on 1 April there was a military coup which reinstated Rashid Ali Qailani in office, this time avowedly as a nominee of the Golden Square. The Regent, Nuri as-Said, and other prominent pro-Treaty politicians fled the country, and a State of Emergency was proclaimed.

The Golden Square Generals were now the effective rulers of the country, with Rashid Ali as nominal Prime Minister. The new Government, which was in close communication with Dr. Grobba, the German Minister in Tehran (Iraq, in accordance with the 1930 Treaty, had broken off diplomatic relations with Germany in September 1939) apparently imagined either that they would receive effective German assistance (there was a widespread impression at the time, not confined to Iraq, that the German descent on Crete was the first move in a well-planned scheme for a lightning German drive through Turkey into the Fertile Crescent) or that British preoccupations elsewhere would prevent any effective British reaction to hostile moves in Iraq. The Golden Square may also have been misled by the ex-Mufti of Jerusalem, who was in Baghdad at the time and a powerful influence in their councils, into believing that sufficiently decisive anti-British action in Iraq would ignite a whole series of Arab rebellions against the British throughout the Middle East. In the event the Iraqi Government stood isolated. No German help was forthcoming; Saudi Arabia and Turkey showed their disapproval; there was no response from the rest of the Arab world. And the British, contrary to expectation, and despite their heavy commitments elsewhere, reacted strongly. In the middle of April the 10th Indian Division was despatched from Karachi to Basra, landed at Basra towards the end of the month and, despite the attempted insistence of the Iraqi Government that they should merely move in transit across Iraq *en route* for Transjordan (the polite fiction that they were in transit had been the original reason given by the British for their landing, since such an operation would have been in accordance with the terms of the Treaty), proceeded to occupy Basra Port and strategic positions around Basra. The Iraqis replied by investing Habbaniya, to which cantonment British wives and children had been evacuated from Baghdad. The British thereupon despatched a column of troops (including a battalion of the Transjordan Arab Legion) from Palestine to the relief of Habbaniya. A state of undeclared war existed between Great Britain and Iraq. There is little doubt that a determined Iraqi Government, backed by a loyal and united Army and an enthusiastic populace, could successfully have defied and defeated the exiguous forces and still more exiguous equipment which were all that the British at that time were able to put into the field against their rebellious vassal. But, in faction-torn Iraq, there was no real unity, no stomach for a fight and no real enthusiasm for the turbulent politician-Generals who had elbowed their way into power. As was to happen so often in the history of Arab nationalism, brave words, unaccompanied by doughty deeds, fell upon the deaf ears of those who were cynically prepared to give two cheers for the winner (whoever he was) as soon as they were certain that he had won. Before the end of May the thirty-day war was over. The Regent was back in Baghdad; a pro-Treaty Government with Jamil al Madfai as Prime Minister was in power; the country was garrisoned by British troops. Rashid Ali, the four Golden Square Generals, and the ex-Mufti of Jerusalem had all fled. And the British, reinstated in Iraq, were proceeding, with their Free French Allies, to the invasion of Vichy Syria.

While the invasion of Syria was proceeding Hitler embarked on the invasion of Russia. It soon became apparent that a Russian collapse would lay the whole Middle East open to a German invasion through the Caucasus. It was vital, from the British point of view, to sustain the Russian Armies by all possible means. The opening of a 'second front' in Western Europe was wildly impracticable; German troops could be and were diverted from the Russian front by offensives in the Western Desert, by commando raids on the European mainland, and by the encouragement of resistance movements in the German-occupied countries of Europe. But what the Russians needed above all were munitions of war. Access to Russia via the Dardanelles and Black Sea was barred by Turkish neutrality and the certainty of effective German reprisals. The Arctic passage to Archangel was hampered both by the weather and by German submarines and surface craft. There remained the possibility of opening a supply route through Iran. Access to this supply route was ensured by British command of the sea and by British control of the Persian Gulf. The use of it would be facilitated by the Trans-Iranian Railway which had just been completed by Reza Shah before the outbreak of war. Such Iranian resistance as might be offered to the violation of her neutrality (in the event of her not accepting to be seduced) could easily be countered by Russian troops from the north and by the British-Indian troops who were still in Iraq after dealing with the Golden Square incident.

Pro-German sympathies in Iran, built up as a result of the rapidly expanding pre-war trade between Germany and Iran, were naturally and ingeniously exploited by German diplomacy, and proved sufficient to preclude any possibility of willing

Iranian acquiescence in the use of their country as a channel for British assistance to Russia against Germany. Consequently, on 25 August 1941, the British and Soviet Ministers in Tehran presented similar Notes to the Iranian Government in which, after expressing regret at Iran's refusal to abandon what the British and Russians regarded as their pro-German neutrality, and after repeating the assurances, usual on these occasions, about respect for Iran's independence and territorial integrity, they announced the intention of British and Russian armed forces jointly to occupy Iran for the purpose of establishing and maintaining a supply route from the Persian Gulf to the Russian frontier. The hope was expressed that Iranian troops would not resist the occupation. Simultaneously with the presentation of these Notes, British and Russian forces entered Iran, joining hands at Qazvin, some 100 miles west of Tehran. Iranian opposition was negligible. Within a few days a new Iranian Government accepted the *fait accompli* and ordered all resistance to cease.

On 30 August the British and Russians presented further Notes to the Iranian Government defining their respective areas of military occupation, demanding the expulsion of all enemy nationals from Iran (this demand was substituted after a few days by a demand for the surrender of all enemy nationals to the British or Russians), and stipulating the provision of all necessary assistance in the movement of troops and the transport of supplies. At the same time the British undertook to continue the payment to Iran of oil royalties in accordance with the 1933 Agreement with A.I.O.C. and promised to evacuate their troops from Iran as soon as the military situation permitted. The Russians gave similar undertakings about the evacuation of troops and the maintenance of existing agreements about fishing rights in the Caspian. These Notes were accepted by the Iranian Government after a little bargaining about the respective zones of military occupation (which left Tehran, and most of the centre of the country, outside these zones).

The principal domestic effect of the Anglo-Russian occupation was to bring to the surface all the underground opposition to Reza Shah which had been accumulating as a result of his increasingly autocratic rule. This opposition, which was now voiced by some of the most reactionary elements in the country, including particularly the big landowners, the tribal leaders and the Mullahs, was, for some extraordinary reason, encouraged by the British as well as by the Russians. It was this factor, rather than the humiliation of his country and the ruin of his neutralist policy, which brought about Reza Shah's abdication on 16 September. He had held effective power in Iran for twenty-one years and had reigned for seventeen. Although increasingly capricious, cruel and autocratic in his later years, he had in earlier years saved Iran from actual chaos and preserved her from probable dissolution. He had cleared the country of foreign invaders and occupiers. He had re-established the authority of the central government over rebellious tribesmen and feudal khans. He had broken the obscurantist influence of the Mullahs. He had improved communications (ironically his Trans-Iranian Railway had contributed to his undoing by enhancing Iran's eligibility as a supply corridor). He had started industry, he had encouraged education, and he had, to some extent, raised the standard of administration from its previous corrupt and chaotic level. He had done all this without recourse to foreign aid. The resentment which he caused was due more to the privileges he had curtailed than to the liberties he had restricted. His army, effective enough for the restoration and preservation of internal security would have been no match for the British and Russian invaders even had its loyalty to him been less qualified than it was.

Reza Shah was succeeded by his son, Mohamed Reza, a boy of twenty-one. The circumstances of his accession would have made it impossible for him to continue his father's dictatorial régime even had he the wish and character to do so. Reza Shah's dictatorship had preserved the façade of the Constitution and, after his fall, the country reverted to that pseudo-democracy which, in so many Middle Eastern countries, provided the rickety framework for a faction-torn, foreign-dominated, administratively incompetent, and usually precarious régime. In the case of Persia, the external defence safeguarded, the economic assistance provided and the ultimate power exercised by the Allies, alleviated the rigours, while increasing the irresponsibility, of this pseudo-democratic régime.

In January 1942 the position of the British and Russians in Iran, which rested on right of conquest and the *diktat* of

September 1941, was regularized by the conclusion of a Tripartite Treaty between Great Britain, Russia and Iran. In this Treaty Great Britain and Russia pledged themselves to 'respect the territorial integrity, sovereignty and political independence of Iran', promised to withdraw their forces from Iranian territory 'not later than six months after all hostilities between the Allied Powers and Germany and her associates have been suspended', and to 'safeguard the economic existence of the Iranian people against the privations and difficulties arising as a result of the present war'. In return Iran undertook to co-operate with the Allies in the provision of all facilities necessary for the Allied war effort, including the recruitment of labour, the requisition of transport and buildings, and the establishment of a censorship, on the understanding that Iranian military assistance was to be 'limited to the maintenance of internal security on Iranian territory'.

By this time the United States had come into the war on the side of the Allies as a result of the Japanese attack on Pearl Harbour, and it was not long before American military establishments appeared in Iran, supplementing and, in the end, almost taking over, the British supply route. This was the beginning of America's supercession of Great Britain as the predominant foreign Power in the Gulf. When the trial of strength with Russia came in Iran, two years after the war, it was a trial not between Russia and Great Britain, but between Russia and the United States. On the other side of the Gulf, as we shall see, simultaneously with the arrival of U.S. military establishments in Iran, the Americans, jealous of British influence with ibn Saud, and apprehensive lest this influence might lead to an alienation of American oil concessions in Saudi Arabia, were taking over and increasing the wartime subsidy which the British were paying to ibn Saud, and were actively developing the oil production in the area of the American concessions.

At the beginning of 1942, however, consideration of the post-war balance of power in the Gulf was overshadowed by the immediate realities of the war, which was going disastrously for the Allies. In Africa a British offensive in the Western Desert had failed, and the British army had started on that long retreat through Libya which was to end at Alamein. In Europe the German armies were nearing the Caucasus. In Asia the Japanese, moving with startling rapidity, had overrun Burma, Malaya, Singapore and the Dutch East Indies and were already threatening the frontiers of British India.

By the end of 1942 the tide of war had turned. The Germans had been defeated at Stalingrad and Alamein. The Americans were holding the Japanese in the Pacific. The industrial centres of Germany were being devastated by aerial bombardment. Italy, with more of her army in prison camps than on the battlefield, was almost out of the fight. Anglo-American forces had landed in North Africa. The Ride of the Valkyries was over and Götterdämmerung had begun.

The Persian Gulf was no longer an actual or potential theatre of war. The immediate urgency of transporting munitions across Iran had lessened sufficiently to enable Iranians, Americans, British and Russians to take stock of future political ambitions and realities. Many of these realities were abundantly apparent. The Allies were going to win. Therefore the temporary occupation had to be accepted with resignation. The wartime alliance between Great Britain, the United States and Russia would be succeeded by a post-war rivalry, possibly resulting in another war, with the United States and Great Britain on one side and Russia on the other. This rivalry would, in all probability, be manifested in a struggle for power throughout Eastern and Central Europe and the Middle East. Therefore each side would require allies and supporters in those areas which were likely to be contested spheres of influence. The British role in the Middle East, as elsewhere, was likely to become more and more subordinated to the American role. Under the impact of these realities political opinion in Iran and in the rest of the Middle East became divided into three broad groups—the pro-western, the neutralist and the pro-Russian. These varying attitudes depended only to a very small degree on ideological conviction or personal sympathy; they were almost entirely a function of the degree of pressure and/or assistance to be apprehended or expected from the rival Great Power groups. As far as Iran was concerned, Russia was in a better position to exert pressure, U.S.A. in a better position to provide assistance. This factor determined the very different methods adopted by the Russian occupiers on the one hand and the Anglo-American occupiers on the other during the last three years of the occupation. The

Russians endeavoured to impress by their power, the Anglo-Americans by their generosity.

It was in this local atmosphere of mutual rivalry, thinly over-laid by the residue of a still only half-achieved common purpose, that the 'Summit' Allied Conference was held in Tehran in November 1943. It was typical of the relationship subsisting between the Allies and Iran under the occupation that Tehran was chosen as the site for the Conference without any consultation with the Iranian Government, that all security arrangements were made without reference to the Iranian Government, and that the Iranian Government was not represented at the Conference. Although the Tehran Conference was of course mainly concerned with the broader aspects of the war, the Declaration on Iran, made at the Conference, and signed by Stalin, Roosevelt and Churchill, recognized the assistance given by Iran to the Allied war effort, promised continued economic aid to Iran, reaffirmed Iran's independence, and reiterated Allied adherence to the principles of the Atlantic Charter.

Before examining the development and American-assisted defeat of Russia's post-war threat to the independence and territorial integrity of Iran, we must turn to the other side of the Gulf and trace the effects of war on the eastern half of the Arabian Peninsula.

In Saudi Arabia the immediate effect of the war was a virtual cessation of the income from the pilgrim traffic and a halt in the expected steady increase in oil royalties due to a war-imposed halt in C.A.S.O.C's plans for expansion. This, combined with the increased cost of essential imports as a result of wartime shortages, brought financial crisis to ibn Saud's kingdom. This crisis was met partly by subsidies from the British Government, partly by advances on future royalties by C.A.S.O.C. But C.A.S.O.C's willingness to make such advances was limited by commercial considerations and, until the United States entered the war towards the end of 1941, ibn Saud had to rely heavily on British subsidies and on British arrangements for shipping essential supplies. In return, ibn Saud, while remaining officially neutral, lent the weight of his influence in the Arab world towards support for and confidence in Great Britain, to such an extent that, by the middle of 1941, C.A.S.O.C. was expressing great anxiety to the U.S. Government lest British ambitions and ibn Saud's needs might reduce Saudi Arabia to the status of a British protectorate and so bring the American oil concessions under British control. At that time the United States Government could not see their way to extending Lease-Lend or any other form of financial aid to Saudi Arabia as a means of preventing it from falling under British influence, and all that was done was to ask the British Government to devote a proportion of the Lease-Lend which the British were receiving from the United States to the needs of Saudi Arabia. As a result, British aid to ibn Saud, which had amounted to about £100,000 during 1940, rose to over £1 million in 1941 and to about £3 million during 1942. By the end of 1942 the scale of British assistance was such that, in order to control the use made of that assistance, there were British plans afoot to establish a central Bank in Saudi Arabia and to bring Saudi Arabia into the Sterling Area. The Americans who, in their Middle Eastern war activities, were always acutely alive to post-war commercial prospects, and who, moreover, were passing through a temporary phase of alarm about the depletion of their indigenous oil resources, now became thoroughly alarmed lest the British, with the use of American money, should, under cover of war, retrieve, at American expense, that monopoly of Middle East oil resources which the Americans had breached during the inter-war years by exploitation both of the Open Door principle and of British commercial timidity.

In February 1943, as a result of almost frantic representations from American oil interests, who had the support of Secretary Ickes, the Petroleum Administrator in the Roosevelt Cabinet, President Roosevelt officially declared that the defence of Saudi Arabia was vital to the defence of the United States and so enabled Lease-Lend funds to be remitted direct from the United States Treasury to Saudi Arabia. This decision marks the end of predominant British and the beginning of predominant American influence in Saudi Arabia. After defeating an attempt by Secretary Ickes to purchase, on behalf of the United States Government, the C.A.S.O.C. concession, for the preservation of which American public money was being spent, the two shareholders in C.A.S.O.C.—Standard of California and Texas—proceeded, with the encouragement and under the protection of the United States Government, to consolidate their position in

Saudi Arabia by expanding their production, thus at the same
time pleasing ibn Saud by an increase in his oil royalties and
building up an advantageous post-war commercial advantage
vis-à-vis British-managed (although partly U.S.-owned) oil
interests in Iraq, Kuwait and Qatar, where expansion was
hindered by lack of equipment.

By the end of the war the United States, as a result of Lease-
Lend aid and of the expanding operations of the American-
Arabian Oil Company (Aramco, the new name for C.A.S.O.C.)
had become firmly established in Saudi Arabia to the virtual
exclusion of the British.[1] To such an extent was this so that
ibn Saud was unable, either then or later, to make any effective protest against American pro-Zionist policy over Palestine,
unprepared as he was to jeopardize his new-found source
of wealth for the sake of any remaining aspirations towards
Arab leadership. As a result of this somewhat unheroic choice
ibn Saud was never able to exercise any very profound influence
on the fortunes of the Arab League, which was formed in
May 1945 and which had, as its primary objective, the defence
of Arab interests in Palestine.

The war had very little effect on the Arab Sheikhdoms of the
Persian Gulf, apart from affecting them with economic shortages and stringencies which were not greatly noticeable in communities which still had a very low standard of living. Shiekhly
autocracy and British protection still insulated them from
the political aspirations and ambitions of Arab nationalism. In Bahrain, oil production was maintained at about its pre-
war level and the oil refinery, fed with crude oil from the Saudi
Arabian fields, continued to expand. As a result Bahrain continued to enjoy a relative prosperity compared with the other
Sheikhdoms. This relative prosperity had the natural result of
encouraging the rise of a politically conscious middle class which
was, before long, to voice its resentment, not so much at British
protection, as at the autocratic rule of the Sheikh of Bahrain
which had, since 1925, been exercised largely through the
medium of his British Adviser and virtual Prime Minister,
Mr. C. D. Belgrave. But, although the Sheikh's rule was no less
autocratic than that of the Rulers of the other Sheikhdoms, it
was, partly owing to Belgrave, and partly as a result of superior
financial resources, a great deal more benevolent. The standard

of living, and the standards of social services in Bahrain, although derisory by western standards, compared favourably with conditions even in relatively advanced Arab States and was immeasurably superior to anything to be seen in the other Persian Gulf Sheikhdoms. But, as has happened elsewhere, these relatively enlightened social conditions hastened the onset of resentment at continued political servitude. And in Bahrain, as elsewhere, certain embarrassments for the British began to become apparent. In a British colony, the Colonial Government, generally speaking, devoted itself not only to securing reasonable standards of equity and justice between ruler and ruled and between man and man, but also to the gradual evolution of self-governing institutions. But in a Protectorate, such as Bahrain, which provided for certain reciprocal obligations between the British Government and the Ruler, the British Government were specifically debarred from any interference in the internal affairs of the Protectorate. The object of the Protectorate, in return for certain obligations assumed by the Ruler towards the Protecting Power, was to safeguard the position of the Ruler, specifically against foreign invasion but also, in practice, against domestic discontents. In Bahrain the British were, in effect, underwriting and lending their countenance to a domestic tyranny which, although sufficiently enlightened and sufficiently efficient to avoid serious scandal, was, perhaps because of that relative enlightenment and efficiency, increasingly resented. And the British, instead of being able, as they would have been in a colony, to open the safety-valve by making some concessions in the direction of self-government, were compelled to accommodate the Ruler by assisting him to sit on it. But, for the time being, all was well, and a visitor to Bahrain might well have been excused for regarding it as something like a paradise amid the almost universal squalor of the Arab world.

In Kuwait, where Sheikh Ahmed as Subah had been Ruler since 1921, oil had already been found by the Kuwait Oil Company before the war and, by 1942, nine producing wells had been drilled. But wartime shortages of steel prevented the development of exports, the British preferring to concentrate on the already developed Iranian oilfields and refinery, and in July 1942 all oil operations in Kuwait were suspended and the wells shut in. This action, particularly when contrasted with the intensified American development of the Saudi Arabian oil-fields during the latter years of the war, naturally caused some local resentment and had the effect (probably intended by the Americans) of underlining the rise of American and the decline of British influence in the Persian Gulf. Sheikh Ahmed, during the course of his long reign, had sustained a number of disappointments from the British connexion. At Uqair, in 1922, he considered, with some reason, that British influence had robbed him of a great deal of territory traditionally belonging to Kuwait which was, by the terms of the Treaty of Uqair, allotted to Nejd. Again, in 1929, British pressure had been exercised in favour of ibn Saud when Kuwait had been prevented by the British from doing anything to embarrass ibn Saud during the course of the Ikhwan revolt. Another cause of grievance against the British was that British influence in Iraq had been insufficient to induce that State to honour the British promise made to Sheikh Mubarak in 1914 to the effect that the Sheikh of Kuwait's ownership of certain date-gardens in the Vilayet of Basra would be guaranteed and held immune from taxation. All these matters combined to convince Sheikh Ahmed that the British were unable or unwilling to protect his interests against his two powerful neighbours. Consequently, Kuwaiti relationships with the British throughout Sheikh Ahmed's long reign were nothing like so intimate as they had been during the days of Sheikh Mubarak. When, in 1948, the export of oil started and Kuwait's New Arabian Nights existence of prosperity began, this intimacy was, to some extent, resumed, and under his successor (Sheikh Ahmed died in 1950 and was succeeded by his son Sheikh Abdullah as Salim as Subah) reinforced by the desirability of preserving Kuwait's new-found wealth from the covetousness of her Arab neighbours. By this time the British Government was less willing than before to sacrifice the interests of Kuwait to those of either Saudi Arabia or Iraq. For Kuwait, if not the brightest jewel in the British Crown, was well on the way to becoming the principal bastion of the Sterling Area by reason of the increasing amounts of foreign currency earned by the British-registered and half British-owned Kuwait Oil Company. In Kuwait, as in Bahrain, the British Protectorate status was later to prove embarrassing to the British Government in that it involved support for the ruling House without any provision for influencing its domestic policies which, as in Bahrain, were uncompromisingly autocratic, without being scandalously tyrannical. (It is to be noted that in Kuwait no Englishman, or indeed no non-Kuwaiti, ever attained a position in the Ruler's councils analogous to that enjoyed by Sir C. Belgrave in Bahrain.)

In Qatar oil had been discovered by the Qatar Petroleum Company in 1939 and, by 1940, about 200,000 tons of oil a year were being produced. But, as in Kuwait, further development was discontinued owing to steel shortages until after the war. As a result conditions in Qatar during the war years under the Ruler, Sheikh Abdullah bin Jasim al Thani, remained in much the same primitive and patriarchal state as described in the last chapter. On the Trucial Coast a British Political Agent was reappointed to Sharja, where an R.A.F. station had been established, at the beginning of the war. But the various Sheikhs continued to fight with each other. The tenure of their rule was precarious as a result of domestic intrigue and the boundaries of their Sheikhdoms fluid as a result of the changes and chances of internecine warfare. (A long drawn out and spasmodic state of war between Abu Dhabi and Dubai persisted until 1948.)

In the Sultanate of Musqat and Oman the mutual observance of the 1920 Treaty of Sib by Sultan Said bin Taimur, who had ascended the throne in 1932, and by Imam Khalili ensured a domestic peace by which the Sultan's suzerainty over the whole of Oman was tacitly recognized without being exercised except in the coastal regions.

CHAPTER EIGHT

A New Era

IN RETROSPECT, THE end of the second world war can be seen as marking the beginning of a new era in the Persian Gulf as definite and as decisive as that ushered in four and a half centuries before by the arrival of Albuquerque in its waters. Several factors contributed towards and commingled with each other in bringing an end to the old order and marking the beginning of the new. First, there was the presence of the United States of America who, under cover of war, had already established themselves as the most powerful foreign influence in Saudi Arabia and as the principal counterweight in Iran to the Russian influence which was once more being insistently asserted from the north. Secondly, there was the emergence of Russia from the war as the second greatest world Power, in potential rivalry with the Western Powers, United States and Great Britain, for the dominion of Europe and Asia, and in close proximity to the oil and the warm-water ports of the Persian Gulf. Thirdly, there was the emergence of India and Pakistan as independent States within the British Commonwealth. The British position in the Persian Gulf had been built up mainly on account of the strategic and commercial importance of the Persian Gulf in relation to the former British Indian Empire, to which the lands bordering the Persian Gulf formed the western approaches. The British Protectorates in the Gulf had been administered as dependencies of that Indian Empire; the Chief Political Resident and the various Political Agents had been servants of the Indian Empire; military reinforcements, when required, had come from India. The Government of India had always exercised a powerful, if not always decisive, voice in matters of British policy affecting the Persian Gulf. This India-ward orientation, absolute up to the beginning of the first world war, had gradually been modified since. The westward destination of

Iraqi oil, the development of Arab nationalism, the rise of Reza Shah and ibn Saud as important entities in their own right, were all of more interest to the Foreign than to the India Office. Thus the break, when it came in 1946, appeared more as the logical end to a long evolutionary process than as a revolutionary change in orientation. This break was signalized by making the posts of Chief Political Resident and the various Political Agents Foreign Office instead of India Office appointments, by transferring the Political Residency from Bushire to Bahrain, and by substituting the Chief Political Resident's bodyguard of Indian troops stationed at Bushire by a battalion of British troops stationed at Bahrain, where a British enclave, consisting of the British Residency, Naval Base and military cantonment was set up on a peninsula on the island of Manama, a few miles distant from the capital.

Fourthly, there was the advent of Arab nationalism (signalized by the formation of the Arab League in May 1945) as a dominant force in the affairs of the Arab Middle East. Arab nationalism, based as it was on a determination to extrude Western political influence from the Arab world, distracted as it was by dynastic, regional and personal rivalries, embittered as it was by the Palestine question, and important as it was by reason of the strategic significance of the Middle East as a potential field of conflict in the struggle for power between Russia and the West which came to be known as the Cold War, was eventually, under Egyptian influence, to become almost obsessed with the idea of using the vast oil resources on the Arab side of the Persian Gulf as a means of exerting successful pressure on the Western Powers. Oil was the fifth, and easily the most important, factor in the new era which was opening for the Persian Gulf. It was oil that explained the American interest in Saudi Arabia; it was oil that explained Russian interest in Iran and American opposition to that interest. It was oil that, in British official eyes replaced the safety of the Indian Empire as an imperative reason for the continued exercise of British influence in the Gulf.

Before the second world war the importance of Persian Gulf oil as a source of supply for the West had been relatively small. In 1938 the total Middle East production amounted to 335,000 barrels per day[1] as against total world production of 5,590,000 barrels per day. In 1947 Middle East production figures were 865,000 b/d against total world production of 8,660,000 b/d. But these figures do not begin to explain the actual and potential importance of Middle East oil to the Western economy after world war two. By 1947 North American production of 5,470,000 b/d was almost entirely consumed in North America, and Caribbean production of 1,540,000 b/d was being increasingly absorbed by the Western Hemisphere, due mainly to the fact that U.S. domestic consumption was beginning to outrun U.S. domestic production. Russian and Eastern European production, amounting to about 640,000 b/d, was almost entirely consumed within the Soviet bloc. Consequently, as Western European production only amounted to 35,000 b/d, U.K. and Western Europe were very largely dependent on exports from the Middle East for the rapidly increasing oil requirements which accompanied post-war reconstruction and industrial expansion. Moreover, figures of known oil reserves in the Western Hemisphere and Middle East respectively, taken together with expected increases in Western Hemisphere consumption, showed quite conclusively that the Middle East was the only known source on which Western Europe could rely in the future for its progressively increasing requirements of oil fuel. Another immediately important factor, as far as Great Britain was concerned, was that, apart from the question of physical availability, it would have been economically (and politically) disastrous to forego the sterling oil obtainable from the Persian Gulf and to replace it with dollar oil from the Western Hemisphere.

By 1947, therefore, the Persian Gulf had become, for the countries of Western Europe in general and for Great Britain (which was the largest consumer of oil products in Europe) in particular, one of the most vitally important strategic areas on the face of the globe. For the United States, where the necessity for sustaining Western Europe in the Cold War gradually, and in some circles reluctantly, began to be recognized as being even more important than the desirability of pursuing commercial rivalries with Great Britain, the Gulf began to assume a similar strategic importance as it became apparent that continued Western European access to Persian Gulf oil was threatened both by a possible Russian desire to deny this oil to Western Europe and by a probable Arab ambition to use it as a counter for political concessions. As it happened, the first threat to these oil supplies came neither from Russia, nor from the Arab nationalists, but from Iran, where the humiliations and political and economic discontents of the war years had bred an over-excited nationalism which was for a time able to maintain itself in power by an access of xenophobia blinding its numerous supporters, as well as the Iranian peoples as a whole, both to the necessities of administrative reform and to the pressure of economic facts. This episode, which resulted in a temporary cessation of oil exports from Iran, and which had the unintended result of increasing the political bargaining power of Arab at the expense of Iranian nationalism, will be the principal theme of the next chapter.

CHAPTER NINE

Iran, 1941–1952

THE ANGLO-RUSSIAN OCCUPATION, the abdication of Reza Shah and the accession of his young and inexperienced son, and the mounting inflation brought about by wartime conditions, all had a disintegrating effect on the political stability which Reza Shah had imposed on Iran. The authority and prestige of the central government, subject as it was to a large measure of Allied control, and unable as it was to do very much to arrest the progress of inflation, waned rapidly. The tribes once more began to assert their regional influences. Opponents of Reza Shah, released from prison or returning from exile, became politically active. The Majlis which, under Reza Shah, had been an obedient servant of the Executive, welcomed the return of 'democracy' by criticisms of the Government which were often intemperate and by obstruction which was frequently irresponsible.[1] The numerous and most venal organs of the Tehran Press, rejoicing like the Majlis in the return to 'democracy', were available as vociferous mouthpieces to any interest, domestic or foreign, which was prepared to subsidize them or to provide them with scarce and expensive newsprint.

In these circumstances the Russians (whose continuing interest in Iran had been succintly stated in paragraph four of the Four Power Pact drawn up in November 1940 between Germany, Italy, Japan and Russia, which reads: 'The Soviet Union declares that its territorial aspirations centre south of the national territory of the Soviet Union in the direction of the Indian Ocean'), had every opportunity for using their military occupation of the northern part of Iran for political penetration. This penetration took several forms. First, the Communist Party, which had existed in Iran since 1918, but which had gone underground in the time of Reza Shah, was reconstituted, under Russian auspices, as the Tudeh ((Masses) Party. This Party, whose proclaimed policy was liberal rather than communist, and which disavowed any direct connexion with the Soviet Union, was, in fact, primarily an instrument of Russian policy in Iran. Secondly, the encouragement of separatist tendencies among various minorities—the Turkish-speaking inhabitants of northern Azerbaijan, the Kurds of south-western Azerbaijan, the Turcomans of Khorassan—in the Russian zone of occupation. Thirdly, the bribery of the Tehran press. Fourthly, propaganda and a manipulation of the Allied censorship. Fifthly, the blackmailing of notables who owned lands in the Russian zone of occupation. Sixthly, a very tight Russian administrative control of the Russian zone of occupation, involving the expulsion of recalcitrant Iranian officials, a close check on entries into and exits from the zone, the withholding of food supplies from the Russian zone to the rest of Iran and so on.

This Russian penetration, which was pursued with more forcefulness than tact, naturally created a reaction by stimulating the evolution of an Iranian nationalist movement based, not on the will of a dictator, but on the desire for a genuine national independence felt by a politically conscious minority. Such a movement which, under the conditions of a foreign occupation, was necessarily limited in scope, first began to manifest itself after the election of a new Majlis in 1943. (It is a remarkable feature of recent Iranian history that, in spite of one dictatorship, several foreign invasions, several military coups and long periods of utter chaos, the Constitution, providing *inter alia* for the election of a new Majlis every four years, which shall approve all legislation and ratify all Treaties and concessions, has never been formally rescinded.) Russian influence provided that the new Majlis contained eight Tudeh Party members elected from northern constituencies. Owing to their discipline they had an influence greater than their numbers in the milling crowd of rival individualists of which the Majlis was principally composed. For, although political parties had been reconstituted after the abdication of Reza Shah, their membership was as fluid as their policies were indistinguishable. Nevertheless, under the influence of Sayyid Zia-ed-Din Tabatabai, who returned from his long exile in 1943 in time to be elected to the new Majlis, something like a coherent group of nationalist, anti-Russian deputies began to become apparent. Partly because of the pro-British sympathies of Zia-ed-Din himself (most of his exile had been spent in the British Mandated territory of Palestine, and he had returned from exile under British auspices), and partly because the British, at the time, were the only available and effective counterweight to Russian penetration, this nationalist group tended, with varying degrees of enthusiasm on the part of its members, to lean towards the British, whose methods during the occupation were a good deal more careful of Iranian susceptibilities than the methods of the Russians, and whose post-war interests, unlike those of Russia, favoured the establishment of a genuinely independent Iran.

There were several principal components of this incipient nationalist movement. There was the Army which, in spite of its rather inglorious performance in 1941, continued to enjoy some prestige and which, in spite of financial stringency, continued to increase in size. There was the young Shah, who had close links with the Army and who, as he gained experience and popularity, was endeavouring to re-establish for the Monarchy the key position which it traditionally occupied in Iran. There were the big landlords who were fearful of the personal results to themselves of an intensification of Russian influence. There were the Shia Mullahs, who had regained some of their influence since Reza Shah's abdication, and who objected to communism on economic as well as on religious grounds. And there were the southern tribal leaders whom both Zia-ed-Din and the British made a point of conciliating. The nationalist group was thus decidely of a right-wing and conservative complexion. This complexion was retained after American influence had helped to abate the immediate Russian menace and after the extrusion of British influence had replaced the extrusion of Russian influence as the principal objective of the Iranian nationalist movement. It was this fact, combined with the anti-Russian origins of the nationalist movement, which was to prevent Dr. Mossadeq's National Front from making common cause with the Tudeh Party in their long drawn out quarrel with Great Britain.

The political influence of the United States was negligible in Iran until about 1944. In 1942 American troops and technicians, later organized into the Persian Gulf Command, came to Iran at the request of the British to assist in forwarding supplies to Russia. (The American military presence in Iran was, incidentally, never formalized by a Treaty.) In the same year, Dr. A. C. Millspaugh, the American financial expert who had been Iran's Financial Adviser during the 1920's, returned to Iran at the request of the Iranian Government to try and reorganize the country's disordered finances. It may have been the expectation of the Iranian Government that the presence of Dr. Millspaugh and his mission would result in the provision of some financial assistance from the U.S. Government. But, in the event, the U.S. Government almost ostentatiously dissociated themselves from Dr. Millspaugh who, without any official American protest, left Iran with his mission in 1944, after almost two years of continual criticism from the Russians and embroilment with the Iranian Government. It was not until the war was over that the United States took over from Great Britain the role of helping Iran to combat the pressure being exercised on Iran by Russia.

This pressure became steadily more insistent as the tide of war receded from the frontiers of Iran. There were in Iran two oil concessions being actively exploited. One was the Anglo-Iranian Oil Co. concession in south-west Iran. The other was a small and unimportant concession at Semnan, in the centre of the country, operated by an Irano-Russian Company called Kavir-e-Kurian. During the course of 1943–4, representatives from Shell, Socony-Vacuum and Sinclair had been negotiating (separately) with the Iranian Government, for a concession in south-east Iran. In September 1944, Kavtaradze, the Russian Assistant Commissar for Foreign Affairs, arrived in Tehran ostensibly for the purpose of discussing matters connected with the Semnan concession. It soon appeared that Kavtaradze was really negotiating for an oil concession covering the five northern provinces of Iran. In October the Prime Minister, Mohamed Said, announced that the Government had decided to reject for the time being all the requests for oil concessions which were being made by American, British-Dutch and Russian interests. In December, Dr. Mossadeq, a Majlis deputy who was subsequently to become better known, introduced into the Majlis a Bill making it a criminal offence for any Minister to enter into negotiations with any foreign party for the purpose of granting an oil concession without the previous agreement of the Majlis. This Bill was quickly passed into law. From that time on Russian propaganda, and the Tudeh Party, began openly to attack the Iranian Government and the British and Americans, alleging that the former were serving the imperialistic designs of the latter to the detriment of the real interests of the Iranian people. From that time too the association between the Tudeh Party and the Russians became open and undisguised.

After this rebuff over the oil concession the Russians appeared to concentrate on the attempted disintegration of the Iranian State by encouraging separatist tendencies in the northern provinces, and particularly in Azerbaijan, where the Tudeh Party was led by Jaafar Pishevari, an Azerbaijani and a veteran Russian-trained communist, who had gone into exile under Reza Shah and who had returned to Iran, under Russian auspices, in 1941.

As soon as the war in Europe came to an end in May 1945, the Iranian Government began to demand the evacuation of Allied troops from Iran. Although the Tripartite Treaty of 1941 only provided for withdrawal six months after the end of war with the Axis, which included Japan, the Iranian Government argued, with some reason, that the continuation of the war with Japan (with whom Russia was not at war) did not involve the sending of munitions to Russia through Iran, which had been the original reason for the Allied occupation. This argument became academic with the surrender of Japan four months later when it became clear that, under the Treaty, Allied troops were obligated to complete their withdrawal from Iran by March 1946. The British and Americans had, in fact, started withdrawing in the spring of 1945. In August the Tehran area was evacuated by both British and Russians. In the same month Iranian forces sent north to Azerbaijan to quell an attempted coup at Tabriz (capital of Iranian Azerbaijan) were stopped at the border of Azerbaijan by Soviet troops. The coup failed through inadequate preparation, but the Russian action naturally intensified suspicions about Russian intentions in Azerbaijan. In September the British Government announced their intention of evacuating Iran, except for the southern oil-fields, by the end of 1945 and suggested to the Russians that they should evacuate all areas except Azerbaijan by the same date. But the Russians expressed their intention of keeping their troops in Iran without limitation until March 1946 as provided for in the Tripartite Treaty. In October Russian troops in Iran were reinforced. In November there was another rising in

Azerbaijan against the central Government, and again the Russians refused to allow the entry of Iranian troops into Azerbaijan to suppress the rising. This time the rising was successful and an Autonomous Republic of Azerbaijan was set up under the Premiership of Pishevari. Simultaneously, a Kurdish People's Republic was set up as the result of a Russian-inspired Kurdish rising in south-western Azerbaijan and formed an alliance with the Autonomous Republic of Azerbaijan.

At the Moscow Conference in December 1945, both the British Foreign Secretary and the U.S. Secretary of State tried, without success, to negotiate a *modus vivendi* between Russia and Iran over Azerbaijan, and in doing so made it clear that neither Great Britain nor the United States were as yet prepared for any strong measures against Russia for the defence of Iranian territorial integrity. In January 1946 the Iranian Government appealed to the Security Council of the United Nations against the Russian action in Azerbaijan. The Security Council adopted what was to become its standard formula for inaction and recommended direct negotiations between the two parties for the settlement of the dispute. Meanwhile, Azerbaijan was completely sealed off from the rest of Iran, thus causing grave economic difficulties, since Azerbaijan was one of the principal grain-growing areas in the country. At the end of January the Iranian Prime Minister, Hakimi, resigned and Ghavam Sultaneh, who was on good terms with the Tudeh Party, was called on by the Shah to form a Government. This looked like surrender, on the assumption that Sultaneh had been chosen as a man likely to be acceptable to the Russians. But, during the next two years, Sultaneh, succeeding to as unenviable a post as could well be imagined, earned, if he did not receive, the gratitude of his country by a remarkable display of diplomatic virtuosity.

Sultaneh's first act as Prime Minister was to dismiss General Ibrahim Arfa, who was regarded as pro-British, from his position as Chief of Staff of the Army. Having thus made an appropriately conciliatory gesture, he proceeded to Moscow in accordance with the Security Council's recommendation for direct negotiations. While he was in Moscow the time limit for the departure of Allied troops from Iran under the Tripartite Treaty expired on 2 March. British and American troops had by that time all been withdrawn. The Russians announced the withdrawal of their forces from Khorassan, Shahrud and Semnan but stated that they intended to leave their troops in the rest of northern Iran, including Azerbaijan, until 'the situation had been clarified'. Great Britain, the United States and Iran severally protested to Russia against this decision and Sultaneh returned to Tehran to face a series of Tudeh demonstrations demanding that the four-year life of the Majlis, which was about to expire, should be renewed, pending new elections. Sultaneh refused this demand and refused new elections as long as foreign troops were in occupation of part of the country. On 11 March the Majlis' term of life expired. Sultaneh again appealed to the United Nations against the retention of Russian troops in Iran in defiance of the Tripartite Treaty. The Russians thereupon announced their intention of evacuating Iran within six weeks 'if no unforeseen circumstances occur'. The Security Council, in default of any strong lead from Great Britain or the United States, agreed 'to defer further proceedings on the Iranian appeal until 6 May', the date on which the Soviet promise to withdraw should have been fulfilled. On 4 April Sultaneh, under strong pressure from Russia, and lacking any support from either Great Britain or the United States, made an agreement with Russia which provided, in return for the Russian promise of evacuation, for some measure of autonomy for Azerbaijan and for the formation of a joint Russian-Iranian Oil Company, with the Russians holding 51 per cent and the Iranians 49 per cent of the shares, which would be granted a twenty-five-year concession for the exploitation of oil deposits in northern Iran. It was provided in the agreement that this concession would be ratified by the (as yet unelected) Majlis within seven months. In May an agreement was made between the Iranian Government and Pishevari for the grant of a large measure of autonomy to an Azerbaijan Provincial Council. Simultaneously the last of the Russian forces were evacuated from Iranian soil. In July the jubilant Tudeh Party organized a general strike in the A.I.O.C. oilfields, and in August Sultaneh reshuffled his Cabinet to provide for the inclusion of three Tudeh members. It looked like a communist victory and it seemed only a matter of time, and a short time at that, before Iran would disappear behind what was already beginning to be referred to as the Iron Curtain.

But the Tudeh-inspired general strike at Abadan had gal-vanized the British Government into action. British troops from India, marking the last instance of British-Indian intervention in the affairs of the Persian Gulf, were ordered to Basra, where their presence was covered by the terms of the 1930 Anglo-Iraqi Treaty. A coalition of Bakhtiari and Qashgai tribesmen, popularly believed to have been sponsored by the British, who maintained several tribal experts among their Consular staffs in Southern Iran, rebelled against the central Government, cap-tured Bushire, Kazerun and several other towns, beseiged Shiraz, the capital of the province of Fars, and demanded the dismissal of the Tudeh members of the Government and auto-nomy for the southern provinces. Sultaneh pacified the rebels by resigning office, and by returning to power with a new Cabinet purged of its Tudeh members and of Muzaffer Firuz, the pre-vious Minister of Propaganda, who was generally regarded as pro-Russian. He then announced that elections would be held and insisted that these elections would be supervised by the central Government all over the country, including Azerbaijan. This was in effect an expression of determination that the new Majlis would be subservient to the wishes of the Government. But the Russians needed elections in order to get the oil con-cession ratified and presumably calculated that political pres-sure and the threat of reoccupation (which might plausibly be justified under the 1921 Treaty) would be sufficient to ensure such ratification.

At about this time Sultaneh's position was greatly strengthened by a hardening of American policy towards Russian designs in Iran. This hardening was signalized by the appointment of a new U.S. Ambassador—George V. Allen—to Iran. One of the new Ambassador's first public actions was a statement of opinion, made to a British Press correspondent, that the despatch of Iranian troops to Azerbaijan to supervise elections was 'quite normal and appropriate'. In the event troops were despatched in December, not to supervise the elections, but to overthrow the Provincial Government, which they did without difficulty. Pishevari fled to the Soviet Union. At the same time the Kurdish People's Republic was liquidated and its leaders brought to Tehran and hanged. Mass arrests were made of Tudeh Party leaders and supporters throughout the country.

After these electoral preparations had been completed, elections were held in January and February. The Democratic Party, created by Sultaneh for the occasion, secured a majority of seats. Two Tudeh Party members were elected, presumably to add verisimilitude to an otherwise unconvincing story, but the main opposition consisted of about twenty-five members, led by Dr. Mossadeq, who looked forward to leading a 'nationalism without tears' movement directed against Great Britain, after Sultaneh had dealt with the Russians.

Immediately after the elections the Russians began to press for the ratification of the oil agreement, which was already overdue, Sultaneh, although openly advocating ratification, cannot have been displeased at the continued reluctance of the Majlis to do so. Matters dragged on until September 1947. During this period of delay the U.S. Government were slowly climbing down from the fence. In April 1947 President Truman enunciated the Truman Doctrine which pledged the U.S. Government to the containment of communism all over the world and to the defence of small nations against communist aggression and infiltration. Specific economic and military aid was pledged to Turkey and Greece; this pledge was subsequently extended to Iran. On 11 September the U.S. Ambassador in Tehran publicly announced that the U.S. Government would understand and support a refusal by the Majlis to ratify the Russian oil agreement. At this point the British Government, presumably aware of the possible implications of a refusal to ratify on the future of the A.I.O.C. concession, advised the Iranian Government to keep the door open for future discussions with Russia on the subject of oil. This cautious British attitude, contrasted with the uncompromising U.S. attitude as enunciated by Ambassador Allen, can be held to mark the end of the British and the beginning of the American role in Iran as the paramount defender of Iran against Russian infiltration. It also marked the beginning of the shift in nationalist feeling from its original anti-Russian to its later anti-British orientation.

The Majlis decided to adopt American rather than British advice. In October they rejected the oil agreement by an overwhelming majority, only the two Tudeh deputies voting in favour of it, and passed a Bill, sponsored by Sultaneh himself (who, encouraged by U.S. support, had come out openly against the agreement which he himself had signed) which provided (*a*) that the oil agreement with Russia be considered as null and void; (*b*) that Iran would not grant any concessions to representatives of any foreign Powers or take such representatives into partnership in any concessions; and (*c*) that Iran would negotiate with A.I.O.C. to obtain a higher share of the profit from the 1933 concession.

The U.S. Government followed up the moral support they had given with material reinforcement. In June 1947, in the midst of the Majlis procrastination about ratifying the oil agreement, Sultaneh signed an agreement with the U.S. Government providing for the sale of surplus U.S. military stores to Iran. This agreement was ratified by the Majlis in February 1948. (By this time Hakimi had returned to the Premiership after Sultaneh had resigned in September.) U.S. Military and Gendarmerie Missions, already in Iran, had their terms of service extended and their personnel reinforced. And in May 1948 the first instalment of what was to prove a massive supply of American financial aid was applied for by the U.S. Government when the Senate Appropriations Committee was asked to approve the delivery to Iran of sixty million dollars worth of 'non-aggressive weapons' in order to 'maintain the international security of Iran'.

Throughout 1948 the Russians continued to protest vigorously against the cancellation of the oil agreement and against the 'militarizing' of Iran by the United States. At one point it appeared that they were contemplating sending Russian troops back into Iran in accordance with the clause in the 1921 Treaty which permitted such action in the event of Iran becoming a base for any attack on Russia by a third party. But gradually the Russians, deeply embroiled in the Cold War in Berlin and in Eastern and Central Europe, drew in their horns and appeared to accept the *fait accompli*, thus paving the way towards the growing anti-British orientation of Iranian nationalist policy which had been foreshadowed in the Majlis Oil Bill of October 1947, providing as it did for an attempted revision of the 1933 A.I.O.C. concession.

During 1948, in spite of the Russian set-back, the power of the Tudeh Party continued steadily to increase. This was due less to Russian influence than to internal conditions in Iran, where many of the measures advocated by the Tudeh Party, and particularly land reform, were precisely those measures which were needed to deal with the deteriorating social and economic condition. The endemic social and economic ills caused by an outmoded system of land tenure and under-capitalization were accentuated by administrative inefficiency and widespread corruption. While the Tudeh Party were agitating on the left, a much less homogeneous opposition to the Government, consisting principally of the Shia clergy, a terrorist organization known as the Fedayeen Islam, and the newly-formed National Front led by Dr. Mossadeq, were bombinating on the right. In the centre, where the Shah was emerging more and more as a leader, genuine efforts were being made to pull the country together economically, as a necessary condition of avoiding a revolution either from the right or from the left. In 1947 the idea of a Seven Year Plan of economic development was conceived and a firm of American consultants retained to work out detailed schemes. It was clear that any such Plan would need large capital expenditure. (A figure of £650,000,000 was mentioned in the first draft of the Plan.) Two possible sources were envisaged for the financing of the Plan: (*a*) an increase in oil royalties; (*b*) loans from the United States.

From this point a more or less coherent pattern begins to become manifest in the Iranian political scene. In the centre were the moderate nationalists, with whom the Shah became increasingly identified, who believed on the one hand in a western orientation of policy in order to secure the necessary financial support, both by way of increased oil revenues and American loans, and on the other hand in such moderate administrative and social reforms in the domestic field as would ensure the productive use of such foreign funds as might be obtained for implementing the Seven Year Plan. On the right were the extreme nationalists—the zealots—who, dominated by a xenophobia applied equally to east and west in their view of foreign policy, and by a dislike of even moderate social reform in their view of domestic policy, were quite prepared to let the economy of the country look after itself rather than incur such dependence on foreign friendship as would be necessitated by an economic policy relying on foreign assistance. And on the left there was a compact disciplined group which believed that the way of economic salvation lay, not by soliciting foreign assistance, but by forcibly mobilizing domestic resources according to the communist pattern.

In February 1949 the growing influence of the Shah in the political life of Iran was underlined by an attempt made to assassinate him. The culprit was almost certainly a member of the right-wing terrorist group, but the blame was laid on the Tudeh Party and the opportunity taken to declare them an illegal body. The Tudeh, in accordance with the well-tried communist technique, then went underground, where they continued as a powerful, unpredictable group, always liable to come to the surface and make themselves felt at times of national disorder. The Government's action in outlawing the Tudeh necessarily increased the relative influence of the nationalist opposition, against whom the moderate centre was, from this time on until the apotheosis of Dr. Mossadeq, fighting a losing battle. It was a losing battle because the moderates, having little or no popular support as compared with the professional agitators of the right and left, could only justify themselves by concrete results in the social and economic fields. And these concrete results could only be obtained, if at all, as the result of massive injections of foreign capital. Of the two available sources, some progress was made, during 1949, in securing the prospect of increased income from A.I.O.C.

In the spring of 1949 negotiations began, at the instance of the Iranian Government, with A.I.O.C. which issued, in July, what became known as the Supplemental Agreement to the 1933 concession. This Supplemental Agreement provided for an increase in the rate of royalty from four shillings to six shillings per ton, for a payment of one shilling (instead of ninepence) per ton in lieu of Iranian taxation, and for a guaranteed minimum annual payment of £4 million in respect of A.I.O.C. dividend payments and transfers to General Reserve.[2] The Agreement also provided for an immediate payment of £5 million in respect of amounts standing to the credit of the General Reserve at the end of 1947 and for additional royalties amounting to some £9 million for each of 1948 and 1949 representing the difference between royalties as calculated under the 1933 and Supplemental Agreements. In accordance with the Constitution the Supplemental Agreement had to be ratified by the Majlis.

This the Majlis declined to do for some months until it was dissolved in May 1950. It could reasonably be expected that its successor would be of even more extreme nationalist complexion.

Meanwhile attempts at coaxing a loan from America proved unsuccessful in spite of a visit to the United States undertaken in the autumn of 1949 by the Shah for that principal purpose. When the new Majlis met in July 1950, it was in a militant mood. During the course of 1949 the Shah had already made some preparations for the imminent struggle with the extreme nationalism represented in the Majlis, and he had secured amendments to the Constitution providing for the creation of a Senate, half elected and half nominated, and for power to dissolve the Majlis at will. Attempts to secure further power for himself from the new Majlis soon ran into trouble. The Shah's policy of domestic reform and friendship with the West was particularly obnoxious to nationalists whose principal leaders were religious fanatics and absentee landlords. These leaders succeeded in attracting to themselves the support of that numerous body of middle-class people who were particularly susceptible to that emotional dislike of the West felt by those upon whom a western education has conferred a kind of second-class western citizenship. Thus, the forces of self-interest, obscurantism and resentment were arrayed against a régime whose subservience to the West could display neither appreciable material dividends nor compensating emotional excitement.

During the spring of 1950 the Prime Minister, Ali Mansour, tried unsuccessfully both to get the Majlis to ratify the Supplemental Agreement and to get the A.I.O.C. to improve on its terms. In June 1950 he was replaced as Prime Minister by General Razmara. In October an American loan of 25 million dollars from the Import-Export Bank was negotiated. This sum was so far below expectations, and indeed needs, if the Seven Year Plan was to be pursued on anything like a realistic basis, that its effect was rather to strengthen the extreme nationalists, who were able to mock at the inadequate results of what they regarded as the Government's subservience. In November a Majlis Oil Commission, which had been set up some months before to make recommendations to the Majlis about the ratification of the Supplemental Agreement, reported against the Agreement on the ground that it did not adequately guarantee Iranian rights and interests. In January 1951 the Majlis accepted this recommendation and asked the Commission to make recommendations as to what course the Government should pursue *vis-à-vis* the A.I.O.C. Dr. Mossadeq had meanwhile recommended to the Commission that the oil industry should be nationalized. This recommendation was not accepted by the Commission, but was adopted by the National Front group led by Mossadeq. There were eight National Front deputies in the Majlis of whom four were on the Oil Commission. There was also a growing and vociferous body of support for the National Front outside the Majlis, which began to conduct an aggressive propaganda campaign in favour of nationalization. Under the influence of this campaign the Oil Commission asked the Prime Minister to report to the Majlis as to whether oil nationalization was practicable. After taking the advice of experts, Razmara reported to the Majlis on 3 March that he had been advised that nationalization was not only impracticable but probably illegal as well. This statement was his death warrant. By this time the demand for nationalization had been taken up, not only by all the right-wing extreme nationalist groups, but by the Tudeh Party as well, until there was virtually a unanimity of popular sentiment in favour of a measure regarded, not as an act of policy but as a gesture of defiance towards Western materialism which, as the nationalists saw it, had not only failed to assist, but was succeeding in the exploitation of, the Iranian nation. On 7 March Razmara was assassinated and the Fedayeen Islam openly lauded the murderer. On the following day the Oil Commission voted unanimously for the nationalization of the oil industry and requested the Majlis to provide for the necessary legislation. On 15 March the Majlis, followed by the Senate five days later, obediently passed a one-clause Bill providing 'for the happiness and prosperity of the Iranian nation and for the purpose of securing world peace' that 'the oil industry throughout all parts of the country without exception be nationalized; that is to say, all operations of exploration, extraction, and exploitation shall be carried out by the Government'.

The Nationalization Bill was the signal for an outbreak of anti-British demonstrations in Tehran and for a strike in the oil-fields. At the end of April a Bill was passed, first by the Majlis and later by the Senate, providing for the details of nationalization and for the creation of a National Iranian Oil Company, to which the assets of the A.I.O.C. were to pass, and which would be the Government Agency responsible for running all aspects of the Iranian oil industry. At the same time Husain Ala, a moderate who had succeeded Razmara as Prime Minister, resigned, and was succeeded by Dr. Mossadeq, who had originally proposed nationalization and who was by that time identified in popular esteem with the struggle against imperialism. The extreme nationalists were now in the saddle and there was little prospect of any compromise.

The act of nationalization naturally provoked protests both from the A.I.O.C. and from the British Government. But the tone of the protests was at first conciliatory, in the belated hope that something might yet be saved from the wreck. But, with the accession of Mossadeq to office and the subsequent moves made to implement the Nationalization Law, it soon became apparent that no compromise was possible. The British attitude stiffened. On 15 May Morrison, the British Foreign Secretary, announced that British paratroops were being held in readiness in the U.K. to protect the lives of British subjects in Iran and to prevent the illegal seizure of British property. This threat to use force in defence of British property was not again mentioned by the British Government, and the paratroops got no nearer Iran than Cyprus (but a British cruiser appeared in the Shatt-al-Arab ready to protect British lives if necessary). On 28 May the British Government appealed to the International Court of Justice to adjudicate on the legality of Iran's act of nationalization. But generally both the Company and the British Government still seemed disposed to try and negotiate a settlement which, while accepting the fact of nationalization, would secure continued control of the oil operation and continued possession of the oil produced. Two such attempts at negotiation took place during the summer and autumn. First, an A.I.O.C. delegation from London tried to negotiate an arrangement which would enable the Company to continue the oil operation as agents of the National Iranian Oil Company (N.I.O.C.) and have at their disposal all the oil produced under such an arrangement (after making provision for meeting Iran's domestic oil requirements) against a payment to Iran of 50 per cent of the net profits of the sales of such oil overseas. In August Richard Stokes, a British Cabinet Minister, made a further attempt at negotiation on the same lines. Both these attempts failed.

The attitude of the Iranian Government may be summarized as follows: (a) They insisted on their sovereign right to expropriate the A.I.O.C. subject to the payment of compensation at a rate which would be determined by the Iranian Courts. (The second nationalization Bill provided that 25 per cent of the net proceeds of oil sales should be set aside to provide a fund for the payment of such compensation as might be so determined); (b) They insisted on entire control of the oil operation (although they were willing to employ the expatriate staff of A.I.O.C. as servants of the N.I.O.C. on the same terms as they had been working for with A.I.O.C.) and ownership and free disposal of the oil produced (although they were willing to guarantee supplies to previous customers of A.I.O.C.).

The attitude of A.I.O.C. and the British Government[3] was that they were prepared to accept nationalization as a matter of negotiation, and not as a *diktat*, provided that the efficiency of the oil operation was ensured by the employment of the Company as managing agents and provided that the Company had an absolute right to the oil so produced, subject to the satisfaction of Iran's domestic requirements (which only formed a very small proportion of the total production).

These points of view were irreconcilable. The break came when the Iranian Government insisted on tanker captains signing receipts which acknowledged the oil to be the property of the N.I.O.C. The tanker captains, by arrangement with the A.I.O.C. refused and oil exports came to a standstill. As a result production ceased and the whole oil operation ground to a halt. By the end of September all British staff of the Company had left the country and the Iranian Government were left in possession of the installations. But, deprived of tankers, customers and overseas marketing organizations, they could turn them to no profitable account.

For the next two years a war of nerves was waged between the British Government on the one hand and Dr. Mossadeq on the other, with the U.S. Government, fearful of the possibility lest popular discontent and economic straits might lead Iran towards communism, agitatedly intervening to try and bring about an accommodation.[4]

It can be seen in retrospect that the paralysis of this great industry came about as a result of an almost total lack of comprehension of the relevant political and economic realities by all the parties concerned. The Iranian nationalists either believed that the British could not do without Iranian oil and that, when it came to the point, they would have to take it on Iranian terms, or else believed that Iran could carry on perfectly well without any oil exports at all. (In fact the economic interests of the Shia clergy and big landlords who made up the majority of the extreme nationalists did not appear to depend on oil and, having very little interest in the economic position of the country as a whole, except in so far as their own personal finances were concerned, viewed with equanimity the prospect of a complete cessation of oil income. They were to learn better later, when they came to realize how the resultant financial difficulties made a breeding ground for communism.) In assessing the importance of the Iranian nationalist movement, it is important to remember that it was a right-wing movement, with no interest whatever in social reform or industrialization. This rendered it extremely vulnerable once its nationalization bluff had been called, as it had nothing else to offer except ultimately self-destructive appeals to nationalist prejudice and incitements to obscurantist violence.

The British, on their side, were unable to appreciate the pressures operating on, and the consequent desirability of sustaining the precarious 'centre' régime in power prior to 1951. (The A.I.O.C. refused to consider a 50/50 profit sharing agreement with the Razmara Government in 1950, although such an offer had been made by the Company, and rejected by Iran, during the course of the Gass-Golshayan negotiations which led up to the Supplemental Agreement and although such an agreement was already being negotiated between Aramco and the Saudi Arabian Government. The announcement of the conclusion of a 50/50 profit sharing agreement between A.R.A. M.C.O. and the Saudi Arabian Government was one of the principal reasons for Razmara's failure to persuade the Majlis to ratify the Supplemental Agreement in January 1951.) The British were also unable to appreciate the extent to which the extreme nationalists were prepared to 'cut off their noses to spite their faces' by foregoing oil revenues altogether. Just as the nationalists overestimated the extent of British reliance on Iranian oil, so the British overestimated the extent of Iranian reliance on oil revenues.

The dispute had an importance far transcending the immediate economic interests of Great Britain and Iran. The fact that a vital British interest in the Persian Gulf had been successfully expropriated, and the fact that the British had not used, or seriously threatened the use of, force in its defence, underlined, as nothing else could have done, the change which had taken place in the relationships between Great Britain and the littoral States of the Persian Gulf. The Gulf was no longer a British lake; British hegemony had been successfully defied. Barely ten years before, the British, with one arm tied behind their back so to speak, had been able to overturn a Government in Iraq and to unseat a dictator in Iran, and to occupy the two countries into the bargain, in both cases with doubtful legality, because the governments of these two countries were pursuing policies inconvenient to the British war effort. Now the case was altered, not because of any diminution in British military strength relative to that of Iran, but because international circumstances—the creation of the United Nations, the necessity for avoiding giving offence to U.S.A., the necessity of not giving any excuse for Russian intervention—had completely changed the pattern of relationships between a Great Power and a small one. Abadan was the first illustration of this. The British Tories, at that time in opposition, clamoured for paratroops and gunboats. Five years later, when they were in power and when a similar expropriation of a vital British interest took place, they tried to use them and learnt a belated lesson.

The Americans, who might have sustained the Razmara Government with financial assistance had they not, with the British, underestimated the pressures to which that Government was subjected and the unreasoning fanaticism of its right-wing opponents, were now seriously alarmed lest the economic difficulties with which Mossadeq was faced might lead him either to an alliance with, or to being overwhelmed by, the communists. This, combined with an atavistic dislike at what they regarded as vestiges of British 'colonialism', and perhaps a business-like desire to obtain for themselves some share of Iranian oil resources, led them to seek for an accommodation with Mossadeq which would save him and his régime from the results of their own excesses and establish them as a popular-based bastion against the threat of communism in Iran.

The Russians now began to realize that the grand object of their Middle East policy, which was to deny the Middle East to the Western Powers either for military bases or as zones of political influence, or, in the event of war, as a source of a vital raw material, could be achieved more immediately, more surely and more cheaply by diplomatic support of nationalist régimes than by attempted interference in the internal affairs of the countries of the Middle East.

The British appealed to the International Court in May 1951, and to the Security Council in September, but they relied principally on the application of economic sanctions either to bring Mossadeq to heel or to drive him from power. In the event the International Court decided that it had no jurisdiction and the Security Council adopted its—at that time—usual gambit of calling on both parties to settle the dispute by direct negotiation. The economic sanctions took the principal form of advising all potential customers for Iranian oil that this oil was regarded as the property of the A.I.O.C. unlawfully seized by the Iranian Government, and that anyone taking delivery of this oil from the Iranian Government would be sued by A.I.O.C. for, in effect 'being in possession of stolen goods knowing them to be stolen'. This threat was effective in preventing any but a negligible quantity of Iranian oil from finding an export market. In addition conversion facilities for Iranian sterling balances were withdrawn, and export licences for all scarce material from U.K. revoked. This uncompromising British attitude led successively to the closing of all British Consulates in Iran (these Consulates had at one time exercised a great influence in Iran and were reputed in Iran to be staffed by agents of the British Intelligence Service, adepts at imperialist plots), and finally, in October 1952, to the severance of diplomatic relations between Great Britain and Iran.

The basic difference between the British and American attitudes was that while the Americans feared the prospect of Mossadeq's downfall and tried to take measures to sustain his government, believing that his fall would lead to communism in Iran, the British hoped for Mossadeq's fall and worked deliberately to bring it about, believing it necessary to demonstrate to Iran and the world that what the British regarded as an act of piracy should be seen to recoil on the heads of its perpetrators. Some British concession to the American point of view was however necessary in order to avoid a position in which the U.S. Government would be providing funds for the purpose of sustaining Mossadeq simultaneously with the British Government withholding funds for the purpose of destroying him. By February 1953 therefore a joint British-American plan had been worked out by which, broadly, the A.I.O.C. would be replaced by a Consortium of oil companies of which A.I.O.C. would be a member. This Consortium would buy oil from the N.I.O.C. and would pay an immediate advance on future purchases. The question of compensation to A.I.O.C. would be determined by an International Court and 25 per cent of the gross proceeds of the sale of oil under the proposed arrangement was to be reserved for the payment of such compensation as might be so awarded. This proposal was submitted to the Iranian Government in March 1953, in a joint Anglo-American Note. It was rejected by Mossadeq. Some weeks later, the U.S. Government, in reply to a request for financial aid from Mossadeq, made it clear that 'so long as Iran could have access to funds derived from the sale of its oil and oil products, and declined such access by a refusal to come to such an agreement regarding compensation and other matters as the U.S. Government considered reasonable, there would be no question of allocating U.S. funds in order to enable the Iranian Government to sustain such a refusal'.

This, although he did not know it, was really the end of Mossadeq. After making personal appearances in New York and the Hague during the autumn of 1951 to present the Iranian case before the Security Council and the International Court, Mossadeq had returned to Iran at the end of November and secured almost unanimous votes from the Senate and Majlis for new elections. For by this time, when it was evident that a long fight lay ahead, Mossadeq was anxious to obtain an emphatic popular endorsement for his oil policy and a Majlis which was as far committed as he was himself to such a policy. The new

Majlis, which assembled in April 1952, voted by a large majority for the reappointment of Mossadeq as Prime Minister (in accordance with the Constitution he had resigned on the election of a new Majlis). Mossadeq, with that euphoria which characterized him, immediately asked the Shah for dictatorial powers for six months in order to enable him to solve the country's economic crisis (which had been brought about as a result of his own actions). The Shah refused this demand and appointed Ghavam Sultaneh as Prime Minister. Immediately, the supporters of Mossadeq, in alliance with the Mullahs, organized violence against the new Government, as a result of which, in Tehran alone, twenty people were killed and about one hundred wounded in the course of the next few days. By coincidence, the International Court announced at this time that it had no jurisdiction in the oil dispute; this was regarded as a resounding triumph for Mossadeq. Sultaneh resigned and the Shah was compelled by popular clamour to recall Mossadeq to the Premiership. From that time onwards Mossadeq abandoned himself wholly to demagogy. On 3 August the Majlis gave him dictatorial powers for a period of six months. He used these powers uncompromisingly to reject any proposal emanating from any quarter for a settlement of the oil dispute. In October he induced the Majlis to vote the Senate, which had been showing some incipient opposition to Mossadeq, out of existence. In November he decreed the dissolution of the Iranian Supreme Court. In January 1953 the Majlis agreed to extend his dictatorial powers for another six months. But Mossadeq was no longer riding on the crest of the wave of his earlier triumphs. Nothing that even he could do in the way of xenophobic demonstration was likely to satisfy the Mullahs; still less was Mossadeq who, to give him his due, was not a bloodthirsty man, likely to satisfy the professional assassins of the Fedayeen Islam. The Tudeh Party's policy was simply to use the extreme nationalists as a battering ram to destroy the last remnants of western influence preparatory to pressing on with a social revolution. But the most significant aspect of the mounting opposition was the regrouping of the moderates under the aegis of the Shah and the Army. Many of the landowners and monied men, who had previously opposed the reforms advocated by the Shah and what they regarded as the Shah's dictatorial tendencies, had now become thoroughly alarmed at the obvious inability of Mossadeq to deal either with the oil crisis or with any of the various economic problems which had been created or accentuated by the cessation of oil exports. That exclusive preoccupation with their personal interests, which had previously led them to support extreme nationalism as a protest against the reformist and dictatorial tendencies of moderate nationalism as represented by the Shah and by such politicians as Sultaneh and Razmara, now led them back to the fold of moderate nationalism in an endeavour to ward off the alternative spectres of communism and theocratic dictatorship towards which Mossadeq's hysterical incompetence seemed to be leading the country.

In March 1953 Mossadeq, in an endeavour to fortify his position against the mounting centre opposition, of which the Monarchy was the symbol and the spearhead, set up a Majlis Commission to study proposed changes in the Constitution which would, in effect, have transferred ultimate authority from the Monarch to the Prime Minister. These proposals split the Majlis and deprived Mossadeq of that virtual unanimity of parliamentary support which he had enjoyed since the election of the Majlis the previous year. In order to try and circumvent this parliamentary opposition Mossadeq instituted a referendum, appealing to the people direct over the heads of the Majlis. This referendum was held in Tehran at the beginning of August and resulted in an overwhelming vote of approval for Mossadeq. The opposition deputies declared the referendum illegal and took possession of the Majlis building. The Shah dismissed Mossadeq and appointed General Zahedi, the C.-in-C. of the Army, as Prime Minister. Mossadeq refused to accept dismissal and called upon the Tehran mob to rise in his support. The Shah left the country. Mossadeq declared the Majlis dissolved. The Tehran mob, which was now Mossadeq's principal, if not his only, basis of support, began agitating for a republic. For the Tudeh Party, it seemed that their moment had almost come. But General Zahedi rallied the Army and moved into Tehran with troops and tanks to restore order. Martial Law was proclaimed, Mossadeq arrested and the Shah recalled. General Zahedi formed a Cabinet and the Senate, which had been dissolved by Mossadeq a year before, was reinstated. A loan of 45 million dollars was rapidly forthcoming from the United States to help shore up Iran's tottering economy. Mossadeq was tried in November and sentenced to three years imprisonment. In December diplomatic relations with Great Britain were restored. Early in the new year negotiations were started with Great Britain and the United States over the future of the Iranian oil industry.

How was it that Iranian nationalism based, like Arab nationalism, on resistance to Western imperialism and on a determination to eliminate western military and political influence should, unlike Arab nationalism, have resulted in a 'moderate' reaction and in a reversion to a régime whose policies came to be subordinated to those of the Western Powers? The nationalist régime was overthrown as a result neither of Western military intervention nor of Western political intrigue. Nor was it overthrown as a result of the economic chaos into which it had thrown the country. Popular based nationalist régimes are well able to survive the results of self-created economic chaos. Nor was it overthrown as a result of a lack of financial assistance from the West, for that is one of the things which nationalist régimes have to learn to do without until they have proved themselves to be firmly established. One answer seems to be that Iranian nationalism, as exemplified by the National Front and by the Mullahs, had no roots in the aspirations of the rising middle-class towards social reform and technical progress. The principal supporters of the movement were big landowners and clergy who were opposed both to social reform and to technical progress and who relied for support principally on the violence of mobs incited by appeals to obscurantist prejudice. They held out no hopes of future material prosperity, no prospects of a new social order. They lived precariously on the heady popular enthusiasms generated by Mossadeq's carefully staged histrionics. Because of this right-wing orientation, the nationalist movement lost to the Tudeh Party most of that constructive enthusiasm for social reform which, in Arab countries, was placed at the service of nationalism. Many Tudeh Party supporters were not in fact communists but liberals who would have rallied to the support of a national movement with any coherent and progressive social content. Another, and perhaps decisive answer is that the Iranian nationalist movement neither sprang from the Army nor at any time gained any substantial support in the Army. As in other Middle East countries the political influence of the Army was in inverse proportion to its efficiency as a fighting force. By this standard the Iranian Army was indeed politically influential. More privileged and more aristocratic than most of the Arab armies it had, unlike the Arab armies, never been, or at all events had never appeared to be, a likely source of revolutionary activity. The Shah had cultivated it carefully ever since his accession to the throne and, on the whole, it remained loyal to him. But he had neither the self-confidence nor the ruthlessness to enable him to make use of that loyalty. The man who eventually used it was not the Shah but General Zahedi, and he used it, like General Monk, to restore the Monarchy and not, like General Qasim, to abolish it.

Mossadeq was the last of the old school of Middle East nationalists—composed of people like Zaghlul—who flourished in days before nationalism needed to be equated with social reform, and before local communist parties existed to steal their extremist thunder and drain off their more constructive potential supporters. The clownish reputation conferred on him by Western journalists was not totally undeserved. He had the clown-like aspect of an anachronism, a man born after his time, who acted the histrionics and mouthed the slogans of a past generation. He created much the same impression, and achieved the same lack of success, as a Marshall Hall would have created and achieved in the English Criminal Courts of the present day. But, for all his intrinsic absurdity, Mossadeq successfully defied the might of the British Empire and signalized the end of 150 years of British hegemony in the Persian Gulf. His record as national leader and would-be dictator was singularly free from bloodshed, and it is satisfactory to record that he did not pay for his failure with his life. Instead, he was sentenced to a comparatively short term of imprisonment, from which he was in due course released. He now lives (1961) in obscurity and, it is said, contentment, on his country estates, of which he was not prepared to jeopardize the ownership by any sponsorship of land reform, and continues to be regarded, if not with veneration and respect, at least with a sort of rueful affection by the majority of the Iranian people.

CHAPTER TEN

Oil, 1940–1954

A T THE BEGINNING of the second world war the Iranian oil industry was still incomparably the most mature and well-developed oil operation in the Persian Gulf area. In 1938 oil exports from Iran exceeded 10 million tons, consisting mostly of oil products refined at Abadan. The production of this refinery, the largest in the world, became particularly important when the war came to the Middle East, when the submarine menace in the Mediterranean developed and when the fuel requirements of the Allied forces in the Western Desert began steadily to increase with the build-up of armoured formations, with lengthening lines of communication and with the increasing use of aircraft. Later in the war the importance of Abadan increased still further as a result of increasing fuel requirements arising from the demands of the war against Japan. Because of this strategic importance, and in spite of difficulties caused by shortages of material and personnel, Iranian oil production, after declining to about 6·5 million tons in 1941, thereafter rose to 9·3 million tons in 1942, 9·7 million tons in 1943, 13·2 million tons in 1944 and 16·8 million tons in 1945. Iranian royalty income increased *pari passu* and, in 1945, attained a figure of £7·1 million compared with about £4 million immediately before the war. A.I.O.C's net profit and dividends had increased correspondingly; from 1941–4 a dividend of 20 per cent was declared every year and from 1945–50 a dividend of 30 per cent. After the war, the presence of an undamaged oil industry, the increasing availability of materials and personnel, and the mounting fuel requirements caused by the process of industrial reconstruction in Europe, ensured a ready and expanding market for Iranian oil. Exports rose to 19 million tons in 1946, 20 million tons in 1947, 24·8 million tons in 1948, 26·8 million tons in 1949, and 31·7 million tons in 1950. In that year A.I.O.C. net profits amounted to £33 million and Iranian oil revenue to £16 million. It was not unnatural that, during these years, the Iranian Government, suffering from severe inflation, desperately in need of funds for development, and feeling that the Iranian Treasury had been inadequately recompensed for the undoubted value of Iranian oil to the war effort and to the requirements of post-war reconstruction, should begin to agitate for an increased share of the golden harvest.

The strength of this agitation greatly increased when it was realized (*a*) that Iranian oil income, under the terms of the 1933 Agreement, was being adversely affected by the policy of dividend limitation which had, for domestic reasons, been imposed on the A.I.O.C. by the British Government, and (*b*) that the British Treasury was actually obtaining more in taxation from the A.I.O.C. than the Iranian Government were obtaining in royalties. In face of this agitation the A.I.O.C., in 1948, agreed to open negotiations with the Iranian Government for a revision of the 1933 Agreement with a view to providing Iran with a greater share of the increasing profits of the oil operation. As a result of these negotiations, extending over a year, a Supplemental Agreement was signed in July 1949. (During the course of these negotiations a proposal was made by A.I.O.C. and rejected by the Iranian Government for a 50/50 division of net profits, on the lines eventually—at the end of 1950—agreed between the Saudi Arabian Government and Aramco. This afterwards became the standard pattern of profit sharing between producing Company and host country in the Persian Gulf.) The Supplemental Agreement provided that the royalty rate should be increased from four shillings to six shillings a ton and that sums equal to one-fifth of those paid to the Company's General Reserve should be paid annually to the Iranian Government instead of being payable only at the end of the term of the 1933 Agreement. The Agreement also provided for an increase of from ninepence to one shilling a ton in tax commutation payment and for a guaranteed minimum of £4 million a year oil income to the Iranian Government. The effect of this Agreement, if it had been ratified, would have been approximately to double the sums receivable by the Iranian Government under the 1933 Agreement. The terms offered were much more favourable than any being at that time enjoyed by any Middle East oil producing country. But, as the delay in ratification lengthened, the terms became relatively less favourable, in that the profitability of oil on a sellers' market continued to increase, and so made the 50/50 proposal, rejected by Iran in 1949 and accepted by Saudi Arabia in 1950, even more favourable. An Iranian suggestion, during the course of 1950, to re-negotiate the Agreement on a 50/50 basis, was rejected by A.I.O.C. But by that time, the rising force of extreme nationalism probably made the ratification of any agreement between the A.I.O.C. and Iran, however favourable to the latter, impossible.

The story of the nationalization of the Iranian oil industry, and the subsequent dispute which resulted in the complete cessation of oil exports, has been told in the last chapter. The sudden loss of some 30 million tons of oil a year threatened to have a catastrophic effect on a world market still hungry for more and more oil. But the loss of Iranian oil was compensated by the rapid development of other oilfields in the Persian Gulf area, and particularly in Kuwait, where A.I.O.C. had a half-share in the concessionary Company, which, in the immediate post-war years, had discovered and had begun to exploit what proved to be the most prolific and most profitable oilfield in the Middle East. The increased exploitation of the vast oil reserves by that time known to exist in Kuwait, Saudi Arabia and elsewhere in the Persian Gulf enabled Great Britain and the Western world generally to do without Iranian oil until such time as Mossadeq, harrassed by deepening domestic crisis and exasperated into folly by rising domestic opposition, was replaced by a Government prepared, on the basis of the *fait accompli* of nationalization, to negotiate a settlement in respect of compensation, management of the oil operation and disposal of the oil. This settlement, which will be described in detail in Chapter 12, assisted as it was by the steadily increasing demand for oil products, not only in the Western world, but also in the lands bordering on the Indian Ocean, enabled Iran, from the end of 1954 onwards, rapidly to resume its place as one of the world's major oil exporters. But in the meantime, the absence of Iranian oil from world markets for three years had greatly stimulated production in Iraq, Kuwait and Saudi Arabia, and enabled

Kuwait and Saudi Arabia to establish themselves as the first and second largest oil producers in the Gulf.

The progress of Iraq's oil industry during the war years had been less happy than that of Iran. At the beginning of the war Iraqi production for export amounted to about 4 million tons, nearly all of which was produced from the Kirkuk field and transported to the Mediterranean by the two pipelines to Tripoli and Haifa. The Vichy régime in Syria (from June 1940 to June 1941) through which the Tripoli pipeline passed, the Rashid Ali régime in Iraq (from April to June 1941), the submarine menace in the Mediterranean (from June 1940 onwards), added to the shortage of men and materials which affected all, and particularly British-controlled, oilfields in the Middle East, combined to limit the development of the Iraqi oil industry. Exports fell to 2·5 million tons in 1940 and to 1·5 million tons in 1941. Thereafter they began to recover, reaching 2·5 million tons in 1942, 3·5 million tons in 1943, 4 million tons in 1944, and 4·5 million tons in 1945. Early in 1942 the threat of invasion from the north, which would have been realized in the event of a Russian collapse, led to the plugging in of all producer wells not actually in operation. This denial exercise had the effect of retarding a post-war increase in the rate of export. In spite of this, post-war development, stimulated, as it was elsewhere, by rapidly increasing demand, was energetically pursued. The limiting factor, until the Basra field in South Iraq came into production (which was not until 1951) was pipeline capacity to the Mediterranean. Immediately after the war two additional 16-inch lines were built to Haifa and Tripoli respectively, thus more than doubling the capacity provided by the existing lines. But hardly had the Haifa line been completed when the Palestine war, the formation of the State of Israel (in May 1949) and the Arab boycott of Israel made it impossible to use either of the Haifa lines. This grave loss of export capacity was made good by the construction of a 30-inch line from Kirkuk to Banias in Syria, which was completed in 1952. By this time the Basra field had come into production and had been linked to the Persian Gulf by a 12-inch, 74-mile long pipeline to Fao (to be supplemented in 1953 by a 24-inch line). In 1951 Iraqi production amounted to nearly 8·5 million tons, or more than double the 1939 figure. The Iraqi Government, like the governments of all other oil producing States in the Middle East, desperately needing extra revenue in order to try and counteract mounting social pressures by social and development works, and acutely conscious of the growing importance of oil to the West and the growing profitability of oil to the concessionary Company, had, ever since the end of the war, been negotiating with I.P.C. for a revision of the 1925 Agreement. By the middle of 1950 agreement was reached for an increase in the rate of royalty from four shillings to six shillings per ton. A dispute then arose about the interpretation of the 'gold' clause in the original Agreement (which was also to be applied to the new Agreement). The Iraqi Government elected to have the dispute adjudicated by a British Court in preference to arbitration, but, while preparations for the case were proceeding, an important new element came into the situation. At the end of 1950 an agreement was announced between the Saudi Arabian Government and Aramco by which the former was to receive 50 per cent of the profit realized on export sales of crude oil. This agreement revolutionized all existing oil agreements in the Gulf and led to the approximate quadrupling of the unitary rates of oil revenue received by the producing States.[1] The attraction of the '50/50 deal' to the producing countries, and its acceptability to the concessionary Companies, derived from the very high current profitability of crude oil, which meant that the '50/50 deal' gave something of the order of £2 per ton profit each to the producing country and the concessionaire. This compared with a figure of something like ten shillings per ton which producing countries were receiving under the four shilling a ton royalty, and with something like twenty-five shillings per ton which they would be due to receive under the six shilling a ton royalty arrangements then being negotiated in Iran and Iraq.

On receipt of news of the 50/50 deal in Saudi Arabia the Iraqi Government pressed for a similar arrangement, and the I.P.C., possibly glad of a way of escape from the troublesome gold clause (which had been further complicated by a recent devaluation of sterling), agreed to negotiate a revised agreement on the 50/50 basis. Such an agreement was arrived at in August 1951 and was applied retroactively from the beginning of 1951. The Agreement, based on the principal of a 50/50 division of net profits before foreign taxation, provided for a minimum production of 22 million tons per annum from the northern fields from 1954 onwards and for a minimum production of 8 million tons per annum from the Basra field from 1955 onwards. It also provided (*a*) as an insurance against low profits, that Iraq would never receive, as its share of the profits, sums less than 25 per cent of the seaboard value of the oil in the case of northern production and 33 per cent of the seaboard value in the case of Basra production; (*b*) that the Iraqi Government could take, at its option as part of its share of the profits, up to one-eighth of the total amount of oil produced under the Agreement as a payment in kind. The effect of the Agreement, with its provisions for increased royalties and increased future production, was that Iraq could, within a very few years, expect to receive sums of the order of £50 million a year in oil revenue as compared with the £5 million approximately which they had received up to 1950. The prospect of this increased revenue meant that the Development Board which had been set up in 1950 and which was entitled by law to receive 70 per cent of all oil revenues, could look forward to the receipt of very considerable sums for financing the ambitious programmes of agricultural, irrigation, social and industrial development, which, up to that time, had been little more than castles in the air.

Meanwhile the I.P.C. shareholders had been passing through a somewhat acrimonious process of readjustment in respect of their interests in I.P.C. During the war, both Compagnie Française des Pétroles (C.F.P.), in view of its Vichy connexions, and Gulbenkian, for some recondite reason, had been declared enemy aliens by the British Government and debarred from receiving either oil or profits from the operations of I.P.C. Gulbenkian's enemy alien status was revoked in 1943 and his claims for compensation settled in 1945. C.F.P's enemy alien status was not revoked until after the liberation of France in 1945, and its consequent litigation against its other partners in I.P.C. not settled until 1950. This litigation was accompanied by another case brought by C.F.P. and Gulbenkian against the American shareholders in I.P.C.—the Near East Development Corporation (N.E.D.C.) consisting of Standard of New Jersey and Socony-Mobil—who, in 1946, informed their I.P.C.

associates that they considered the 1928 Red Line Agreement as null and void and that they proposed respectively to acquire a 30 per cent and a 10 per cent share in Aramco. It will be recalled that the Red Line Agreement, which the N.E.D.C. companies had, with some difficulty, been induced to sign in 1928, bound the shareholders in I.P.C. not to seek concessions elsewhere in the Red Line area (which, *inter alia*, included all the western shores of the Gulf except for Kuwait) except in conjunction with their I.P.C. associates. The N.E.D.C. which had, twenty years before, with the assistance of the U.S. Government, invoked the Open Door principle as a means of acquiring an interest in Iraqi oil, now, again with the support of the U.S. Government (and with the agreement of the British Government) invoked U.S. Anti-Trust legislation as a means of escape from the restrictive agreement which had been an original condition of their admission to I.P.C. It appears that N.E.D.C. had already committed themselves to participation in Aramco when they denounced the Red Line Agreement in 1946. But the objections of C.F.P. and Gulbenkian made it necessary to delay for two years their formal assumption of shareholding in Aramco (who needed the capital which the two Companies could provide both for increasing oil operations being undertaken and, more particularly, for the pipeline which was about to be constructed to the Mediterranean). The difficulty was solved by the two Companies guaranteeing bank loans to Aramco until, in November 1948, a settlement was arrived at with C.F.P. and Gulbenkian which released N.E.D.C. from their obligations under the Red Line Agreement and permitted them officially to enter the Aramco enterprise. This settlement marked the end of the Red Line Agreement and left all the shareholders in I.P.C. free to develop their concession-hunting separately outside Iraq.

We have already seen how, in Saudi Arabia, the Americans, nervous about the diminution of their indigenous oil reserves, and suspicious of British designs on the Aramco concession, embarked on a vigorous policy of developing Saudi Arabian oil resources during the war with the double object of safeguarding U.S. post-war oil requirements and, by means of the increased income accruing to ibn Saud from oil royalties, of replacing the British Government as ibn Saud's principal financial patron. As a result of this forward policy Saudi Arabian production, by the end of the war, was running at a rate of nearly 3 million tons a year as compared with about half a million tons a year immediately before the war. The impetus of wartime development enabled post-war plans to get under way very rapidly. Large new fields were discovered and exploited and a 30-inch Trans-Arabian pipeline (TAPline) constructed to the Mediterranean terminal of Saida in Lebanon. A refinery was erected at Ras Tanura on the coast of al-Hasa, the Caltex-owned refinery at Bahrain enlarged, and the line connecting it to the Saudi fields doubled to enable it to refine greater quantities of Saudi crude. Production soared upwards with amazing rapidity. 7·8 million tons were produced in 1946, 11·8 million tons in 1947, 18·7 million tons in 1948, 22·8 million tons in 1949, rising to no less than 46 million tons in 1954, making Saudi Arabia the second largest producing country in the Persian Gulf (Kuwaiti production in 1954 just exceeded that of Saudi Arabia) and the third largest exporting country in the world (after Venezuela and Kuwait). Income to the Saudi Arabian Government, calculated in accordance with the 50/50 Agreement concluded at the end of 1950, reached an equivalent of nearly £100 million in 1954. The revolutionary nature of this enormous accession of wealth can be imagined when it is remembered that the total Saudi Arabian budget in 1938 had amounted to some £3 million, and that in 1942 the finances of the Saudi kingdom were almost entirely sustained by a subsidy of £3 million from Great Britain.

The 50/50 Agreement of December 1950 set a pattern for the revision of oil concessions all over the Persian Gulf. The Agreement was arrived at as a result of pressure from the Saudi Arabian Government for a revision of the pre-war concession. There was the same controversy over the gold clause as in Iraq and it was solved in the same way. But Aramco got in first with their 50/50 Agreement (something of the same sort was already in force in Venezuela) and so, on the one hand, gained the propagandist advantage *vis-a-vis* the producing countries of having pioneered a more generous division of profits as between producing countries and concessionaires and, on the other hand, incurred the odium, *vis-à-vis* British, Anglo-Dutch and French oil companies, of having given away more than was immediately necessary and thus having forced the hands of other oil companies currently engaged in similar negotiations.

Before the conclusion of the 50/50 Agreements in Saudi Arabia, the Americans had already introduced a new element into the search for oil and negotiations for oil concessions in the Persian Gulf. In 1945 the U.S. Government advanced the claim that riparian States should have sovereignty over mineral deposits underlying the 'continental shelf' or shallow area of sea lying off their coasts. Applied to the Persian Gulf this meant that riparian States could claim sovereignty outwards from their coasts to a line midway between the Iranian and Arabian shores. In the shallow waters of the Persian Gulf prospecting and drilling for oil was practicable over most of its marine area. In 1947 Aramco relinquished the concessionary rights which they had acquired from the Saudi Arabian Government over the undivided Saudi share of the Neutral Zone (demarcated in 1922) between Saudi Arabia and Kuwait, in exchange for exploration and exploitation rights over the 'continental shelf' off al-Hasa. In 1949 the British Government advised the Persian Gulf Sheikhs under British protection formally to claim sovereignty over their 'continental shelves'. This led to an interesting piece of litigation over the Qatar continental shelf, a concession for the exploration and exploitation of which was awarded by the Sheikh, in 1949, to the Superior Oil Company. His right to do this was challenged by the mainland concessionaires (Petroleum Developments (Qatar), later the Qatar Petroleum Company, a subsidiary of I.P.C.). As a result of arbitration proceedings the Superior concession was upheld and the rights of the mainland concessionaire held to extend to the three-mile limit only. (Subsequently, Superior transferred their concession to Shell.) Later, continental shelf concessions were awarded (*a*) by the Sheikh of Abu Dhabi to Abu Dhabi Marine Concessions Ltd., owned as to 70 per cent by the British Petroleum Co. (the new name for the Anglo-Iranian Oil Company after 1951) and as to 30 per cent by the Compagnie Française des Pétroles; (*b*) by King Saud and the Sheikh of Kuwait over the continental shelf of the Neutral Zone; (*c*) by the Iranian Government, who, in 1957, gave three 'continental shelf' concessions off the Iranian coast; and (*d*) by the Sheikh of Kuwait

173

who, in 1960, awarded a concession to Shell for the exploitation of the Kuwait continental shelf.

The development of the oil resources of the Sheikhdom of Kuwait proceeded even more rapidly than in Saudi Arabia, and the impact of hitherto undreamed-of incomes from oil produced an even more revolutionary effect on its 200,000 inhabitants. As we have seen, nine producing wells had already been drilled in Kuwait by 1942 when wartime shortages compelled a suspension of operations and the shutting-in of the wells. Work was resumed by the Kuwait Oil Company in 1945 and the first shipment of oil took place in 1946. In 1948 production amounted to 6·3 million tons. By this time it was apparent that Kuwait possessed some of the richest oilfields in the world which, owing to the comparatively shallow depth at which the oil was located, and the proximity of the fields to the sea, could be very economically exploited. Kuwait's big chance came with th Iranian shut-down in 1951. The economical production costs or Kuwaiti oil, the fact that British Petroleum Co. (ex-A.I.O.C.), as 50 per cent owners of Kuwait Oil Co. were naturally anxious to offset the loss of the oil denied to them in Iran, and the fact that Gulf, the other 50 per cent owner, had a supply contract with Shell, who were deprived of large quantities of Iranian oil previously obtained from A.I.O.C., all combined to ensure that Kuwait would be the principal beneficiary of Mossadeq's oil policy. Kuwaiti production, which was 17 million tons in 1950, rose to 27·8 million tons in 1951, 37 million tons in 1952, 42·6 million tons in 1953, and 46·9 million tons in 1954. In December 1951, the original Agreement, which provided for a royalty of Rs. 3 per ton plus As. 4 per ton in lieu of taxation (this, after the devaluation of the rupee in September 1949, was the lowest per ton rate of payment among all the Persian Gulf concessions), was amended to provide for the by now conventional 50/50 division of profits. As a result Kuwaiti oil revenue which, in 1950 amounted only to about £5 million, had, by 1954, increased to something like £90 million per annum.

It has been related that Aramco, in August 1948, abandoned their concession over the undivided Saudi half of the 2,000 square miles of mostly uninhabited territory between Saudi Arabia and Kuwait known as the Neutral Zone. Just before that the Sheikh of Kuwait had awarded a concession for the undivided Kuwaiti half of the Neutral Zone to a group of small American oil companies who had formed the American Independent Oil Company (Aminoil) on terms very much more favourable to the producing country than any other concession operative in the Middle East at that time. The royalty was fixed at 2.50 dollars a ton plus a one-eighth share of net profits to the Kuwaiti Treasury; provision was made for a bonus of 7 million dollars on signature of the Agreement and for a rent of 625,000 dollars a year thereafter. In January 1949 the relinquished Aramco concession in the Saudi Arabian half of the Neutral Zone was awarded to another American Company, the Pacific Western Oil Corporation, on terms even more favourable than those offered by Aminoil. The royalty was fixed at 4 dollars a ton plus one-eighth share of net profits, an initial bonus of 9½ million dollars and an annual rent of 1 million dollars. The two concessionaires formed a joint organization for working the two concessions in the undivided area. After a long and frustrating period of fruitless exploration, commercial oil was struck in 1953 and commercial production started in 1954.

This was the first successful incursion of any oil Company other than the eight 'majors' (Standard of New Jersey, Royal Dutch-Shell, British Petroleum, Gulf Oil, Standard of California, Texas Oil, Socony-Mobil, and Compagnie Française des Pétroles) into the field of oil concessions in the Persian Gulf. It was not the last. The generous terms offered, first by Aminoil and later by Western Pacific in 1948–9, were the prelude to the 50/50 Agreement concluded between Saudi Arabia and Aramco in 1950 and afterwards to the other oil concessions in the Persian Gulf. Thereafter the Governments of the producing countries realized that it might be possible to obtain from relatively small independent oil companies better terms than the 'majors' were prepared to offer, and to use such terms as a lever with which to revise existing agreements with the major companies. There were disadvantages in this procedure for the producing countries as well as for the major oil companies. The independents, by reason of inferior capital, equipment and manpower resources compared with the major companies were generally not able to exploit their concessions as rapidly as the 'majors'. And when they found oil, lack of marketing facilities and the desire for a quick 'pay-off' were liable to lead to price cutting and to over-production, both of which had a disturbing effect on the profitability of Persian Gulf prices as a whole. Since, under the 50/50 agreements, the producing countries were directly interested in profitability, this was a potentially serious consideration which, in the full flush of the sellers' market which lasted until about 1958, was not always taken fully into account by the governments of the producing countries.

In Bahrain, where the oil concession was owned 50/50 by Standard of California and Texas, the fortunes of the Bahrain Petroleum Company (B.A.P.C.O.), the concessionary company, came to depend less and less on the limited crude production, which rose to the maximum of about 1·5 million tons in 1948 and thereafter became stabilized at about that figure, and more and more on the refining of Aramco crude pumped over from the mainland. By 1954 the through-put of the refinery exceeded 10 million tons, most of which was Saudi Arabian oil. The terms of the original Agreement, by which the Government of Bahrain received a royalty of Rs. 3 per ton on all oil produced, were amended in 1950 to provide for a royalty of Rs. 10 per ton. In 1952 a further amendment was negotiated providing for the implementation of the 50/50 profit sharing arrangement on the by now usual pattern in the Gulf. Provision was also made for a royalty payment in respect of the Saudi Arabian oil entering Bahrain for refining. As a result of these amendments Bahrain's oil income which, up to 1950, had been of the order of £0·5 million a year, rose, in 1950 and 1951, to over £1 million a year, and thereafter to between £3 and £4 million a year. Such an income, insignificant compared with that being received from oil by Kuwait and Saudi Arabia, and applied to an economy much more mature than those of Kuwait and Saudi Arabia, naturally had a much less drastic effect on that economy. In Bahrain the oil income, small in amount and developing slowly over the years, made a beneficial addition to rather than a revolutionary change in standards and ways of life.

In Qatar, as we have seen, oil development was suspended owing to wartime shortages in 1942 although, by the end of 1940, three producing wells had been drilled. Operations were not resumed until 1947, and the first export took place at the end of 1949. Production during 1950 amounted to 1·5 million tons, rising to 4·7 million tons in 1954. Meanwhile, as has been related, a concession was awarded by the Sheikh of Qatar in 1949, covering the 'continental shelf' to the Superior Oil Co. who subsequently transferred it to Shell. But, by the end of 1960, no commercial oil had been produced from this concession. The terms of the mainland concession, operated by the Qatar Petroleum Company, a subsidiary of I.P.C., were amended in 1950 to provide for an increase in royalty from Rs. 3 to Rs. 10 a ton, and in 1952 to provide for the implementation of the 50/50 profit-sharing principle. As a result Qatar's oil income which in 1950 amounted to £400,000, rose in 1951 to £1·75 million and by 1954 amounted to between £8 and £9 million a year. Although small compared with Kuwaiti and Saudi Arabian incomes, the impact of this wealth on a primitive country with a population of about 30,000, ruled by a family whose ways of life and general outlook had been that of minor tribal sheikhs, was revolutionary and, in some respects, catastrophic. Sheikh Ali al Thani, who succeeded his father in the Sheikhdom in 1949, was determined to retain the patriarchal and despotic nature of sheikhly rule, and regarded the increasing oil income primarily as an accretion to his own personal fortune. However, he was induced to appoint a British Adviser and, in practice, half the oil income was devoted to governmental services, a quarter to the Ruler's privy purse, and a quarter to provide incomes for his numerous relations.

Oil exploration in the Trucial Coast and in the Sultanate of Musqat and Oman by various subsidiaries of I.P.C. did not lead to the production of any commercial oil. But this exploration had one important political consequence. The desert boundaries between the Trucial Sheikhdoms and the Sultanate of Musqat and Oman on the one hand and the Kingdom of Saudi Arabia on the other were, for the most part, vague and undefined and, until the possibility of oil deposits was known to exist, little importance had been attached to the question of sovereignty over the few oases to be found in these borderlands, which were used as watering-places by the various wandering tribes of the area in accordance with traditional custom, sometimes disputed and occasionally fought over. One of the largest of these oases is Buraimi, situated in the indeterminate triangle where the Kingdom of Saudi Arabia, the Sultanate of Musqat and Oman and the Sheikhdom of Abu Dhabi meet. The oasis consists of eight villages, of which six are claimed by the Sheikh of Abu Dhabi and two by the Sultan of Musqat and Oman. In August 1952 one of the two villages claimed by the Sultan of Musqat was occupied by the Saudis, who advanced a claim to sovereignty over the whole oasis based on its possession by the Wahhabis during the first half of the nineteenth century. (The Wahhabis had been evicted by the Sultan of Musqat in 1869, but effective control of the oasis had never been exercised from Musqat—mainly owing to difficulties of communication—and in the twentieth century the oasis came under the effective control of Abu Dhabi.) The British Government, acting on behalf of Musqat and Abu Dhabi, took the dispute to arbitration. Arbitration proceedings, which took place at Geneva, broke down in 1955 and combined forces of Oman Levies and Trucial Scouts (British-officered military forces under the nominal control of the Sultan of Musqat and the Trucial Sheikhs respectively but under the effective control of the British Chief Political Resident stationed at Bahrain) forcibly evicted the Saudis and reoccupied the oasis. Saudi Arabia then broke off diplomatic relations with Great Britain and has not since resumed them. Thus the Buraimi dispute, during the course of which (in 1953) Abdul Aziz ibn Saud died and was succeeded by his eldest son who assumed the style of King Saud, marked the end of some forty years of consistently amicable relations between Great Britain and the House of ibn Saud. From the Treaty of Darin in 1915 to the Treaty of Jidda in 1927 ibn Saud had been virtually a British client. From 1927 to 1943 Great Britain had continued to be the paramount foreign Power in Saudi Arabia and, during the first part of World War Two, had assumed the burden of financing the poverty-stricken State, whose income from the Pilgrimage had been reduced to nothing as a result of the war. Thereafter, as we have seen, British was rapidly replaced by American influence as a result of large American oil investments and American aid from Lease Lend funds which replaced the previous British subventions. From then onwards ibn Saud found that he could do without the British. His increasing absorption with oil caused him to ignore, not only his previous ambitions for Arab leadership, but also his previous and long-standing ties with Great Britain. His own death in 1953, followed by the departure from Saudi Arabia of Philby, his British adviser and friend who had been intimate with him for upwards of twenty years, severed the last remaining links of friendship between the two countries. King Saud's western contacts had been much more with American than with British and he had never been friendly with Philby, who was in any case, by this time, *persona non grata* with the British Government. Thus the severance of diplomatic relations as a consequence of the Buraimi dispute was the culmination of many years of increasing estrangement.

In 1949 the Sheikh of Abu Dhabi awarded the exploration concession for the Abu Dhabi 'continental shelf' to the International Marine Oil Company. After the award of this concession had (as in Qatar) been unsuccessfully contested by the owners of the Abu Dhabi mainland concession (a subsidiary of I.P.C.), the International Marine Oil Co. (in 1952) transferred its concession to Abu Dhabi Marine Concessions Ltd., owned 70 per cent by British Petroleum and 30 per cent by Compagnie Française des Pétroles. (Both these Companies were shareholders in I.P.C. who, after the dissolution of the Red Line Agreement in 1948 were entitled to obtain independent concessions in the previous Red Line area.) In 1958 oil was found near Das Island, in the area of this concession.

Both absolutely and relatively the importance of Persian Gulf oil had increased enormously between 1939 and 1954, both as a factor in world oil supplies and as a factor in the economies of the producing countries. In 1938 total oil production in the countries of the Persian Gulf amounted to about 16·5 million tons, of which Iran accounted for about 10·5 million tons, out of a total world production of some 280 million tons. In 1954 total Persian Gulf production amounted to some 137 million tons, of which Iran accounted for only 2·9 million tons, out of a total world production of some 800 million tons. The increased importance of Persian Gulf oil for Western Europe had, by 1954, become very great. In 1938 less than one-fifth of Western Europe's oil supplies had come from the Persian Gulf area. By 1954 this proportion had risen to three-quarters. The potential importance of Persian Gulf oil was even greater. In 1954 it was calculated that some two-thirds of the world's proven oil reserves were in the Persian Gulf area; it was apparent that Western Europe would become more and more dependent on supplies of oil from the Persian Gulf area unless other substantial oil reserves could be found—as they have since, to some extent, been found in North and West Africa. This increasing dependence on Persian Gulf oil for actual peacetime and potential wartime uses by the countries of Western Europe made the Persian Gulf and the oil lanes between the Persian Gulf and the Mediterranean (the Red Sea and the Suez Canal, and the pipeline routes across Saudi Arabia, Jordan, Lebanon and Syria) a vital strategic area for the Western alliance at a time when nationalist influence bearing on the area from within and communist influence threatening to bear on the area from without were tending to subvert Western relations both with Iran and with the Arab world, thus endangering the free availability to the West both of the oil itself and of the means of transporting it. The Iranian oil dispute, of which an account has already been given, was an indication of what might be in store for the West. The growth of Arab nationalism, of which an account will be given in the next chapter, seemed likely to endanger the continued availability of that Arab oil, an increase in the production of which, as we have seen, had made up for the loss of Iranian production to the West during the years 1951–4. The Iranian oil dispute was patched up during 1954 (see Chapter Twelve) and Iranian oil started to flow again to the West. But what Iran had done, might be done again by governments of oil-producing States actuated by or exposed to similar nationalist ambitions and xenophobic resentments.

The importance of increasing revenues to, and the effect of these revenues on, the economies and social structure of the oil-producing States, was not less than the importance of the oil itself to, and its effects on the policies of, the countries of Western Europe. The impact of these revenues naturally varied with the proportion which these revenues formed of the country's total income and of its government's total budget. Generally, oil revenues only began to have an important effect on the social life and economy of the States concerned from 1950 onwards, when rapidly increasing production and the larger share of profit accruing to the producing countries under the 50/50 profit-sharing agreements combined greatly to increase the annual sums received. In Iran, where the oil operation virtually came to a halt at a time when a greatly increased income from oil was within the grasp of the Iranian Government, the effect was seen in terms of the non-availability of the income which might otherwise have been theirs—in the delay necessarily imposed on development schemes and in the economic stagnation and political ferment resulting from the loss of Iran's principal export and major source of foreign currency. In Iraq the increased revenue received after 1950 enabled a rapid implementation of the ambitious plans adumbrated by the Development Board, which had been set up in 1949 and which received 70 per cent of Iraq's oil income. These plans, which consisted for the most part of long term irrigation and drainage schemes, did not have that immediate impact on living standards which less ambitious and shorter-term projects might have done, and failed in what was perhaps their primary objective—that of reconciling the people of Iraq to the domestic and foreign policies of the governing régime. The benefits of the money invested will perhaps be reaped by the successors to that régime.

But the greatest impact of oil revenues, on a hitherto undreamt-of scale, was felt in those Arab States—Kuwait, Saudi Arabia and Qatar—which previously had been in an endemic state of extreme, primitive and perhaps not altogether discontented indigence and unsophistication and to whose governments these oil revenues represented almost the only, and incomparably the greatest, source of revenue they had ever known. All three of these States were despotically governed by absolute hereditary Rulers who were accustomed to make little or no distinction between their own personal income and the income of the State. In all three States therefore the oil income became in effect the property of the Ruler, and the principal limitation on his free disposal of it arose from the exigencies of the Ruler's (usually very numerous) relatives. In Saudi Arabia virtually all of the vast oil revenues accruing to the Ruler were disposed of by the Ruler and his relatives in the building of palaces, in overseas investments, in high living abroad and in the financing of complicated intrigues and plots at home and in the rest of the Arab world. Very little benefit was obtained by the ordinary citizen, except by the (often foreign) contractors who built the palaces, the merchants who furnished them, and by the innumerable hangers-on of the various scions of the

Royal House. Anything done in the way of communications—like the railway from Dharan to Riadh completed in 1952 or the road which parallels the Trans-Arabian pipeline across the Peninsula—or schools, or bore-holes for water, or agriculture, or any other form of development, has been financed and carried out by Aramco as part of the oil operation (and thus, after 1950, deductible from the shared profits of the oil operation). This state of affairs lasted until 1957, when the personal extravagances of King Saud, combined with his inability to control the exigencies of his relatives and hangers-on, had reduced the finances of the State to such chaos that he was compelled to give his brother Feisal, who became in effect his Prime Minister, power to separate the State Budget from the Privy Purse, and to control and limit the amount of expenditure under both heads.

The social impact of foreign technicians and foreign techniques on an extremely primitive society was minimized by a policy of 'apartheid', encouraged by a régime anxious to avoid the spread of dangerous thoughts which might lead to undesirable speculations. Even Moslem Arabs from Egypt, Syria and Iraq, who came in ever-increasing numbers to Saudi Arabia as contractors, teachers, etc., were not encouraged to mix much with the native Saudis. But many thousands of Saudis were necessarily taught a variety of industrial trades and skills, and many hundreds went abroad on various courses of instruction. A new generation of children, whose parents were mostly illiterate, were taught to read and write in Aramco schools. All these things were bound to have their long-term effect, which would make it impossible for the Rulers of Saudi Arabia to benefit from the results without eventually exposing themselves to the implications of an industrial revolution.

Most of the 200,000 inhabitants of the Sheikhdom of Kuwait were concentrated in one town, and on this town was concentrated the full benefit of the golden shower which was falling on the tiny Sheikhdom, Sheikh Abdullah as Subah, who succeeded his father, Sheikh Ahmed, as Ruler in 1950, is a wise, prudent and reasonably benevolent Ruler, who has no unduly extravagant tastes himself, and restrains any undue extravagances on the part of his relatives and hangers-on. Moreover he and his advisers take care to see that too much of Kuwait's oil wealth does not get into the hands of the army of Lebanese and other contractors, entrepreneurs and foreign adventurers who descended on Kuwait in the early 1950's. Kuwaiti money was, as far as possible, to be kept in the Kuwaiti family; foreign contractors had to take Kuwaiti partners; foreign nationals, whether or not they were Arabs, found it virtually impossible to qualify for Kuwaiti citizenship. Apart from the reasonably modest requirements of the Ruling House, Kuwaiti income is partly spent on the creation of a comprehensive Welfare State, with up-to-date hospitals, free schooling (Kuwaiti parents are actually paid to send their children to school), retirement pensions, etc., and partly invested (mostly in London) against the time, still far distant, when Kuwait's oil resources will have become exhausted.

In Kuwait, as in Saudi Arabia, the social impact of Western techniques and Western manners has been minimized by a deliberate policy of 'apartheid' (the whole oil operation, including the administrative offices, is tucked away in the desert, some twenty-five miles from Kuwait town) but, as in Saudi Arabia, the long term impact of technical training, knowledge of English (necessary for administrative positions in the oil Company) and almost universal literacy on the part of the coming generation of adults, is already beginning to make itself felt among the students and younger generation generally.

In Qatar, the Sheikh, in his treatment of oil revenues, endeavoured to follow the example of Saudi Arabia rather than that of Kuwait, although the influence of a British Adviser provided that half of these revenues were devoted to social works designed to improve the living conditions of the 30,000 Qataris generally by the construction, equipping and staffing of schools and hospitals, etc. The other half was spent according to the caprices of the Ruler and his relatives; as in Saudi Arabia these caprices took the form of numerous palaces, numerous and expensive motor-cars, mountain villas in Switzerland and Lebanon, and so on. The insensate extravagance of Sheikh Ali who, by 1959, was receiving a personal income of some £4 million a year and spending considerably more than that, was cut short by his abdication in that year. This abdication was arranged by the Chief Political Resident Persian Gulf and was marked by the appearance of a British gunboat off Doha, the capital of Qatar. He was succeeded by his son Ahmed who seems likely to institute a wiser and more enlightened régime than that maintained by his father.

In Bahrain, the much more gradual and much more limited effect of oil revenues on a community which was much the most socially advanced in all the Persian Gulf Sheikhdoms, was analogous to the impact of these revenues on Iraq. That is to say, they created the possibility of social and economic development rather than entirely changing a previous way of life. Sheikh Salman bin Hamad al Khalifa who succeeded his father, Sheikh Hamad, in 1942, is, like Sheikh Abdullah as Subah of Kuwait, a wise and relatively enlightened man.[3] He traditionally receives one-third of the oil revenues for his own use and that of his family, one-third is allotted to the Government Budget and one-third is invested. In Bahrain, the effect of oil revenues in stimulating literacy, the acquisition of technical skills, and knowledge of foreign countries and foreign ways, superimposed on an already higher cultural standard than that existing in the other Sheikhdoms in pre-oil days, has already had its effect on social and political attitudes, and there had already appeared, to a far greater extent than in Kuwait or Saudi Arabia, or of course Qatar, signs of political consciousness and resentment against the (reasonably benevolent) despotism of the Ruler.

This political awakening in Saudi Arabia and in the oil-bearing Sheikhdoms, stimulated as it was by the financial, technical and social implications of oil production, tended to find a focus in the movement of Arab nationalism, which will be the theme of the next chapter.

CHAPTER ELEVEN

Arab Nationalism in the Persian Gulf

AFTER THE DEFEAT of the Iraqi Army, the collapse of the Golden Square, the flight of Rashid Ali, and the return of the Regent in June 1941, Jamil al Madfai, a 'pro-Treaty' politician, formed a Government which, like its immediate successors, was, owing to wartime conditions and the fact that Iraq was once more virtually a conquered country, very much subject to the authority of the British Government. Although not again to be an active theatre of war, Iraq became strategically important to the Allies from two points of view. First, together with Iran, it was to form a base for the transport of supplies across Iran to Russia. Secondly, in the event of a Russian collapse—a possibility which continued to exist until the German retreat from Stalingrad at the end of 1942—Iraq would probably be in the line of advance of German armies making for the Persian Gulf and Suez Canal. Thus, southern Iraq became covered with Allied supply depots, northern Iraq with Allied fortifications, and the whole of Iraq with Allied military officials. All this, together with the accompanying inflation, the security regulations which imposed a virtual ban on all political activity, and the necessarily 'collaborationist' nature of the régime, resulted, as in Egypt, and as in Iran, in the build-up of a heterogeneous opposition, consisting, in the case of Iraq, principally of the pre-war 'anti-Treaty' politicians, and of emerging middle-class groups, ranging ideologically from fascist to communist and united only in their opposition to the régime and to the British connexion. Although the Majlis remained in being throughout the war (there were elections in 1943) this opposition was extra-constitutional. For the Majlis did not reflect the real opposition but only the shadow boxing of factional intrigues and petty rivalries within 'the pro-Treaty' establishment. These intrigues and rivalries led to numerous changes of Government during the war years. Jamil al Madfai resigned in October 1941 and was succeeded as Prime Minister by Nuri as Said who had, for the previous six months, been Iraqi Minister in Cairo. Nuri as Said remained as Prime Minister for 2½ years, heading three successive Cabinets, until, in May 1944, he was replaced by the veteran Hamid al Pashashi. During this period Nuri established himself, and until his death in 1958 was to remain, the outstanding figure in Iraqi political life and the principal Iraqi champion of a consistent Arab policy of which the main and related ingredients were: (a) continued alliance with Great Britain; (b) the formation of an association of Arab States in alliance with Great Britain which would use that alliance to secure from Great Britain a satisfactory solution of the Palestine problem and which would, generally, be a development of the 'Arab State or Confederation of States' under a British aegis adumbrated during and aborted after the first world war; and (c) the development of the Iraqi economy, by the use of the increasing oil revenues and the preferential treatment for Iraqi oil, as well as by means of British and American grants and loans which, it was hoped, would result from a policy of alliance with Great Britain and the West. This policy was a logical extension of the 'pro-Treaty' position in that, in the light of increasing opposition to that position in Iraq, it endeavoured to fortify it (a) by broadening its base to include an alliance with other Arab States pursuing the same policy, and (b) by extracting the maximum economic and political advantages from the West as the price of a western alliance in order to appease popular opposition with evidence of solid advantages being derived from the alliance. In the event this policy was to fail. Nuri was unable to carry a majority of other Arab Governments with him in a 'pro-Treaty' policy and Arab nationalists became more and more identified with a neutralist, which meant in effect an anti-British, position. Economically, although in the post-war years oil revenues rose beyond all expectation, Nuri never succeeded in applying these oil revenues in such a way as to assuage the popular discontent or to counteract the propaganda from communist and Arab nationalist sources provoked by the political aspects of his policy. This failure was undoubtedly to some extent due to Nuri's failure to extract from the British, as the price of his

186

friendship, a settlement of the Palestine question satisfactory to Arab nationalist aspirations (which meant, in effect, a policy based on the 1939 White Paper which was still, at the end of the war, the official policy of the British Government). It is arguable that, had Nuri been able to demonstrate, both to his own fellow-countrymen and to the other Arab Governments, the benefits of a British alliance in the shape of a British Palestine policy which showed that the British Government was prepared seriously to take Arab nationalist views into account, he would have attracted sufficient support, both domestically and in other Arab capitals, successfully to combat the tide which was beginning to run so strongly against the British connexion, and successfully to confuse that identity which was establishing itself in the public mind both in Iraq and in the rest of the Arab world between Arab reaction and British imperialism. As it was, the Arab humiliation over Palestine, the politically repressive nature of the Nuri régime in Iraq, and the paucity of immediate and obvious economic advantages accruing to the people from the oil revenues (which, it was generally realized, would have been forthcoming anyway, owing to Western Europe's need for oil, irrespective of the nature of the régime), confirmed Arab opinion, both in Iraq and elsewhere, in its trend towards neutralism and in its identification of domestic reaction with the British connexion. In retrospect it can be seen that Nuri was fighting a losing battle. Even if British policy in Palestine had been other than it was, even if Abdul Nasr had not risen in Egypt to rally the forces of Arab nationalism to the cause of neutralism and social reform, it is doubtful whether Nuri's policies could have survived the withering aura of the Zeitgeist stalking through the Arab world. For Arab nationalism, unlike the Iranian nationalism epitomized by Dr. Mossadeq, was identified, not with social reaction, but with social reform, not with religious obscurantism, but with secular enlightenment. It was moving, or endeavouring to move, with the times in a way that Iranian nationalism was not. The 'collaborationist' forces in Iran, as epitomized by the Shah, were no more associated with 'feudalism', no more inefficient, no more corrupt (probably less so) than the extreme nationalists. The Mossadeq régime was a cul-de-sac and not a logical stage in the process of social and economic development. But Arab nationalism, as it developed, was in the mainstream of history and those who, like Nuri and Eden, attempted to obstruct and divert it were swept away.

But to return to our story. When Nuri became Prime Minister in October 1941 the war was going most unfavourably for the Allies. The Russian armies were being pushed back across the Ukraine and towards the Caucasus. It seemed not improbable that victorious German armies might ere long be erupting through Turkey into Iraq on their way to the Persian Gulf and the Indian Ocean. In the Far East the Japanese were over-running the various British, Dutch and American possessions and were soon to capture Singapore, the symbol and bastion of British power in South-east Asia. The power of the U.S.A., unwillingly dragged into the struggle as a result of the Japanese attack on Pearl Harbour, had not yet begun to make itself felt. In these circumstances Nuri had more than the usual difficulty in getting colleagues to associate themselves with, and in getting the people as a whole to accept, the virtual cessation of political activity, the security restrictions, the presence of Allied troops, and, in general, that identification with the British cause which was implicit in his policy. Diplomatic relations with Vichy France and with Japan were broken off. At the beginning of 1942 a Resolution of the Chamber was obtained in favour of the United Nations Charter and in October 1942 a reconstructed Ministry, with Nuri remaining as Prime Minister, declared war against Germany, Italy and Japan. The adherents of the Golden Square were pursued, tried when they could be caught, and punished, sometimes with death. Others suspected of pro-Axis sympathies were interned. By the end of 1942 the tide of war had turned, and the Germans were in full retreat in Russia and North Africa. Nuri's pro-British policy was to that extent vindicated and his opponents were correspondingly discomforted. But the issue was a good deal wider and more fundamental than one of pro-British sympathies on the one hand and pro-Axis sympathies on the other. Pro-Axis sympathizers had simply backed the German horse as a means to an end; the fact the German horse had lost did not mean that they were going to cease their efforts to put an end to those two things with which Nuri was becoming particularly identified and which were, in consequence, becoming identified with each other—the British connexion and the existing social order.

Meanwhile, Nuri was concentrating more and more on the concept of Arab unity and spent much of his time travelling to and fro between Arab capitals. It had by now become vitally necessary for him to reinforce his position and that of the Monarchy in Iraq by trying to swing the Arab world as a whole into line with his policy of alliance with Great Britain. There were other reasons too why Iraq, whatever policy the Government stood for, should make its weight felt in the Arab world, and try and gather as many and as powerful allies as possible in the Arab world. For the Iraqi economy was very heavily dependent on free access to the Mediterranean for her oil through the pipelines running through Syria. The National Bloc, the predominant political party in Syria, was strongly anti-Hashemite. Ibn Saud, who had close connexions with the National Bloc, was also, for dynastic reasons, anti-Hashemite. It was therefore prudent policy to try and offset this potential threat from the two Arab countries whose borders marched with those of Iraq.

Partly by reason of his frequent absences abroad Nuri tended to lose his grip of the situation at home and, in March 1944, he fell from office. He was succeeded by Hamid al Pashashi who remained in power during nineteen turbulent months. There were serious disorders in Kurdistan. There were strikes, partly brought about by communist influence, in the oilfields and elsewhere. The release of the wartime internees added to the difficulties of a Government headed by a Prime Minister who lacked Nuri's ruthlessness and sense of purpose. During the lifetime of the Pashashi Government the negotiations, which had been proceeding in Arab capitals for the previous two years, and in which Nuri had played a leading part, bore fruit in the Alexandria Protocol of October 1944, at which the delegates of seven Arab States, including Iraq, meeting in Alexandria under the chairmanship of Mustafa Nahas Pasha, the Egyptian Prime Minister, laid down the ground rules for a League of Independent Arab States. The Pact of the Arab League, drawn up as a result of the Alexandria meeting, was signed by the seven signatories of the Alexandria Protocol in May 1945. The Arab League, as formulated in the Pact, was a loose association of sovereign States which bound themselves to joint consultation and joint action in matters of common interest. Partly as a result of Nuri's absence from the centre of affairs, the League, whose headquarters were in Cairo and whose first Secretary-General was an Egyptian, fell from the start under Egyptian influence and became in fact what Nuri was most concerned to prevent it from becoming—a neutralist alliance under Egyptian leadership whose principal object was to defeat those policies with which Nuri was identified.

The two most immediate problems faced by the Arab League were: (*a*) the French insistence on Treaties with Syria and Lebanon—on the Anglo-Egyptian and Anglo-Iraqi model—as a condition of ending their Mandates over these countries and of evacuating them militarily; and (*b*) the British tendency to run away from the 1939 White Paper on Palestine as a result of Zionist violence and American political pressure. The first was settled by a forcible British intervention in Syria and Lebanon which secured the unconditional evacuation of French troops from both countries and the termination of the French Mandates without their being replaced by Treaties. This British achievement raised the British Government momentarily to an unusual height of popularity in Arab capitals. As an earnest of British devotion to the Arab cause it might reasonably have been thought to mitigate nationalist objections to that pro-British orientation which was the basis of Nuri's foreign policy. But, in fact, British intervention in Syria and Lebanon deprived the French of precisely those relationships with their ex-Mandatories that the British, as the whole basis of their Middle East policy, were trying to perpetuate, with the support of the Arab 'pro-Treaty' politicians, in Egypt, Iraq and Transjordan Timely British assistance to the Arab cause in Syria and Lebanon therefore did nothing to weaken, and may indeed have helped to strengthen, the demands already being heard in Cairo and in Baghdad for an abrogation of the Treaties with Great Britain. It is unlikely that any British action in Palestine, however pro-Arab, would have had much effect in moderating such demands, although a similar rescue operation carried out on behalf of the Arabs of Palestine might well have strengthened the hands of those who supported the British connexion against their domestic opponents. In the event, British policy in Palestine, although designed to help the Arabs, assumed erroneously that the Arabs were also willing and able to help themselves. But internal dissensions, military unpreparedness and widespread corruption prevented the States of the Arab League from taking advantage of the opportunity which the British, by their evacuation of Palestine, had presented, and they suffered a humiliating defeat at the hands of the Israelis. As a result it became an article of Arab nationalist belief that the British, by failing actively to assist, had deliberately betrayed the Arab cause. This belief was to prove fatal to any possibility that the British connexion, advocated by Nuri, would prove an acceptable basis for Arab foreign policy either by the people of Iraq or by the peoples and governments of the other Arab States.

Meanwhile, in Iraq, the Pashashi Government fell in January 1946 and was replaced in February by a Government under the premiership of Taufiq as Suwaidi, another 'pro-Treaty' politician. Under this Government the censorship and martial law were (rather belatedly) revoked and political parties allowed to resume their activities. The immediate result was an outbreak of press polemics and verbal violence which led, in May, to the fall of the Suwaidi Government and to its replacement by a much more authoritarian Government headed by Arshad al Umari, who immediately reimposed many of the restrictions which the Suwaidi Government had taken off. In November 1946 the Umari Government resigned in favour of a 'neutral' Government under the premiership of Nuri as Said which was charged with the task of supervising the forthcoming elections for the Majlis. So effective was this supervision that the elections, held early in 1947, returned a Majlis consisting almost entirely of Nuri's supporters. After the elections the Nuri Government (the ninth of which Nuri had been Prime Minister) resigned and was replaced by a Government headed by Saleh Jabr, a nominee of Nuri's. The new Government, sure in the support of an obedient Majlis, proceeded to adopt a repressive attitude towards the opposition Press and towards the opposition political parties. Several newspapers were suppressed. Political parties were declared illegal. Several communists were arrested, tried and sentenced to long terms of imprisonment. The result of all this activity was to drive the opposition on to the streets from where, before long, it was to make itself felt.

With the probable support of the newly elected Majlis it became possible for the Jabr Government to negotiate a new

Treaty with the British Government which, while preserving the special British connexion, would, it was hoped, contain sufficient concessions to the nationalist point of view to prove reasonably acceptable to public opinion in Iraq. Under the terms of the draft Treaty negotiated, the British bases at Habbaniya and Shaiba were to be handed back to Iraqi control and the British Military Mission replaced by an Anglo-Iraqi Council. In general, everything done to meet Iraqi susceptibilities within the framework of an alliance with Great Britain which would permit the British reoccupation of Iraq and British use of Iraqi facilities in the event of war or the threat of war. The Treaty was initialled at Portsmouth by the Foreign Ministers of the two countries in January 1948. The news of this event was the signal for serious rioting in Baghdad and for demonstrations by the various opposition parties. The Regent promptly disclaimed the Treaty (which he had previously approved) and the Jabr Government resigned. It was an impressive demonstration of anti-British, anti-Treaty and anti-Nuri opinion in Baghdad and in Iraq generally.

A new Government, headed by Sayyid Mohammed as Sadr, an 'anti-Treaty' politician, repudiated the Treaty, which was never ratified, and dissolved the Majlis on the ground that it had been illegally elected. On the election of a new Majlis in June the Sadr Government was replaced by one headed by Muzahim al Pashashi which found itself fully occupied with the situation in Palestine resulting from the end of the Mandate, the formation of the State of Israel and the attack on that State by the armies of the Arab League States on the day after (15 May 1948) that on which the British Mandate came to an end. The Iraqi army only played a minor part in the campaign but it shared in the general Arab humiliation at their defeat at the hands of the Israelis. The expenses of the campaign, and the effect on oil revenues of the closing of the Kirkuk–Haifa pipeline caused a serious economic crisis. This, added to disaffection and indiscipline in the army as a result of the failure of the Palestine campaign, was too much for a weak Government to cope with and, at the end of January 1949, Nuri as Said, *l'homme des mauvaises heures*, was back in office as Prime Minister to clear up the mess. From that time onwards, driving sometimes from the front seat as Prime Minister and sometimes from the back seat as a private individual, Nuri as Said was to control events in Iraq until the revolution, and his murder, in 1958. His first act on regaining power was to organize formal political support in the shape of a new Party, the Constitutional Union, which was joined by most of the Independent majority in the Majlis.

From 1950 onwards Nuri's domestic position was greatly strengthened by progressively increasing oil revenues which, as a result of the 50/50 Agreement (see Chapter Ten) and rapidly increasing production were, in 1954, to attain a figure of £50 million, an amount undreamt of in the early post-war years. On the Arab League front the confusion following on the Palestine defeat (which led to a series of military coups in Syria, to a series of internal crises in Egypt and to the almost complete withdrawal of Saudi Arabia from active participation in Arab affairs) put an end, for the time being, to any serious activity by the Egyptian-dominated Arab League. The Collective Security Pact of the Arab League, signed in 1950, was formed ostensibly for the purpose of mutual defence against the mythical possibility of Israeli aggression but was in fact an Egyptian-inspired and Saudi-supported manœuvre to counter any Hashemite attempt, emanating either from Jordan or from Iraq, to bring the distracted State of Syria into the Hashemite orbit.

During the years 1950–4 Arab nationalism was licking its wounds, regrouping its forces and nourishing its rancours. During these years, Syria, after reeling from one military dictatorship to another, reverted to a precarious constitutional life. Egypt experienced a military coup which resulted in the deposition of Faruq and the emergence of Gamal Abdul Nasr who, after divesting Egypt of the links that still bound her to Great Britain under the terms of the 1936 Treaty, emerged as the leader of a resuscitated and militant Arab nationalism. Ibn Saud died in 1953 and his son and successor, King Saud, involved in a quarrel with the British over the Buraimi oasis, and inheriting a family feud against the Hashemites, divided his subservience about equally between the United States and Egypt.

Towards the end of 1954 Nuri, the whole basis of his 'pro-Treaty' policy threatened by the Anglo-Egyptian Agreement of July 1954 which provided for the withdrawal of British forces from the Canal Zone and for the supercession of the 1936 Anglo-Egyptian Treaty, and despairing of the possibility of any accommodation with the Egyptian dictator, who was already attracting Syria and Saudi Arabia into his orbit, sought to break away from the Arab world and find security from the twin menaces of communism and Arab nationalism in an alliance with Turkey which, since Turkey was a member of N.A.T.O., would bind Iraq more tightly and, it was hoped, from the point of view of Arab public opinion, more respectably, to the western system of alliances. The British, having apparently 'written off' Egypt as a possible ally, favoured the new alignment. The U.S. Government, obsessed at that time with the idea of military alliances directed against the internal and external menace of communism, seemed certain to welcome it. Consequently, in February 1955, Iraq signed a mutual assistance Agreement with Turkey which became known as the Baghdad Pact. In April Great Britain joined the Baghdad Pact which replaced the 1930 Treaty as the instrument of alliance between Great Britain and Iraq. In September, Pakistan, and in November, Iran also joined the Pact which thereby became a regional alliance affiliated to N.A.T.O. through the common membership of Great Britain and Turkey, and aligned to anti-communist western strategy in the Middle East in the same way that S.E.A.T.O., of which Pakistan was also a member, was in the Far East. The principal difference from S.E.A.T.O. was that U.S.A., although a member of S.E.A.T.O., did not join the Baghdad Pact, apparently in order to avoid what the State Department regarded as the risk of driving Adbul Nasr into the communist camp.

The formation of the Baghdad Pact completed the estrangement which had been growing up on the one hand between Great Britain and Egypt and on the other hand between Iraq and Egypt. Although formally designed as an instrument of defence against Russian communism, the Pact was in fact regarded, both by the British and by the Iraqi Governments, as a means of preserving British influence in the Middle East by way of sustaining the Iraqi Government against its opponents both inside and outside Iraq.

Domestic opposition to the Nuri régime was stifled during the course of 1954 by the dissolution of all political parties and

194

by a ban on almost all political activity. From then onwards, until the revolution in 1958, Iraq was a police State, where criticism of the Government, whether by organizations or by individuals, was kept within strictly limited bounds by the operation of a severe censorship, an efficient security force and capacious prison accommodation. The opposition, thus driven underground, crystallized into two broad tendencies about equal in strength. On the one hand there were followers of the Arab nationalism preached by Abdul Nasr; on the other hand there were communists.

Abdul Aziz ibn Saud had been one of the earliest apostles of Arab unity over Palestine and had been a powerful influence in the negotiations with the British Government which led to the issue of the 1939 White Paper. After the war he had taken a leading part in the formation of the Arab League and joined Egypt in attempting to limit Hashemite influence in the League. His public utterances on Palestine were hardly less uncompromising and no less optimistic than those of other Arab statesmen. But, when the fighting started, he was almost unrepresented on the field of battle. Thereafter, he detached himself almost entirely from Arab affairs outside Saudi Arabia and became absorbed in the fascinating process of self-enrichment. When he died in 1953 his son and successor, Saud, possibly as a result of the influence of his abler younger brother Feisal, soon came under the influence of Egypt to such an extent that a part of the proceeds of oil revenues were diverted from the uses of the ruling family to the financing of Arab nationalist propaganda and (some whispered) to the procurement of political assassinations in the Fertile Crescent. But the active expression of King Suad's nationalist sympathies and dynastic rancours was limited by the prime importance which he attached to his relationships with the United States, which were analogous with the relationships between his father and Great Britain some twenty-five years previously. Thus his relationships with Abdul Nasr were warmest at times when the State Department were wooing Abdul Nasr; when the State Department were displeased with Abdul Nasr, as in the days of the Eisenhower Doctrine in 1957, King Saud tended to cool off, refusing to help Egypt in denying the Gulf of Aqaba to Israeli shipping and paying ostentatious visits of friendship to Amman and Baghdad.

The worthless character, and the corrupt and extravagant administration of King Saud, precluded Saudi Arabia from any important influence either in the Arab world or the Persian Gulf after 1953 except in so far as the changing requirements of U.S. foreign policy from time to time permitted or withheld the use of Saudi Arabian oil revenues for the purpose of subserving the policies of Gamal Abdul Nasr.

The possibility of oil deposits, and the fear of Saudi cupidity, caused a strengthening in the relationships between the Sultanate of Musqat and Oman and the Trucial Sheikhdoms on the one hand and Great Britain on the other during the early 1950's. A new Treaty of Friendship, Commerce and Navigation was concluded between Great Britain and Musqat and Oman in December 1951 which provided for the recognition of the British Consul General in Musqat as the only foreign diplomatic representative (except the Indian Consul) in the Sultanate, for the exercise of jurisdiction by the British Consul General over British nationals in the Sultanate, for the provision of some financial assistance from Great Britain, for the employment of British officials in the Administration, and for the recruitment of British officers into the Oman Levies, the Sultan's military force.

We have already given some account of the Saudi occupation of two villages in the Buraimi oasis and of the reoccupation of the oasis by a joint force of Omani Levies and Trucial Oman Scouts (see below). The next Saudi-inspired attack on the Sultanate came in 1954 when, after the death of the Imam Abdullah with whom the Treaty of Sib had been concluded in 1920 (see Chapter Ten), his successor to the Imamate, Ghalib bin Ali, proclaimed the sovereign independence of Oman, declared invalid the oil concessions covering the area which had been awarded by the Sultan, and applied in the name of an independent Oman for membership of the Arab League. The Sultan thereupon marched into the interior and occupied Nizwa, the principal town in the Imam's territory, without meeting any resistance. The tribal chiefs all submitted to the Sultan and the Imam fled to Saudi Arabia. Three years later, in 1957, revolt again broke out in Oman under the leadership of Talib bin Ali, the Imam's brother, this time with open encouragement both from Egypt and from Saudi Arabia. This revolt, actively assisted as it was from Saudi Arabia, was more serious than the 1954 demonstration and the Sultan was obliged to call for British armed assistance under the terms of the 1951 Treaty. This was provided and the rebels were again defeated. On this occasion ten Arab member States of the United Nations tried to arraign Great Britain before the Security Council, alleging British armed aggression against the independence, sovereignty and territorial integrity of the Imamate of Oman (which, incidentally, in spite of the Imam's application in 1954, had not been admitted to the Arab League). This Arab Resolution failed to secure the necessary seven votes in support and the Security Council consequently took no action. At the beginning of 1959 a third revolt took place which again required the intervention of British troops, which again attracted the support of the U.A.R. and Saudi Arabia, and which was again defeated.

In the Trucial Sheikhdoms the possibility of oil deposits, the presence of a predatory neighbour and the existence of vague and undetermined inland boundaries clearly demanded some common action and some common means of defence between the seven Trucial Sheikhdoms (Dubai, Abu Dhabi, Sharja, Ras al Kheima, Ajman, Umm al Qaiwan and Fujaira). In 1950 the Protecting Power approved the creation of a local levy to maintain order. At the beginning of 1955 a British-officered force, known as the Trucial Oman Scouts was raised with its headquarters at Sharja to take part in the reoccupation of the Buraimi oasis in October of that year. (The importance of the Buraimi oasis to the Sheikhdom of Abu Dhabi can be gauged from the fact that the ten villages of the oasis claimed by Abu Dhabi contain an estimated 20,000 out of an estimated population of 25,000 for the whole Sheikhdom.) The Trucial Scouts also assisted the Sultan of Musqat and Oman in the 1957 and 1959 campaigns against the Omani rebels referred to above. In 1952 a Trucial Council, where all the seven Rulers meet periodically for the discussion of matters of common concern, was established under British advice. The British Government, in order to assist in the economy of the Sheikhdoms, which had collapsed owing to the decline of the pearling industry and owing to the enforced desuetude of the previous principal occupation of piracy, established a development fund of

£2 million to provide for agricultural and technical training and for the establishment of an experimental farm which was set up in Ras al Kheima.

These British reactions to threatened Saudi penetration are an earnest of the extent to which the British Government is prepared to go to defend British interests in that thin red line of British-protected territories stretching from Aden in the south-west to Kuwait in the north-east which now forms the last ditch of British influence in the Middle East and which has achieved a new and vital importance arising from its actual and potential oil wealth.

With the signature of the Baghdad Pact there started a vociferous bombardment of radio, newspaper, and word of mouth propaganda emanating from Cairo, assisted from time to time by bribery from Saudi Arabia, and directed to the Arab lands of the Fertile Crescent and the Persian Gulf. In the Persian Gulf, the impact of this propaganda was assisted by the presence of Palestine refugees who came seeking employment, and of Egyptian technicians and schoolteachers seconded by the Egyptian Government, who had come to the Persian Gulf as a result of the employment opportunities created by the educational and other development programmes called into being by the new oil revenues. Much as the Rulers themselves, much as the British Government, and much as the oil companies would have liked to insulate the inhabitants of the Sheikhdoms from this propaganda, which attacked British influence, sheikhly despotism and the terms of the oil concessions with equal vigour and venom, they were unable entirely to do so. In Kuwait and in Bahrain particularly there were many eager listeners, in the clubs, in the schools, and in the oil company canteens. To the educated and half-educated youth of these States, this propaganda from Cairo seemed to open up the prospect of wider and freer horizons than those narrow vistas to which the paternal rule of their British-protected Sheikhs had so far restricted them. In Kuwait the fewness of the inhabitants and the richness of the oil revenues, which ensured that the garden in which they were enclosed, although small and subject to tiresome regulations, was at least a very luxurious one, tended to minimize the attractions of an association which would involve the sharing of Kuwaiti wealth with other less fortunately situated. But in

198

Bahrain, where the oil income per capita was insignificant compared with Kuwait, and where legitimate political aspirations on the part of some quite responsible and mature people were not very wisely handled, either by the Ruler or by his British Adviser, there was a certain amount of trouble. Previous political trouble in Bahrain had almost always taken the form of quarrels between Sunnis and Shias, representing (broadly) the Persian and Arab-descended inhabitants between whom the population of the islands were divided. In 1954, however, a Higher Executive Committee was formed, consisting of both Sunni and Shia members, which made a series of demands on the Ruler calling for the establishment of Trade Unions, the introduction of a proper legal system and the promulgation of a Labour Law. As these demands were rather reluctantly and tardily granted, fresh demands were made for a Legislative Council, for official recognition of the Higher Executive Committee and for the dismissal of Sir Charles Belgrave, the British Adviser. These demands, too, were acceded to tardily and in part, and Sir Charles Belgrave retired in 1957. Before that, however, news of the Suez incident had touched off anti-British riots which caused some damage to British property and necessitated the intervention of British troops. Several members of the Committee of National Union (which the Higher Executive Committee had renamed itself after having been accorded official recognition) were arrested and tried on charges of having been concerned in these riots. Whether they were really guilty, or whether the opportunity of the riots was taken as a means of breaking up a body which was beginning to become a nuisance both to the Ruler and to the British authorities, is uncertain. At all events several of them were convicted and, by arrangement between the Ruler and the British Government, were sent to the British colony of St. Helena to serve their sentences, thus confirming in the eyes of a great many unfriendly witnesses, the identification between British imperialism and local despotism.

The effect of the Suez incident on the whole of the Arab side of the Persian Gulf was profound. In Iraq every circumstance of the incident combined to discredit and to disarm the Baghdad Pact policy, which had already been seriously undermined by eighteen months of propaganda from Cairo and by eighteen months of tyranny in Baghdad. The collusion with Israel, the armed attack on a comparatively weak country and, above all, the military and diplomatic defeat incurred by Great Britain, reduced the case for collaboration with Great Britain to moral and material bankruptcy. The economic loss imposed on Iraq by the destruction of an I.P.C. pumping station in Syria and by the consequent stoppage of Iraqi oil exports through Syria, deliberately prolonged as it was by the refusal of the Syrian Government to expedite repairs, was of secondary importance. Nuri tried to save what he could from the wreck. He denounced the Anglo-French action, expressed his support for Abdul Nasr, broke off diplomatic relations with France (but not with Great Britain) and acquiesced in the exclusion of Great Britain from the next Baghdad Pact meeting. But he had already burnt his boats and was tied to the British connexion. The operation of the Eisenhower Doctrine and the disintegration of Syria during 1957 was to give him some reprieve, but the end was in sight.

The behaviour of the Saudi Arabian Government during and after the Suez incident was circumspect and unheroic. They broke off diplomatic relations with France (they had already broken off diplomatic relations with Great Britain over Buraimi). They made no attempt to interfere with the flow of Aramco oil through TAPline (although they must have known that this greatly reduced the effectiveness of the oil blockade created by the blocking of the Suez Canal and the cutting of the I.P.C. pipelines). For some inscrutable reason they stopped the much less important flow of oil going to Bahrain for refining. After the withdrawal of Israeli troops from Sinai they refused to collaborate with Egypt in blockading the entrance to the Gulf of Aqaba, with a view to preventing Israel from using the port of Elath, after having been warned that Israel would resist any such attempted blockade by force. This performance was perhaps not entirely dictated by greed and cowardice. Subservience to U.S.A. may also have played a part. For the State Department was once more becoming alarmed about the possibility of communist penetration in the Middle East and was once more becoming interested in the possibilities of helping to sustain 'sound' i.e. pro-Western, Governments. The Eisenhower Doctrine, first propounded in January 1957 was ostensibly an offer of financial and other assistance to any state in the Middle East threatened with and prepared to resist communist infiltration; in fact, it was an offer of financial assistance to any Arab State prepared to resist Abdul Nasr, whom U.S. policy was beginning once more to equate with communism. King Saud, who was visiting the United States at the time, and who may have been beginning to wonder what the ultimate effect of Abdul Nasr's propaganda might be on his own ramshackle and spendthrift régime, gave a characteristically equivocal assent to the Eisenhower Doctrine in return for a promise of military assistance, and, on his return to Arabia, made some ostentatious gestures of friendliness towards Iraq and Jordan (which was by this time back in the Western camp). He also appears to have tried to secure by bribery the assassination of Gamal Abdul Nasr. The resultant difficulty of trying once more to collaborate with Abdul Nasr after the Eisenhower Doctrine had foundered and after Syria had been incorporated into the United Arab Republic, was eased by the fact that King Saud had by that time been relegated to the puppetry for which nature had intended him, and the conduct of affairs taken over by his brother Feisal, as a result of the chaos to which he had, in four years, and in spite of increasing oil revenues, reduced his kingdom, by his extravagance, weakness and incompetence. (It is characteristic of him that, late in 1960, after Feisal had succeeded in restoring some semblance of order into the financial affairs of the State, he should have dismissed him from his post as Prime Minister and taken over the conduct of affairs himself with results which will, no doubt, soon become dismally apparent.)

Kuwait was the one part of the Persian Gulf in which a really serious reaction to the Suez incident might have represented a catastrophe for Great Britain and a decisive triumph for Abdul Nasr. The Sheikh of Kuwait, partly owing to the obligations which Kuwait had assumed towards the British Government under the 1899 Treaty, by which Kuwaiti foreign policy had to be conducted in accordance with that of the British Government, and partly owing to native prudence, had successfully avoided becoming involved in the intricacies and dissensions of pan-Arab politics. In 1955 Nuri as Said had anxiously but vainly tried to persuade him to join the Baghdad Pact. After Suez there were attempts, inspired from Cairo, to persuade him to apply for membership of the Arab League. At the time of Suez, therefore, there was no serious danger that the Sheikh himself, however much he might deplore the British action, and however fervently he might go through the verbal motions of solidarity with his brother Arabs, would of his own accord take any action which might seriously estrange him from the British Government or seriously jeopardize the continued receipt and continued control of the mounting oil revenues. But there had grown up in Kuwait a vociferous body of more or less educated public opinion, which found its principal expression in the graduate and student clubs and in the local press, which was strongly Arab nationalist. Thus public opinion could be expected violently to denounce the British action, as in fact it did. Such denunciation of the British was also, by implication, a criticism of the Ruling House, which was in alliance with Great Britain. There was a possibility of serious disturbances which would have faced the Ruler with the alternatives of calling for British military assistance or of repudiating his Treaty relationship with the British. In the event, matters passed off without the necessity either for repression or for concession. (One reason, then and afterwards, for Kuwait's relative freedom from serious political trouble arising from the ambitions and resentments of its educated youth, can be seen in the extent to which the Ruler has been successful in creating, both in his own Administration and, to some extent, with the Oil Company, opportunities for lucrative and responsible employment for the educated youth of Kuwait.)

For a time, during 1957, it seemed possible that the operation of the Eisenhower Doctrine, whose intended effect was to shore up the shattered fabric of the Baghdad Pact in the Arab world, might put an end to that isolation from the rest of the Arab world which had been imposed on Iraq as a result of the failure of the Suez expedition. But the Union between Egypt and Syria in February 1958 both ended the effective operation of the Eisenhower Doctrine and confirmed the isolation of Iraq. For the Union between Iraq and Jordan (which had become detached from Cairo during the course of 1957) accentuated rather than relieved that isolation.

The Iraqi revolution of July 1958 was at first assumed, in the West, to be another Nasserite coup. But what developed, after the bloody preliminaries which involved, *inter alia*, the murders of young King Feisal II, the Regent, and Nuri as Said, was a struggle for power between the Arab nationalists and the communists. General Qasim, the nominal Dictator, whose coup had released all those subversive political energies which had for the last four years been bottled up by Nuri's security organization, having sought the assistance of the communists in order to defeat Arab nationalism, soon found himself struggling to avoid the absorption of the new régime by the communists. By the end of 1959 it became apparent that Qasim had, with the assistance of the Army and of some of the leaders of the non-communist National Democratic Party, which had been pro-scribed by Nuri as Said, succeeded in establishing a more or less stable authoritarian régime, which was neither Arab nationalist nor communist and which appeared to be capable of maintaining itself against both communist and Arab nationalist elements in Iraq.

In its external relationships the Qasim régime left the Baghdad Pact (which, renamed CENTO, continued as before, minus the membership of Iraq), announced a policy of neutrality between East and West, maintained diplomatic relations with the United States, Great Britain and Russia and, although bitter mutual hostility developed between Cairo and Baghdad, continued to be an active member of the Arab League. During the course of 1959 Abdul Nasr, in addition to fomenting an abortive military revolt against the Qasim régime, made repeated and unsuccessful attempts to organize the member States of the Arab League against the Qasim régime on the ground of its alleged communist tendencies. When it became apparent (*a*) that the other Arab States were unenthusiastic, (*b*) that the Qasim régime was not communist and unlikely to become so, and (*c*) that the Qasim régime was firmly established, the strength of Cairo's hostility, and in consequence the strength of Baghdad's counter-hostility, began gradually to abate until, by the middle of 1960, relations between the two countries were not more acrimonious than is usual between two member States of the Arab League, and considerably more friendly than they had been in the days of Nuri as Said.

The emergence, in the Arab world, of a reasonably stable and reasonably viable alternative to the British connexion, which was neither Arab nationalist (in the Nasserite sense) nor communist, but neutralist and nationalist in its own right, was a fatal blow to Abdul Nasr's ambitions for hegemony in the Arab world. As such the emergence of this alternative was bitterly attacked throughout the Arab world by all the propagandist weapons at Abdul Nasr's disposal. This propaganda was audible in the Arab States of the Persian Gulf, as was the communist and other counter-propaganda emanating from Baghdad and Moscow.

The effect of this ideological warfare was significant. In Saudi Arabia and in the Persian Gulf Sheikhdoms the serious set-back suffered by Abdul Nasr in Iraq seemed decisively to break the spell which the concept of Arab nationalism, as preached by Abdul Nasr, had begun to cast over the imaginations and the ambitions of the educated youth and the emergent middle class. At the same time, the failure of the communists to consolidate their early successes in Iraq prevented communism from becoming a serious counter-attraction. Nothing fails like failure. The course of the Iraqi revolution therefore had the effect of reducing those social and political pressures which the attractive force of Arab nationalism was beginning to build up in Saudi Arabia and in the Persian Gulf Sheikhdoms.

After the fall of Mossadeq at the end of 1953, relationships between Iran and Iraq, although for historical reasons never particularly cordial, became progressively closer as the result of a widening area of common interests. Both countries were constitutional monarchies in a largely republican Middle East. Both countries had much the same reactionary social order, both countries were politically aligned with the West and both countries had to contend with domestic oppositions which objected both to the social reaction and to the Western alignment. Both régimes feared and disliked Gamal Abdul Nasr, though for different reasons—the régime in Iraq because Abdul Nasr was trying to overthrow it, the régime in Iran because it disliked the prospect, posed by Abdul Nasr's ambitions, of a powerful Arab Union confronting it on the other side of what Abdul Nasr's supporters were already referring to as the Arabian Gulf. After the revolution, first the Arab nationalist, then the communist, threat presented by Iraq could not but be disturbing to the Government of Iran. Such relief as they felt as the danger, first of the one and then of the other, was removed by the course of events, was considerably mitigated by the sudden belligerence shown by Qasim, in December 1959, towards Iran over the question of the Shatt-al-Arab frontier between the two countries.

By the terms of the Treaty of Erzerum, concluded in 1847 between the Ottoman Empire and Persia, the Shatt-al-Arab had been fixed as the boundary between the two countries from the head of the Persian Gulf up to a point just below Basra, but since the existence of the port of Basra depended on its access to the Persian Gulf, it was provided that the boundary, instead of following the line of the *talweg*, as is usual with international river boundaries, should run along the low water line on the Persian side of the Shatt, thus leaving the navigation channel in Turkish territory. This boundary was confirmed by the international Boundary Commission in 1914 and was inherited by the State of Iraq when it was formed after World War One. In 1937 a modification of this boundary was agreed to between Iraq and Iran by which a rectangular area of water opposite the Abadan jetties was ceded by Iraq to Iran to provide that vessels loading or discharging at the Iranian port of Abadan should do so in Iranian waters. In December 1959 Qasim denounced this agreement, as having been arrived at by an Iraqi Government under 'imperialist' influence, and claimed Iraqi sovereignty over the Shatt in accordance with the Treaty of Erzerum. He also made some vague claims to Iranian territory on the Iranian bank of the Shatt. These claims produced a furious Iranian reaction. It was pointed out that navigation on the Shatt was still controlled entirely by and dues paid to the Basra Port Authority in spite of a provision in the 1937 Agreement for setting up a joint Iranian-Iraqi Board of Control; it was alleged that part of the navigation dues collected by the Port Authority was being misappropriated by the Iraqi Government. The area of the quarrel spread and embraced the Shia pilgrim traffic which was accustomed to proceed from Iran to visit the holy cities of Nejaf and Kerbela, but which had been stopped after the Iraqi revolution, as well as the alleged ill-treatment of the large number of Iranian nationals resident in Iraq. Diplomatic relations between the two countries were suspended and the press and radio polemics which were emitted by both sides would, in other times, have been regarded as unusually violent if exchanged between two nations at war with each other. However, a common hostility towards Abdul Nasr who, in July 1960, broke off diplomatic relations with Iran owing to that country's refusal to stop the shipment of Iranian oil to Israel, served for the time being, to compose the quarrel, without leading to any settlement of the points at issue.[2]

What Iran regarded, not unnaturally, as the threat presented by Arab nationalism to Iranian interests in the Persian Gulf caused successive Iranian Governments assiduously to develop friendly relations with the Rulers of many of the Arab Sheikh-doms and particularly with the Rulers of Qatar and the Trucial Sheikhdoms, in many of which there was a sizeable Iranian population. Relations with Kuwait and Bahrain were less cordial. Although there was much trade between Iran and Kuwait (about three-quarters of Kuwait's imports of meat, fresh vegetables and fruits come from Iran), there is perennial Iranian dissatisfaction about the treatment of Iranian nationals in Kuwait; moreover Iranians can never forgive Kuwait for having, during the period of Mossadeq's Premiership, usurped Iran's position as the largest oil producer in the Middle East. Relations with Bahrain are bedevilled by Iranian persistence in claiming sovereignty over the archipelago, a fact which makes any friendly intercourse between the two Governments impossible.

Relationships between Iran and Saudi Arabia are good, although Saudi recognition of the *status quo* in Bahrain is a perpetual, if minor, irritant. There is no common boundary and few points of contact between the two countries and the present absence of any Saudi naval ambitions in the Persian Gulf removes the only foreseeable potential cause of friction between the two countries.

The Iranian anger which is manifested at any reference to the 'Arabian Gulf' is more than a mere matter of nomenclature. With the decline of that British hegemony which had, for some 200 years, provided for the impartial policing of the waters of the Persian Gulf, the relative naval strengths of the various riparian Powers began to assume some importance. The triumph of Nasserism in the Arab world, leading to effective Egyptian control of the Arab shores of the Gulf, would almost inevitably have meant an Egyptian attempt to make of the

Persian Gulf an Arab lake. To Iranians this intention was forecast in Arab nationalist references to the 'Arabian Gulf'. The failure of Abdul Nasr's wider ambitions was therefore a source of unmitigated satisfaction in Iran, where it was realized that the term 'Arabian Gulf' represents, not the shadow of an impending reality, but the ghost of a lost cause.

CHAPTER TWELVE

Iran Since Mossadeq

THE MOSSADEQ EPISODE had not done anything irreversible.
The Shah was still on his throne, the Constitution was still
in being. Iran had not disappeared behind the Iron Curtain. Even the stoppage of the oil revenue had not seriously
affected the mass of the people. The break with A.I.O.C. had
taken place before Iran had started to draw the greatly increased
revenues which would certainly have eventuated had not
Mossadeq forestalled the course of events by expropriation. The
most important effect of the dismissal of Mossadeq and the
restoration of the Shah was that Iran became almost irrevocably
bound to the Western cause. The new Government urgently
needed both immediate financial assistance and an oil settlement which would give Iran terms not less favourable than those
being enjoyed by other Persian Gulf oil producers. The United
States was prepared to provide the one, and Great Britain and
the United States were, between them, willing to negotiate the
other. Both Great Britain and the United States wished to sustain the new régime and to help build it up as a barrier against
the xenophobia epitomized by Mossadeq on the one hand and
the communism represented by the Tudeh Party on the other.
From the point of view of the West the reason for wanting to get
the oil flowing again was much more political than economic.
The gap in supplies caused by the stoppage of Iranian exports in
1951 had long since been made good and it was more important
to put Iran in the way of earning some money than it was to put
Western Europe in the way of getting more oil. An American
loan of 45 million dollars was almost immediately forthcoming
—the precursor of a long series of loans and gifts to Iran from
U.S. sources which, by the end of 1960, was to amount to about
1,000 million dollars in the way of gifts and 600 million dollars
in the way of loans. The process of restoring the flow of oil took

rather longer. On the one hand the British Petroleum Company (ex-A.I.O.C.) insisted on a proper settlement of the compensation issue, and other oil companies who were approached insisted on a commercial arrangement if they were to participate in a rescue operation. On the other hand it was necessary to consider the reputation of the new Iranian régime *vis-à-vis* public opinion. It was impossible for the Iranian Government to accept less than Mossadeq had been offered; it was impossible for the oil companies to agree to more than they could justify to their shareholders. After some hard bargaining, in which the Iranian, British and U.S. Governments and eight international oil companies participated, an agreement was arrived at. Iranian *amour-propre* was preserved by retaining the principle and to some extent the reality of nationalization, by providing for Iran an income per ton of oil produced similar to that being received by other Persian Gulf States, and by guarantees under which Iranian exports would be restored to something like their previous level within a short period of years. The interests of B.P. were secured by arrangements for compensation over the loss of their concession; a payment of £25 million was to be made, in instalments, by the Iranian Government; an additional sum, amounting to a total of £252,400 was to be paid to B.P., also in instalments,[1] out of the profits of the other oil companies participating in the new Agreement,[2] which was ratified, without undue enthusiasm, by the Majlis in October 1954.

The Agreement was made between the Iranian Government and a Consortium of international oil companies of which B.P., with a 40 per cent interest, was the largest shareholder. The others were: Royal Dutch-Shell (14 per cent); Standard of New Jersey, Socony-Mobil, Gulf, Texas and Standard of California (7 per cent each); Compagnie Française des Pétroles (6 per cent); and a group of nine 'independent' American oil companies with 5 per cent between them. The terms of the Agreement were in line with the offers that had been made to, and refused by, Mossadeq at various times after the act of nationalization. The fact of nationalization was recognized and the new twenty-five-year concession (with the option of renewal, subject to certain conditions, for three further periods of five years each) took the form of a lease granted to the Consortium by the National Iranian Oil Company of land and assets in the

Agreement Area (an area of about 100,000 square miles in Southern Iran covering Abadan Refinery and most of the areas previously exploited by the A.I.O.C.) for the exploitation of the oil resources in that area. The concession was to be operated on behalf of the Consortium by two Operating Companies—an Exploration and Producing Company and a Refining Company —whose Head Office was to be in Iran and who were to be entirely responsible for day-to-day management, with the Consortium members providing the capital in accordance with their shareholding, and also technical advice. What were termed 'non-basic' functions, such as housing, medical services, etc., were to be provided and managed by the National Iranian Oil Company. The various member Companies of the Consortium were to receive the oil produced (less Iran's domestic requirements on which N.I.O.C. had first call) in proportion to their shareholdings and were to fix the f.o.b. prices at which it was to be sold. The Iranian Government was to receive 50 per cent of the net profits of all oil sold for export. Although, in the Agreement, some regard had been paid to the fact of nationalization, decisions about the level of production and the price of the oil remained, as in the case of the other Persian Gulf oil agreements, firmly in the hands of the shareholders and the Agreement did not differ fundamentally from the pattern which had been set elsewhere in the Gulf. The international nature of the Consortium, which was imposed partly out of deference to Iranian susceptibilities and partly as the result of an American determination to penetrate still further into the Persian Gulf oil business, was similar to that of the I.P.C. But, unlike the I.P.C., whose management was British, the Consortium was not only internationally owned but internationally managed as well.

The Agreement soon served its immediate purpose of putting Iranian oil back on to world markets and of putting money into the Iranian Treasury. In 1956 Iranian oil income was over £40 million, and in 1960 over £100 million. This income, together with some U.S. loans, enabled a serious start to be made on some development schemes which, in Iran, were administered by a Government agency known as Plan Organization, analogous to the Development Board in Iraq. As in Iraq before the revolution, a proportion of oil income was annually voted to Plan Organization;[3] the increasing demands of the national

Budget, accentuated by inflation, caused this proportion to be a steadily decreasing one although, thanks to the buoyancy of the oil income, the annual amounts voted to Plan Organization increased at the same time as their proportion to the whole decreased. But inflation, caused in part by an influx of foreign currency and a consequent influx of imports unaccompanied by any increase in productivity (except in oil) largely nullified the benefits of increasing wealth by driving up the cost of living. American financial assistance (apart from loans negotiated direct by Plan Organization) was largely concentrated on attempts to underwrite the stability of the régime by financing the requirements of the Army whose continued loyalty was basic to the continued survival of a régime which the Army had restored to power. Of the 1,000 million dollars approximately which the U.S. Government has contributed to the Iranian Treasury since the war, some 400 million dollars has gone to the armed forces.

Relying on the West as it did both for financial insurance against domestic discontents and for military and political insurance against Russia, it is not surprising that the Iranian Government, in October 1955, joined the Baghdad Pact, of which Great Britain, Turkey, Iraq and Pakistan were already members and with which the United States was closely associated. Thus Iran became a kind of country member of N.A.T.O. and an associate of the Western system which sought to contain communism by a mixture of military deterrent and economic betterment. In Iraq, as we have seen, the Baghdad Pact was regarded both by its friends and by its enemies in terms of British support for the Nuri régime against Abdul Nasr. In Iran its connotation was entirely different. It was seen in terms of a departure from Iran's traditional policy of neutrality as between Russia and the West, and as an association with the West, and particularly with the United States, in the cold war between the West and Russia, in return for the expectation of financial aid from the United States. From the military point of view it behoved Iran to walk warily over this departure from neutrality. The 1921 Treaty with Russia had given Russia the right to send troops into Iran in the event of any other Power using Iran as a base from which to launch an attack upon Russia. This clause in the 1921 Treaty precluded Iran from making a bilateral defence treaty with Iran (a project mooted in 1959) and has also precluded her from agreeing to the establishment of any U.S. military bases on Iranian soil. Russia was swift to react to Iran's membership of the Baghdad Pact (to which Iran continued to adhere, after the defection of Iraq early in 1959, when the Pact was renamed CENTO) and from the end of 1958 until about the beginning of 1960, maintained a constant propaganda warfare against Iran accompanied, there can be no doubt, by attempted subversion through the once-more-proscribed Tudeh Party.

General Zahedi, the author of the coup which brought down Mossadeq and restored the Shah to his throne, remained as Prime Minister until April 1955. By that time he was an ageing and sick man; when he resigned the Premiership his place was taken by Husain Ala, who had been Mossadeq's predecessor as Prime Minister in 1951. From that time onwards the Shah began to emerge as the most considerable single political force in the country. He was then in his middle thirties. The circumstances of his reign had not, so far, been such as to enhance his prestige. The first four years had been spent under the shadow of a foreign occupation; the next four had been marred by the Azerbaijan troubles and by serious internal difficulties. The Mossadeq episode had followed, during which time his advice had been ignored, his person treated with scant respect, and his country committed to policies of which he disapproved. Finally, he had missed the opportunity of himself leading the Army against Mossadeq and had instead been beholden to General Zahedi for quelling the anti-monarchist riots which Mossadeq had incited and for bringing him back from the exile which he had chosen. This was not an encouraging background for one who aspired to lead his country in fact as well as in name. He had neither the personality, nor the dynamism, nor the ruthlessness of his father, the great Reza Shah. But he had a very shrewd idea of what had to be done if Iran was to avoid the three principal evils—communism, mob rule, and western domination —which seemed to threaten her. He realized, far better than most of his Ministers, and far better than any of his wealthier subjects, that a steady process of social and political reform was the only ultimate alternative to revolution. He tried to give an example of the first in the field of land reform by distributing part of the Crown Lands to the tenantry. He induced the Government of Dr. Iqbal, who succeeded Husain Ala as Prime Minister in April 1957, to present to the Majlis a Land Reform Bill, which was bitterly attacked by the landlords in the Majlis and only passed into law after having been emasculated beyond all prospect of effectiveness. In the field of political reform he encouraged the creation of constitutional political parties with the object of having future Majlis elections fought on issues of policy instead of on issues of personality. Here again he failed, and the 1960–1 elections, conducted between the two parties which had obediently and cynically been formed in deference to the Shah's wishes, were so farcical that the first ballot was annulled, after Dr. Iqbal had resigned as a result of the Shah's criticisms of the way in which the elections had been rigged, and the second ballot, at which only about 10 per cent of the electorate voted, regarded with open derision by nearly everyone.[4]

The Shah also realized two things about his country which his American allies and paymasters did not. First, that the forces of opposition to the régime—the supporters of communism and the supporters of the National Front—were both too popular and too powerful to make a really free 'democratic' régime—without security police, without a censorship and without arbitrary imprisonment—possible, at all events until the results of the money being spent on development had begun to become apparent in increased productivity, better social services and higher standards of living for the people as a whole. He also realized that the comparative ineffectiveness of such political and social reforms as were introduced, and the wastefulness and delays which accompanied some of the economic development programmes, were due, not so much to 'corruption', as the Americans facilely imagined, as to the sheer inability of defective administrative machinery to translate plans into action, particularly when these plans were opposed, as they often were, and as they often are in other countries besides Iran, by passive resistance on the part of those to whom they were applied. (The fact that in U.K. and U.S.A. people usually pay their taxes, and usually obey the law in such matters as building licences, statutory declarations and so on, is not because people in U.K. and U.S.A. are less 'corrupt' or more public-spirited

213

than they are in Iran but because the machinery of administration is, by and large, effective enough to ensure that people cannot 'get away with' not paying their taxes and disobeying the law generally, however much they might dislike doing so.)

The failure of Mossadeq's 'dash for freedom' in the matter of oil had been a bitter blow to Iranian pride, even among those Iranians, and they were probably the majority among educated Iranians, who had not approved Mossadeq's policies. It was therefore necessary for the Shah to demonstrate at all times his determination to extract as hard a bargain, on behalf of his country, as could be obtained in respect of the exploitation of his country's oil resources. It was particularly necessary to demonstrate that Iran was driving at least as hard a bargain *vis-à-vis* foreign oil interests as were the neighbouring governments of oil producing States. For these reasons much was made of oil agreements arrived at during the course of 1957 for the granting of oil exploration concessions to three foreign oil companies—A.G.I.P. Mineraria, the Italian Company directed by Signor Mattei, Pan American Oil Company, and the Canadian Sapphire Oil Company—which, in addition to the usual 50/50 profit-sharing arrangement, provided for the setting up of local Companies for operating the concessions in which N.I.O.C. would have a 50 per cent share. It could thus be plausibly represented that Iran would receive a 75 per cent share in the profits of these enterprises, once they had started producing oil commercially, without stressing the fact that the additional 25 per cent would be obtained at the price of contributing 50 per cent of the capital required for financing the enterprise. For similar reasons the Iranian Government was the first Middle East Government to react to the second decrease in the export prices of crude oil brought into force by the major oil companies in August 1960; on this occasion the Shah publicly and forcibly protested against the fact that the producing countries had not been consulted about these price reductions.

These and other gestures of nationalist fervour became more and more necessary as it became more and more apparent that neither the material benefits accruing from, nor the moral regard felt for, nor the fear inspired by, the régime were sufficient to check, not so much the discontent but the cynicism and apathy with which the régime was regarded. There were obvious similarities, but there were also basic differences, between the post-Mossadeq régime in Iran and the pre-revolutionary régime in Iraq. Both were allied with the West; neither enjoyed any great measure of popular support; both strove and on the whole failed to gain this popular support as a result of the benefits to be derived from what was intended to be a wise and prudent use of the oil revenue. But whereas the Nuri as Said régime was assailed not only by propaganda from Moscow but also by Cairo-inspired propaganda with which a large proportion of educated Iraqis were in sympathy, the Shah's régime was only subjected to propaganda from Moscow (and from a communist-inspired radio station calling itself the 'Free Voice of Iran') which probably had very little effect on such of his subjects as contrived to listen to it. Also, although the Shah's régime was certainly autocratic, it was a good deal less harsh than that of Nuri as Said. A third important difference was that the principal opposition within Iran—the opposition from the National Front which consisted broadly of supporters of Mossadeq and his policies—had none of the dynamic and little of the popular support that might have been conferred by a policy of social reform. In fact, the opposition had no dis-coverable policy at all, and it was popularly regarded with much the same apathy and cynicism as the régime itself.

It was incompatible with the general policy of the Govern-ment to do anything seriously embarrassing to the interests of the Western Powers, but this did not preclude the exploitation of every situation that arose in a way calculated to obtain from the West the maximum of reward in return for, and as a condi-tion of retaining, Iran's existing commitments to the West. Thus, disagreements with the West over the prices of oil or the terms of financial loans were usually followed by some ostenta-tious flirtation with Russia. This tactic, pursued during 1960, secured a momentary truce in the war of verbal abuse with Russia which had started on the radio after Iran had joined the Baghdad Pact in October 1955, and which was renewed after Iran had confirmed her adhesion to CENTO at the begin-ning of 1959. But, for good or for ill, the régime stood committed, almost as irrevocably as Nuri as Said had been, to the western connexion. Its chances of survival seemed very much better than those of Nuri as Said. First, there appeared to be no very formidable enemy within the gates; secondly, the leader of the régime being a Monarch, and not merely a Minister, there remains the possibility, if circumstances should dictate it, of an adaptation to the wind of change which was not open to Nuri as Said. The régime's commitment to the West is almost, but probably not quite, irrevocable. The Iranians have an amiable habit of never quite burning their boats.

CHAPTER THIRTEEN

Oil, 1955–1960

BY THE BEGINNING of 1955 the supply of oil from the Persian Gulf had become an essential item in the Western European economy. Out of Western Europe's total oil requirements of some 140 million tons per annum, about 100 million tons per annum came from the Persian Gulf area. Of this some 67 million tons per annum came through the Suez Canal and some 33 million tons per annum by pipeline to the Mediterranean and thence by tanker to its destination. Up to the end of the war Western Europe had received most of its oil supplies, either from the Middle East or elsewhere, in the form of refined products which had been refined from the crude at or near the point of production—at Abadan, Bahrain or Haifa in the Middle East, or at Curacoa in the Caribbean, or at one of the refineries in the United States. After the war, for a variety of reasons—strategic, economic and technical—the countries of Western Europe began to build their own refineries and to import oil in its crude form for processing. This development was hastened first by the non-availability of Haifa Refinery for the processing of Middle East crude from 1949 onwards and, more importantly, by the non-availability of Abadan refinery, which had processed most of the Iranian crude before export, after 1951. There was no refinery of comparable size to Abadan in the Middle East, and Kuwait, which succeeded to a large part of Iran's export markets, had no refinery at all, except for a small topping plant to meet local needs of refined oils. Thus, by 1955, something over 80 per cent of Western European oil imports were in the form of crude. (When Iranian oil again began to be exported, towards the end of 1954, most of the oil was exported in this form and exports of refined oil never rose above 17 million tons per annum while annual exports of crude oil, had by 1960, risen to over 30 million tons per annum.)

The importance of oil to the Western European economy was not confined to its use as fuel. British, Dutch and French investments in Middle East oil amounted to a considerable sum, from the point of view both of the money actually invested and of actual and potential profits deriving from these investments. Also, for the British particularly, the sales of British-owned and British-controlled Middle East oil represented a very valuable source of foreign exchange. (In so far as Middle East oil was imported into Great Britain it was a question of saving rather than of earning foreign exchange.) For the United States, Middle East oil was a good deal less important, as the United States were only marginally dependent on supplies of Middle East oil. Similarly, the utility of the foreign exchange earned was only marginal for the American economy. But the American investment in Persian Gulf oil was considerable; after the acquisition of a 40 per cent share in the Iranian Oil Consortium in 1954, the total American stake in Persian Gulf oil exceeded that of the British, Dutch and French interests combined. Although this was relatively less important to the United States than the smaller British, Dutch and French shares were to these countries it still represented a large investment, even by American standards.

The principal difference between the American and the British attitude towards Middle East oil, as exemplified over the Iranian crisis and, later, over Suez, was that the American interest was primarily political while the British interest was primarily economic. The United States were prepared to jeopardize supplies and investments (particularly other people's supplies and other people's investments) in order to avoid political differences which might, in the State Department's view, lead to communist penetration. (The U.S. Government were continually entreating the British Government to make some settlement with Mossadeq as they were obsessed with the idea that the only possible—or rather the most likely—alternative to a Mossadeq-controlled régime in Iran was a communist-controlled one.) The British, on the other hand, as well as the French, to whom the economic aspect was vital, were prepared to take political risks over what they regarded, almost literally, as a matter of life and death. To the Americans, Persian Gulf oil was, in the last anaylsis, expendable in the interests of global strategy. To the British and French it was not so expendable.

Important as the oil revenue had become to the oil producing States, they were not vital. The abilities of societies to tighten their belts in case of necessity varies inversely with the maturity of their economies; and the economies of even the more advanced Persian Gulf States—such as Iran and Iraq—were still primitive by Western standards. The example of Iran had just shown that oil revenues could be foregone, with inconvenience certainly for a minority of the inhabitants, but without very much effect on the majority. In Iraq a total cessation of oil revenues would almost certainly have been fatal to the régime, but would not necessarily have been disastrous to the economy as a whole. In Saudi Arabia and the Arab Sheikhdoms a cessation of oil revenues would have meant an awakening—unpleasant but not catastrophic—from a golden dream.

Nevertheless, in 1955, it seemed unlikely that any of these States, even in the event of a change in any of the generally pro-western régimes which were governing them, would take any action seriously to jeopardize the prospect of continuing to receive these ever-increasing revenues. The cautionary tale of Dr. Mossadeq had been taken to heart. The vulnerable area lay, not in the oilfields themselves, but in the transport lanes along which the oil was conveyed to the west—in the Suez Canal and in Syria.

By the terms of the Anglo-Egyptian Agreement of July 1954 the British had undertaken to evacuate the Canal Zone Military Base, thus in effect relinquishing that control over the Suez Canal which they had held uninterruptedly since 1882. Successive Syrian Governments had refused any sort of alliance with the West, and the civilian régime to which Syria had reverted in 1954 after five years of military dictatorship was moving towards an alliance with Egypt whose military dictator was becoming identified with the policy of 'positive neutrality' which—in the Middle East context—meant rallying the Arab world in opposition to the Baghdad Pact and to the remains of British hegemony in the Middle East. In this context the accidents of geology and geography presented Egypt with the maximum of temptation combined with the maximum of opportunity. The accident of geology had denied to both Egypt and

Syria those rich reserves of oil which had been bestowed on the States of the Persian Gulf (Egypt in fact is an oil producer to the extent of about 3 million tons per annum). The accident of geography (combined with the results of human engineering) provided that the shortest and most convenient routes for oil between the Persian Gulf and the markets of Western Europe lay through the Suez Canal and through the pipelines which had been laid across the Syrian desert. Thus, as middlemen in a literal sense, Egypt and Syria were in a position to exert pressure both on the Persian Gulf producer and on the European consumer. Arab nationalism, as inspired by Abdul Nasr, involved, as a long term policy, the incorporation of the Arab oil-bearing States into an Egyptian-controlled Arab Union and, as a short term policy, using control of the transport lanes as a means of dealing with resistance to the long-term policy whether proceeding from Western Europe or from the oil-producing States. As it happened, the development of this policy was precipitated by two quite extraneous matters—the American withdrawal of their promised loan to Abdul Nasr for the construction of the High Dam, which led to Abdul Nasr's nationalization of the Suez Canal, and the Israeli invasion of Sinai, which led to the Anglo-French attack on Egypt, the blocking of the Suez Canal and the cutting of the I.P.C. pipelines through Syria. We are only concerned here with the results of these events on the oil economy of the Persian Gulf. These results were, in the long run, quite other than what might have been expected. In the first place the peoples of the producing countries, alarmed at the implications of Abdul Nasr's ambitions and unimpressed by the military prowess of the Egyptian Army as revealed in the Sinai Desert, began to have second thoughts about the attractions of Arab nationalism. (The expression 'peoples' is used advisedly; the point is that the—delayed—lesson of Suez helped to ensure that any future popular revolutions in the Persian Gulf States would not be Nasserite ones. The identification between Nasserism and social reform, if not still-born, died very soon after birth from a disease contracted as a result of sudden exposure to reality at about the time of Suez.) In the second place, British and French interests, defeated in their attempt to remove Abdul Nasr from the scene, and alarmed at what appeared to be the prospect of Abdul Nasr's growing influence

in the Middle East, began feverishly (and remarkably successfully) to explore the possibilities of finding oil on the right, or
western, side of the Suez Canal. As a result, within the next
three years, considerable oil deposits were discovered in French
North Africa, in Libya and in Nigeria. The effect of these discoveries was two-fold. In the short term they contributed
towards the development of a surplus of oil supplies on the
world market, which put an end to the sellers' market for oil
existing since the end of the war, and led (in February 1959 and
August 1960) to two substantial reductions in the f.o.b. prices
for Persian Gulf crude oil and oil products. In the long run
these discoveries decreased, although they did not eliminate, the
previous reliance of the West on the Persian Gulf as a vital
source of supply for an essential commodity.

The lessons of Abadan and of Suez were apparent in the attitude adopted by the revolutionary régime in Iraq towards the
I.P.C. There was no attempt at nationalization, and no serious
interference with the Company's operations. Only a steady
pressure exercised with the object of acquiring increased control
and increased remuneration. Almost equally significant was the
fact that the U.A.R., although seriously at odds with the régime
in Iraq, made no attempt to use its control of the transport lanes
to hinder the flow of Iraqi oil to European markets.

Generally, the post-Suez objects of oil policy pursued by the
governments of the various oil-producing countries were (*a*)
increased participation, (*b*) increased control, and (*c*) increased
profitability. Irrespective of political orientation, each oil producing country concentrated on attempts to use, rather than be
used by, the concessionary oil companies.

Neither the consciousness of political risks, nor the development of oil resources elsewhere, deterred foreign oil companies
from the intensive exploitation of existing concessions and from
the active and competitive quest for new concessions in the
Persian Gulf area. World demand for oil was still increasing at a
rate of something like 5 per cent per annum. In spite of developing conditions of over-supply prices were still profitable enough
to attract newcomers to the field, particularly in those areas, like
the Persian Gulf, already known to be rich in oil. And some of
the major companies, whose refining facilities and marketing
outlets were greater than their sources of crude, were anxious

to redress the balance and avoid the competitive disadvantage of having to rely, for part of their supplies of crude, on oil bought from outside. Since most of the likely land areas in the Persian Gulf were already covered by concessions, the quest for new concessions was concentrated on the continental shelf. By 1960 concessions had been awarded and drilling was taking place in the continental shelf areas off Iran (by an Irano-Italian and an Irano-American company), Saudi Arabia (by Aramco who had exchanged their Neutral Zone mainland for a continental shelf concession), the Neutral Zone (by a Japanese Oil Company), Qatar (by Shell) and Abu Dhabi (by a Company owned jointly by B.P. and C.F.P.). Oil in varying quantities had already been struck by nearly all the various concessionaries and facilities for storage and loading for export were already in hand. At the end of 1960 the concession for the Kuwait continental shelf was awarded to Shell in the face of keen competition.

The competition for these concessions was reflected in the prices which the bidders were prepared to pay in order to obtain them. We have already referred (see Chapter Twelve) to the details of the offshore Iranian concessions awarded in 1957. The Japanese company undertook to pay 56 per cent of net profits (including refining and marketing profits) to Kuwait and 57 per cent to Saudi Arabia in respect of each half of the oil produced under the Neutral Zone offshore concession. Companies already holding interests in existing concessions were unwilling (because of the existence of explicit or implicit 'most favoured nation' clauses in their existing concessions) to depart formally from the 50/50 profit sharing principle in their new bids, but offered instead substantial bonuses and the chance of local participation. (The Shell concession for the Kuwait continental shelf provided for a bonus of £30 million and gave an option of participation of up to 20 per cent to the Government of Kuwait or its nominee in the event of oil being found in commercial quantities.)

Progressive increases in production more than offset the reduced unit profitability resulting from decreases in the price of crude oil which came into effect in February 1959 and August 1960. In 1960 total oil production in the Persian Gulf area approached 250 million tons, or about a quarter of total world production. Of this quantity Kuwait accounted for about 80 million tons, Saudi Arabia 60 million tons, Iran 50 million tons, Iraq 45 million tons, and Qatar 8 million tons. The oil revenues accruing to these States came to about £160 million, £120 million, £100 million, £90 million and £16 million respectively.

Competition between the oil companies for concessions was paralleled by competition among the producing countries for markets. Kuwait had taken full advantage of the cessation of Iranian oil exports during 1951–4 to establish itself as the premier producing country in the Persian Gulf. Iran, partly as a result of the destruction of the I.P.C. pumping station in Syria in 1956, improved her position at the expense of Iraq in 1956–7. The Governments of all the producing States impressed on the concessionary companies the desirability of increasing exports at the expense of their neighbours, although their powers of insistence were limited by the fact that both level of output and of prices were controlled by the shareholders of the concessionary companies who, in many cases, were also shareholders of concessionary companies in neighbouring countries. This realization of dependence on the shareholding companies was sharpened by the developing buyers' market, adumbrated by the February 1959 and underlined by the August 1960 price reductions, and producing countries began to think in terms of consultation and common action in defence of their common interests. The first Arab Petroleum Congress, held in Cairo under the auspices of the Arab League in March 1959, was the first overt indication of this desire for a united producing country front. The Congress was not fully representative of Middle East oil interests—Iran, not being an Arab State, was only represented by an observer, and Iraq, seriously at odds with U.A.R., was not represented at all. The proceedings of the Congress underlined the growing demand which existed in the producing countries for financial participation in and for greater control of the exploitation of their oil resources. It was clear that the old 'plantation' days, when oil companies regarded their Middle East concessions as a means of obtaining secure access to a cheap source of raw material, were over and that producing countries were beginning to expect an increasing share in the development of their greatest national asset. The Second Arab Petroleum

Congress, held in Beirut in October 1960, at which Iraq was represented, as well as all the other Arab producing States (but at which Iran was not even by an observer), provided a somewhat acrimonious repetition of the demands and aspirations voiced in the First Congress. But just before this—in September 1960—a rather more significant meeting had been held in Baghdad. At this meeting, which was attended by official delegates from the world's principal oil exporting countries— Venezuela, Kuwait, Saudi Arabia, Iran and Iraq—decisions were taken which led to the setting up of a permanent Organization of Petroleum Exporting Countries (O.P.E.C.) having as its primary object the 'stabilization' (i.e. the maintenance) of oil prices in face of a buyers' market and in face of the control over oil prices exercised by the shareholders of the concessionary companies. Although the overt demand was for 'consultation' between the oil companies and the governments of the producing countries in the event of the former wishing to introduce any price change, it was clear that the price and production control envisaged, whether exercised by the Organization as a whole or by the member countries individually, could only be implemented as a result of the assumption of measures of control over the oil operations by the governments of producing countries which would (at all events in the Persian Gulf countries) involve a radical change in the pattern of existing concessions.

The most immediate result of O.P.E.C., as far as the Arab member States were concerned, was that it superseded the Arab League as the principal policy making organization for oil matters. In other words, it appeared that these States had decided to regard their oil resources as economic assets to be developed and not as political assets to be used for the furtherance of such vendettas as the Arab League might for the moment be pursuing.

In 1955 the oil revenues were still to a large extent regarded by the Governments of the producing States as an agreeable extra; they had not yet become built into the Budget and into the State economy generally. By 1960 all this had changed. The economies of the oil producing States had become geared to the receipt of large and increasing oil revenues and any sharp reduction, let alone complete cessation, of these revenues would have provoked severe financial crises in, at all events, Iran, Iraq and Saudi Arabia. Finance Ministers even got into the habit of budgeting for automatically increased oil revenues, and the revenue for the previous year tended to be regarded as a basic minimum. In fact, the 1955 position had been reversed in that, by 1960, the oil producing States needed the revenue more than the Western European consumers needed the oil. This was the principal reason why the histrionics of the early fifties, when the oil revenue represented an unexpected piece of good fortune which could be staked on some glorious nationalist spree, tended to be replaced by hard bargaining and sober calculation. 'Expenditure rises to meet income.' Except in the case of Kuwait, which was receiving upwards of £150 million per annum to be divided among a population of about 200,000, the financial difficulties of every oil producing State tended to increase proportionately to its oil income. It has already been related how, in 1957, King Saud had to retire temporarily from the direction of affairs in order to enable his brother Feisal to clear up the financial mess which his extravagance and incompetence had created. Iran, by the end of 1960, had saddled herself with an enormous load of foreign debt and was faced with a severe credit and foreign exchange crisis. The revolutionary Government of Iraq was compelled, by reasons of financial stringency, to spend more and more of the oil revenue on everyday expenses and less and less on development works, which almost came to a stop. In Qatar, Sheikh Ali al Thani, who was in receipt of a personal income of some £4 million a year, contrived to get himself into debt to such an extent that, in 1960, he was compelled to abdicate.

Why is it that these oil revenues—except in Kuwait—have been so comparatively ineffective in raising living standards? In Saudi Arabia and Qatar the principal reason has been the unscrupulous greed of the Rulers of these States, and the fact that the tribal traditions of these States made no very clear distinction between State revenues and the Ruler's privy purse. In Iran and Iraq the explanation is different. Neither country had the administrative machinery with which to control and direct the effects of a large annual influx of foreign currency. The development plans were not always very well conceived. The foreign experts were too numerous, and not always very well qualified. There was no attempt to limit the flow of inessential imports, many of which competed with local produce. Creeping inflation steadily diminished the real value of the sums received. In Iraq after the Revolution, disproportionately large sums were spent on the Army, on the security services, and on Government propaganda, both at home and abroad. In Iran, where Reza Shah had built the Trans-Iranian Railway without any assistance either from oil revenues or from foreign loans, Plan Organization floundered deeper and deeper into debt without having anything very impressive to show for it in the way of completed and beneficial work. But in these two countries, and in Saudi Arabia, although the receipt of oil revenues seemed to bring no appreciable nourishment, their cessation, or even their sensible diminution, would have meant chaos.

CHAPTER FOURTEEN

Conclusion

AT THE BEGINNING of the twentieth century three great Empires converged in the Persian Gulf area. To the north there was the Tsarist Russian Empire, to the East the British Indian Empire, and to the west and north-west, the Turkish Ottoman Empire. The international importance of the area was entirely strategic, and derived from the relationships between these three Empires, and from the relationships between the Ottoman Empire and the various European Powers. The only two sovereign States in the area were Persia and Afghanistan, which the British wished to preserve as independent buffer States between India and the developing Russian colonization of Central Asia. The rest of the area, apart from the British-protected Sheikhdoms of the Persian Gulf and the Sultanate of Musqat and Oman, which was technically a sovereign State but in fact a British Protectorate, consisted of outlying parts of the Ottoman Empire, subject to varying degrees of administrative control from Constantinople. The increasing influence of the crescent German on the declining Ottoman Empire was reflected in the German plans for an extension of the German-owned Anatolian Railway through Iraq to the head of the Persian Gulf. The threat of German expansion in the East and elsewhere led to the association of Great Britain with the Dual Alliance of France and Russia and, consequently, to a truce in the eastern rivalry between Great Britain and Russia. In 1907 this truce resulted in the virtual partition of Persia between Great Britain and Russia. Soon afterwards, Anglo-German rivalries in the Ottoman Empire were apparently compounded in an Anglo-German Agreement which provided for British participation in the proposed railway extension to the Persian Gulf.

Then the first world war put everything into the melting pot.

At the end of it Tsarist Russia and the Ottoman Empire had both disappeared, and Germany had been eliminated as a Great Power. Communist Russia was, for the time being, too busy with internal consolidation to have strength enough for imperial expansion on the communist model. But the British still remained masters of India, had conquered the ex-Ottoman territory of Iraq, were in military occupation of part of Persia and had, to all intents and purposes, inherited the previous Ottoman suzerainty over the various princes of the Arabian Peninsula. It seemed that the Persian Gulf area was in process of being incorporated into the British Empire.

But appearances were deceptive. Ideas of self-determination had been nourished by President Wilson's Fourteen Points and by various promises and pledges made by the Western Allies to the Arabs and others during the course of the war. It soon became clear that the 'liberated' areas of the Middle East, and any territories which happened to be conveniently adjacent to them, could not be regarded as 'colonial' territories to be disposed of entirely according to the will of the conqueror.

In Persia a Treaty was concluded in 1919 between the British and Persian Governments which, in effect, provided for a British Protectorate over Persia. But the Majlis refused to ratify the Treaty and, in 1921, after the coup by Sayyid Zia-ed-Din and Reza Khan, it was formally denounced. Thereafter, under the leadership of Reza Khan (afterwards Reza Shah) Persia was able to divest herself of the capitulations and various other derogations from sovereignty and to become a genuinely independent State. In Iraq nationalist agitation and tribal rebellion caused the British Government to modify their original plans and to acquiesce first in the autonomy and later (in 1932) in the sovereign independence of Iraq. In Arabia, the original relations of protector and protected which existed between the British Government and ibn Saud were substituted, in 1927, after ibn Saud's annexation of the Hijaz, by a Treaty which acknowledged, in theory and in fact, the sovereign independence of ibn Saud as Amir of Nejd and King of the Hijaz. Only the protectorate relationships between Great Britain and the various Arab Sheikhdoms remained unchanged, as did the alliance between Great Britain and the Sultanate of Musqat and Oman.

Conclusion

Thus, by the beginning of World War Two, British influence in the Persian Gulf area, although still paramount, principally by reason of British sea power, had been considerably modified by the course of events between the end of one world war and the beginning of the next.

By the end of World War Two the position had changed again and was in some ways analogous to the position before World War One. Russia, once more a Great Power as a result of its victory over Germany, was once more exerting its influence over Persia. The influence of the British Indian Empire had been replaced by the influence of the Anglo-American alliance in which the two parties, although often at odds with each other were always at one in their determination to combat the spread of Russian influence through Iran and down to the Persian Gulf. The influence of the Ottoman Empire had been replaced by the rising influence of Arab nationalism. And in the same way as the European Powers had tended to use the declining Ottoman Empire as a catspaw for the furtherance of their own designs, so Great Britain and Russia were attempting to harness Arab nationalism to their own purposes. In the event both failed to do so and Arab nationalism emerged as a genuine 'Third Force' in the struggle for power which developed over the Persian Gulf.

In this struggle for power there were two great differences between the pre World War One and post World War Two positions. Before World War One the peoples of the Persian Gulf were pawns in the game of power politics, having little desire and no means at all to assert themselves against the Great Powers which surrounded them. Thirty years later, after World War Two, both the desire and to some extent the means existed. Iran, Iraq and Saudi Arabia were all independent sovereign States, members of the United Nations, who had secured and retained their independence of the British after World War One, and who had preserved or regained that independence after World War Two. Moreover, each of these countries was in possession of oil deposits which provided them with incomes to render them economically viable and with bargaining counters in their struggle for independence. The second difference, which also militated in favour of the continued independence of these States in face of pressures from outside, was the fact that, owing to the invention of the A-bomb, and later of the H-bomb, and their possession by both sides in the cold war between east and west, the existence of superior military forces as a means of exerting pressure was almost discounted as a result of the known reluctance of those possessing that military force to use it, at all events in the explosive Middle East area, for fear lest they might be inviting reprisals from the other side which would precipitate their own destruction. This discounting of military force both strengthened the ability of small States to resist dictation from either of the Great Power blocs, and diminished the effect of the military inferiority of Arab nationalism in its rivalry with the other two forces—communism and Anglo-American imperialism—which were competing with it for hegemony in the Persian Gulf.

Thus the position which developed in the Persian Gulf after world war two was that of four forces, each interacting on the other, struggling for political control. First there was the force of local nationalisms within each State, which wished to establish, protect and develop the sovereign independence of that State in face of the three exterior forces—Russian communism, Anglo-American imperialism and Arab nationalism—which were actually or potentially threatening that sovereign independence. (Sometimes the struggle against these three exterior forces involved a temporary alliance with one or more of these forces against what was regarded as a particularly imminent threat from one or more of the others.) Secondly, there was Russian communism which, pursuing its ultimate aim of communising the whole area, often found it convenient to ally itself temporarily either with some local nationalism or with Arab nationalism in order to defeat the immediate aims of Anglo-American imperialism. Thirdly, there was Anglo-American imperialism which often found it convenient to ally itself with some local nationalism, and occasionally with Arab nationalism, in order to defeat the ultimate objects of Russian communism. Fourthly, there was Arab nationalism which often found it convenient to ally itself either with some local nationalism, or with Russian communism, in order to defeat the immediate objects of Anglo-American imperialism. Since, for the reason stated, the use of military force was almost ruled out, this complicated struggle for power was fought out in terms of financial assistance and propaganda, or to put it more shortly, in terms of bribes and lies, the three exterior or imperialist forces being the donors and the indigenous forces of local nationalism being the recipients in each case.

In this complicated cold war certain definite patterns emerged. Iran obtained the alliance of Anglo-American imperialism against the threat of communism. Iraq, before the revolution, obtained the support of Anglo-American imperialism against the threat of Arab nationalism. After the revolution Iraq obtained the support of Russian communism against the threat of Anglo-American imperialism. Saudi Arabia obtained the support of both Arab nationalism and Anglo-American imperialism against the threat of Russian communism. The Arab Sheikhdoms obtained the support of Anglo-American imperialism against Arab nationalism.

This struggle was fought, not for a general strategic advantage, but for a specific asset—oil. The Russians wanted to be in a position to deny both the profits from the oil and the oil itself to the Anglo-Americans. The Anglo-Americans wanted both to safeguard their investments and to secure their oil supplies. The Arab nationalists wanted to transfer control of the oil and control of the profits deriving from oil from the individual Arab States owning the oil and from the Anglo-Americans exploiting it to an Arab Federation under Egyptian control. The individual States wanted to control the oil and the profits from it themselves. In this struggle the individual States enjoyed a tremendous initial advantage. They had the oil and the ruling out of military force meant that no exterior Power could take it from them by violence. All they had to do was to resist the propaganda directed towards them and to use, instead of being used as a result of, the natural advantages with which nature had endowed them.

This brings us to the theme of this concluding chapter.

A power vacuum may be defined as an area where one or more politically immature, socially backward or militarily defenceless States, occupying an area which is either militarily important or rich in some vital raw material, or both, provide a standing temptation for intervention by some outside Power. The Persian Gulf area is a power vacuum, and thus constitutes a continuing menace to the peace of the world and to the security of its inhabitants unless this power vacuum can either be abolished or policed. Its abolition can be achieved either by its occupation by a Power able to make it defensible militarily and viable economically, socially and politically, or by the development of its component States, either independently or in association, in such a way as to make them, from their own resources, defensible militarily and viable socially, economically and politically. (These attributes of genuinely independent States are necessarily relative; none but the largest States, and perhaps not even these, can be defensible militarily, or viable economically, socially and politically, in an absolute sense. The sort of minimum defensibility and viability necessary to abolish a power vacuum is that inhering in the larger South American Republics or in the Kingdoms of Scandinavia.) The policing of the power vacuum can either be achieved, as it was achieved in the days of British hegemony between World War One and World War Two, by placing a shield of protection round the area, or by a self-denying ordinance on the part of all exterior Powers to guarantee the neutrality of the area and to refrain from intervention in it. Since any attempt by any exterior Power to fill the power vacuum by occupying it or to police it by placing a shield of protection round it could and would be effectively resisted by other exterior Powers, and since none of the exterior Powers seem likely to combine together to guarantee the neutrality of the area, it is apparent that the only effective way of dealing with the power vacuum is by the development of the component States of the area, either independently or in association, in such a way as will, with the qualification mentioned, make them defensible militarily, and viable economically, socially and politically.

It is assumed therefore that such development is desirable both in the interests of the inhabitants of the area and of the world in general. The purpose of this final chapter is briefly to discuss the chances of such development in each of the component States of the Persian Gulf. In this discussion it cannot be assumed that any of the three exterior forces converging on the area will cease to exert the various economic and propagandist inducements and pressures directed by them towards the area. For, even though each of the three forces may (possibly) be prepared to recognize the desirability of a genuine independence for the area, none of these exterior forces has sufficient confidence in the others, to enable them to arrive at, let alone to observe, a genuine self-denying ordinance in respect of the area (which would have to include joint plans for financial and economic assistance to the area).

It will therefore be assumed not only that pressures and inducements from the three exterior forces continue but that the inducements are potentially capable of enabling the States of the Persian Gulf to resist the pressures. It will also be assumed that, for reasons already stated, the use of military force for offensive purposes by any of the three exterior forces is unlikely except as part and parcel of a third world war.

In Iran, the largest and most populous State in the area, exterior pressures and inducements from Arab nationalism are non-existent. Here the problem is to build up a viable independence in face of Russian proximity and propaganda on the one hand, and of commercial, financial and military reliance on the West on the other. Leaving aside the possibility of Russian military intervention, Russian influence is exerted through propaganda and through the activities of the (underground) Tudeh Party. The effect of this influence is inversely proportional to the successes achieved by the régime in dealing with Iran's social and economic problems. In dealing with these problems the régime depends heavily on (a) oil revenues received from the Western oil companies, and (b) financial assistance and technical aid received from the United States. Although there is no *a priori* reason why heavy dependence on the proceeds of an essential raw material exported mainly to the West should spell economic dependence on the West, the form of the principal oil concession does in fact mean that the oil industry in Iran is effectively controlled, not by the Government of Iran but by the Western oil companies. The reliance on financial assistance and technical aid from the United States is basically due to the fact that the oil revenues are not being used productively enough to enable social and economic development to proceed at a speed sufficient to ensure the stability of the régime without additional assistance. This additional assistance, intended as it is, by furthering social and economic development (and by enabling the Army to be paid and equipped on a scale adequate to preserve and strengthen its loyalty to the régime) to make the régime less vulnerable to communist and other hostile propaganda, actually makes it more vulnerable to that propaganda by assisting communists and others to convince local nationalist opinion that the policy of the régime is to make Iran a satellite of the West. The remedy consists of (a) administrative improvements providing for a more efficient use of the money received and, in this way, providing for the possibility of doing without any such assistance as implies, or involves, subordination to Western policies, and (b) social and political improvements providing for the more equitable and more widespread distribution of the benefits accruing from the administrative improvements. The application of these remedies is blocked by a social system which inhibits both social and administrative improvement. It is an inhibition, not of means, not of intellect, but of will. It is an inhibition which can be overcome, if at all, either by an evolutionary process, operating through the will of the beneficiaries of the system who forego immediate benefits for the sake of ultimate survival, or by a revolutionary one, operating through the will of the victims of the system goaded beyond endurance by the greed and stupidity of the beneficiaries. It should not be assumed that the revolutionary process is necessarily quicker or more certain than the evolutionary one. Revolution does not inevitably lead to social reform; at best revolution is a process of *reculer pour mieux sauter*, and it may take several jumps even to regain the ground lost as the immediate result of a revolution.

Iraq is a good illustration of the fact that the revolutionary process is neither a certain nor a quick way of bringing about political and administrative improvements previously inhibited by an obsolete social system. Iraq is in receipt of an oil income which, although in total slightly less than that received by Iran, is much greater per head of population (about £5 per annum per head of population in Iran; about £13 per annum per head of population in Iraq). As in Iran the terms of the principal oil concession mean that ultimate control of the oil industry in Iraq is in the hands, not of the Iraqi Government, but of the Western oil companies. Before the revolution Iraq was in a similar position to Iran at present in that the use of the oil revenue was too inefficient to ensure the stability of the régime and to make it less vulnerable to the outside pressures being directed against it. As in the case of Iran this revenue was supplemented by financial and technical assistance from the West which, so far from decreasing the vulnerability of the régime to outside pressures, increased that vulnerability as a result of the subservience to the West which this assistance involved or implied. In Iraq the communist and Arab nationalist pressures directed towards the régime resulted in a revolution. The effect of this revolution was not to secure the victory either of communism or of Arab nationalism. Instead it resulted in a victory for a régime which, although it dispensed with any aid from the West, was still dependent on the West to the extent that it received its oil revenue from the West on terms which left the West largely in control of its oil industry. The new régime was subject to even stronger pressures from communism and Arab nationalism than the previous régime had been. In spite of the revolutionary social changes which, in theory, removed the previously existing inhibitions standing in the way of administrative and political improvements, there is as yet no sign either that the oil revenue is being more productively used (and many signs that it is being less productively used) or that the benefits are more widely or more equitably distributed than before.

Iran and Iraq are in approximately the same stage of social, political and economic development. That is to say, they are in much the same stage of social, political and economic development as Western Europe in the middle of the eighteenth century. And in the same way as the discovery of new mechanical processes and the evolution of new systems of thought have revolutionized the social, political and economic systems and have greatly increased the wealth and power of the countries of Western Europe since the middle of the eighteenth century, so the discovery of oil and the potential wealth accruing therefrom, consisting not only of money from oil exports but of cheap and readily available power, together with the evolution of new systems of thought (derived principally from the accumulation of outside contacts achieved during the course of the twentieth century), have provided these countries with the possibility of a similar revolution in their social, political and economic systems, and a similar increase in their wealth and power. For this fortuitous wealth from oil has provided these countries with possibilities of capital accumulation, and thus of increased productivity per head, which simply did not exist, other than by way of forced accumulation by starvation and forced labour on the communist model, so long as it was a question of trying to achieve capital generation from a subsistence economy. Thus, in these two countries, oil offers the opportunity of a transition from a subsistence to an industrial economy, with all that that means in terms of increased living standards, without the necessity of recourse either to the forcible accumulation characteristic of communism or to the interested and probably inadequate benevolence of foreign Powers, or to forcible accumulation under capitalism by means of sweated labour (as in Japan). The probable alternative to the use of oil for this purpose is not a continuance of the old subsistence economy, mitigated in detail by such minor alleviations as a haphazard use of oil revenues may bring about, but an inexorable popular pressure in the direction of forcible accumulation on the communist model, partly and perhaps temporarily offset by an increasing reliance on financial assistance from the West.

The position in Saudi Arabia is entirely different from that in Iran or Iraq. The population of Saudi Arabia consists principally of Bedouin or ex-Bedouin. The basic economy of the Bedu is pastoral—camel, sheep and goat breeding—and their social structure is tribal. Here the problem is not one of transition from a subsistence agricultural to an industrial economy but from a pastoral economy to an agricultural one. This, in Saudi Arabia, involves using the oil revenue for an intensive development of the limited water resources, for land reclamation and settlement, for the building and equipping of villages, for the stocking of farms and for agricultural training. Here, as in Iran and Iraq, the obstacles are administrative, social and political. But, whereas in Iran and Iraq, it is the social structure which inhibits political and administrative improvement, in Saudi Arabia it is the political tradition of absolution which inhibits social and administrative improvement. Here again, revolution will not necessarily be either quicker or more certain than evolution, and in fact, the tradition of absolutism has, by a process of evolution, been considerably modified over the last ten years. As in Iran the inefficient use of oil revenue (incomparably greater per head per annum than in either Iran or Iraq—about £40 per head per annum as compared with £13 in Iraq and £5 in Iran), combined with the insensate extravagance of the Ruling Family, has necessitated reliance on financial assistance from the United States and a consequent measure of subordination to the policies of the United States. This in its turn has led to Arab nationalist-inspired political discontent with the régime among the educated class, whose growth has been stimulated by the requirements of, and the money furnished by, the oil industry. Of the exterior pressures directed at Saudi Arabia, Arab nationalism is the most important in that, as an influence subversive to the existing social and political order, it is far more potent than communism, and is not seriously resisted by the Americans, who probably regard it, in the Saudi Arabian context, as a prophylactic against communism.

Kuwait is a special case in that the scale of oil revenue (amounting to something like £750 per annum per head of the population) is almost automatically sufficient, whatever the extent of the maladministration (and in Kuwait oil revenues are fairly well administered), palpably and largely to benefit everyone and thus minimize such injustices and inequalities as may arise from a social and political system which, although it shows a surprising capacity for peaceful evolution as compared with Saudi Arabia and the other Persian Gulf Sheikhdoms, is still fairly primitive. As in Saudi Arabia, the principal external pressure on Kuwait comes from Arab nationalism, which pressure, as in Saudi Arabia and possibly for the same reason, is not resisted by the Western Powers. (There is also the external threat from Iraq.)

Arab nationalist influence in the Persian Gulf Sheikhdoms and in Saudi Arabia has a significance different from that which it has in Iraq. In these States this influence is probably a necessary condition of social and political progress since they have, in view of their small populations and social backwardness, no adequate indigenous human potential with which to implement such progress. As in the case of American financial assistance to Iran, it is for the Governments of these States to try and ensure that they use for their own purposes the human and other resources provided by the other Arab countries, instead of being used as a result of receiving them. Under the conditions of absolutism prevailing in these States, this depends mainly on the character and capacity of the various Rulers and their Advisers who are not, as yet, subject to any uncontrollable popular pressures or institutionalized by the operation of unwieldy bureaucratic machines. Here again, it is a question, not of means or of intellect, but of will.

In the interests of their inhabitants, and in the interest of world peace, the two desirable objectives for the government of any Persian Gulf State are (*a*) to become efficient enough to avoid having to ask for financial assistance from any foreign Power and thus to avoid incurring the reality or the suspicion of having become subservient to that foreign Power, and (*b*) to become popular enough to ensure that no considerable body of citizens will prefer the prospect of foreign domination to the fact of indigenous rule.

If these objectives are attained, governments unfettered by obligations abroad and fortified by support at home will be able to withstand the exterior pressures directed towards them. But it is idle to imagine that independence of foreign pressures can be secured with the assistance of foreign Powers. It is of no use to succeed in resisting pressures from one direction at the price of incurring obligations in another. *Timeo Danaos et dona ferentes* should be inscribed over the mantelpiece of every Head of a Persian Gulf State.

Navigation in the Persian Gulf

THE FIRST MAN who is known to have navigated the Persian Gulf from end to end is Alexander's Admiral Nearchus who, in the years 326–325 B.C., sailed his fleet through the Gulf from the mouths of the Indus to the mouth of the Tigris. The first evidence of navigation aids in the Persian Gulf appears in the writings of the Arab historian Masudi, who lived in the tenth century A.D. and who noted that 'There are marks of wood erected for sailors in the sea, at Hezara, on the side of Uballa, and Abadan, which look like three seats in the middle of the water, and upon which fires are burnt by night, to caution the vessels which come from Oman, Siraf and other ports, lest they run against the Hezara; for if they run there they are wrecked and lost'. Other references to these primitive lighthouses are made by Idrisi, an Arab geographer, and Nasir-e-Khusraw, a Persian writer, writing about a century later. Idrisi says, 'The Khashabat (wooden structures) are situated exactly at the place where the Dijla (Tigris) discharges its waters into the Sea of Fars (Persian Gulf). They are pile work, on which stand huts or cabins occupied by coast guards with boats which enable them to get to their cabins or go ashore'. Nasir-e-Khusraw says, 'they are erected for a double purpose; firstly for lighting during the night, by means of lights enclosed in glass to protect them from the wind, to warn vessels to take precautions in these dangerous waters; and secondly, to show the navigator his position, and to warn him against possible pirates'. (These quotations are taken from A. T. Wilson's *Persian Gulf*, George Allen & Unwin, 1954 impression, p. 59.)

The first attempt at surveying the Persian Gulf was made by the Indian Navy in 1772 when the coast off Makran and Persian Baluchistan was surveyed. In 1788 Lieutenant McCluer of the East India Company's Marine surveyed the north-east waters of the Gulf and the Shatt-al-Arab up to Basra and made plans of the harbours of Basra and Musqat. In 1817 a survey was made by Lieutenant Tanner of the Bombay Marine of the ports and pearl banks of the Bahrain archipelago. But it was not until the pirate menace had been checked as a result of the various expeditions described in Chapter One that it was possible, in 1820, to start a really systematic survey. Between 1820 and 1836 the first complete survey of the waters of the Gulf was made by the Indian Navy. Between 1835 and 1840 surveys were made of the Tigris, Euphrates and Karun by a British expedition commanded by Colonel F. R. Chesney. The harbour of Kuwait was surveyed in 1839. The general survey begun in 1820 was revised and corrected between 1857 and 1860. The Indian Navy was disbanded in 1863 and their work taken over by the Royal Navy. But it was not until 1903 that systematic survey work was resumed, mainly on the initiative of Lord Curzon, at that time Viceroy of India.

Responsibility for the safety of navigation, in the same way as responsibility for controlling and trying to suppress the slave trade, piracy and traffic in arms was undertaken by the British in the Persian Gulf as a necessary consequence of that position of paramountcy which they had attained in these waters by the end of the eighteenth century.

The lighting and buoying of the Gulf waters was at first undertaken as a private enterprise by the British India Steam Navigation Co. which, during the second half of the nineteenth century, had something approaching a monopoly of commercial steam navigation in the Persian Gulf. At the beginning of the twentieth century, when foreign competition came on to the scene which the B.I. were unwilling, in effect, to subsidize by giving them free the benefits of the service they had set up and had been maintaining, the Persian Gulf Lighting Service, as it was termed, was taken over by the Government of India and placed under the control of the Chief Political Resident at Bushire who collected tolls from the various shipping lines using the Gulf to pay for the maintenance of the service. (The headquarters of the Lighting Service were transferred from Bushire to Basra in 1920.) This arrangement continued until 1946, when the authority of the Government of India in the Persian Gulf was transferred to the British Foreign Office and the headquarters of the Chief Political Resident transferred from Bushire to Bahrain. The Persian Gulf Lighting Service was taken over from the Government of India by a non-profit-making commercial organization made up of the tanker owners and shipping companies who were the principal users of the service, which was provided free to locally-owned dhows and other small craft. Its headquarters were transferred from Basra to Bahrain and the Chief Political Resident was given a seat on the local Board. Since 1946 continuous and, on the whole, harmonious co-operation has been achieved between the Lighting Service and the relevant Customs, Port and Naval authorities of the various riparian States regarding the maintenance of navigation aids and the safety of navigation generally.

In 1960 the Persian Gulf Lighting Service, in consultation with these authorities, decided to adopt the Decca Navigator System, to enable vessels fitted with the system easily and accurately to pinpoint their exact location. By this time a new and important set of customers for navigation aids had come on the scene in the Persian Gulf. By 1960 no less than six oil companies were looking for oil under the sea—mostly in the northern part of the Gulf—and exact pinpointing of marine location was obviously an important matter to them. The Decca Navigation System is based on three land-based stations placed in a triangle round the periphery of the marine area covered, sending out radio signals which are picked up and plotted by ships in the area carrying the necessary receiving and plotting equipment.

The principal maritime traffic passing through the Persian Gulf now consists of oil tankers either proceeding up the Gulf in ballast towards oil loading ports or down the Gulf loaded with oil. All of the oil ports—Abadan, Bandur Mashur and Kharg in Iran, Fao at the mouth of the Shatt-al-Arab in Iraq, Mina al Ahmadi in Kuwait, Ras Tanura in Saudi Arabia, Awali in Bahrain and Umm Said in Qatar—have been especially constructed by the oil producing companies for the export of oil, and most of them can accommodate the largest tankers now afloat. Apart from the oil ports, Basra, which handles all Iraq's maritime imports and exports, other than oil, is easily the largest. Khorramshahr on the Shatt-al-Arab and Bandar Shapur on the Khor Musa are Iran's two largest non-oil ports. The other big ship ports of the Persian Gulf, none of which have quayside accommodation for large vessels, are Bushire, Lingeh and Bandar Abbas in Iran, Kuwait, Uqair in Saudi Arabia, Manama in Bahrain, Doha in Qatar, and Musqat. There are in addition a number of small boat harbours such as Sharja, Dubai and Ras al Kheima on creeks along the Trucial Coast.

The Pattern of Oil Concessions in the Persian Gulf

THE ANGLO-PERSIAN OIL COMPANY, which took over the d'Arcy Concession, the first oil concession in the Middle East which had succeeded in producing oil in exportable quantities, became one of the world's major oil companies as a result of its Persian concession. The refining, marketing and transport interests which it subsequently acquired, were acquired for the purpose of marketing the Persian oil whose production had been the original object of the Company's formation. The various concessions awarded after world war one were operated on a different pattern. They were obtained by groups of two or more existing international oil companies and operated through companies formed *ad hoc* for the purpose of exploiting the concession by the companies who had obtained the concession, who were the sole shareholders in the operating companies so formed, who provided the necessary finance for the operating companies, and who received from the operating companies, f.o.b. the nearest port, the oil produced in proportion to their shareholding. The operating company was in fact the agent of the shareholders and its business was to manage the concession in accordance with the requirements of the shareholders (and in accordance with the terms of the concession) and to hand over the oil produced to the shareholders. The object of these arrangements, from the point of view of the shareholding companies, was to provide these companies with a secure source of their own crude (and in some cases refined) oil for their marketing operations instead of having to rely on the open market for their raw material. The reasons for combination between international companies for the obtention of these concessions were various. As we have seen, the shareholding in I.P.C. was dictated by political considerations. The Bahrain and Saudi

243

Arabian concessions were originally obtained by a single Company—Standard of California—which afterwards sold a half share in each concession to the Texas Oil Company in order to facilitate the marketing of the oil produced through the large Texas marketing interests in Asia. Subsequently, two other Companies—Standard of New Jersey and Socony-Mobil—were admitted to shares in the Saudi concession as a means of obtaining extra capital for this enterprise. The Kuwait concession was exploited jointly by Gulf and Anglo-Persian because Anglo-Persian, at that time, were unwilling to 'go it alone' in what was regarded as a very speculative enterprise. In Iran the Oil Consortium which, in 1954, was awarded a concession in approximately the same area from which A.I.O.C. had been extruded in 1951, consisted of no less than seventeen shareholders—one British (British Petroleum, ex-A.I.O.C.), one Anglo-Dutch (Shell), one French (C.F.P.), five major U.S. Companies (Standard of New Jersey, Standard of California, Gulf, Socony-Mobil and Texas) and a 'consortium within a consortium' of nine U.S. 'independents' having a 5 per cent share between them. This grouping, like that of I.P.C., was dictated by political considerations.

Other post world war two concessions followed something of the same pattern as the post world war one concessions, but with two important differences. The post world war one concessions had almost invariably been awarded to and exploited by groups consisting of two or more of the eight or nine major international oil companies. Several of the post world war two concessions were awarded to and exploited by small independent companies singly. This was due (*a*) to the fact that the speculative element in the investment had diminished as a result of the discoveries already made in the vicinity by the major companies, and (*b*) to the very profitable prices at which crude oil could be sold in the sellers' market which prevailed for the first fourteen years or so after the war. The second difference was that many of the post world war two concessions gave to the government of the producing country the option of participation by its nationals in the shareholding of the operating company. For example, concessions awarded by the Iranian Government to Agip, Pan American and Sapphire provided for the creation of Operating Companies (S.I.R.I.P., I.P.A.C. and I.R.C.A.N.

respectively) in which N.I.O.C. had a 50 per cent shareholding. The concession awarded to Shell in 1960 covering the Kuwait 'continental shelf' gave the Government of Kuwait the option of up to a 20 per cent share in the operating company to be formed in the event of oil being found. (The Abu Dhabi 'continental shelf' concession was, however, on the old conventional lines, being awarded to a combination of two 'majors' (B.P. with 70 per cent and C.F.P. with 30 per cent) without the option of local participation.)

More immediately important than the form of the new concessions was the drastic revision of the old ones in respect of the award accruing to the producing States. In all the original concessions this reward had taken the form of a fixed royalty per ton on all oil produced plus various annual payments in respect of rents, compounded taxes, etc. (Except for the original d'Arcy concession which provided for a 16 per cent royalty on net profits; this was amended to a fixed royalty per ton in 1933.) These payments varied and were from time to time adjusted upwards. Immediately prior to 1951 they amounted, on an average, to about ten shillings per ton on all oil produced, irrespective of the price at which it was sold. As a result of the revisions in the terms of all the major concessions which took place between 1950 and 1952, and which provided for a 50/50 division of net profits between concessionary company and producing country based on the f.o.b. price of all crude oil sold, these payments suddenly increased to something of the order of £2 per ton. (Under the new arrangement the rate of payment depended, of course, on the selling price of the oil which was not necessarily constant.)

A common feature of the non-participating concessions, which was not removed by the so-called 50/50 'partnership' arrangements, was that both the rate of production and the prices at which it was sold were determined entirely by the various oil companies who were shareholders in the concessionary companies and who became, in proportion to their shareholding, owners of the oil produced. And since the oil produced was produced almost entirely for the requirements of the refining and marketing affiliates of the shareholders, both level of production and f.o.b. prices tended to reflect (at all events in the eyes of the producing countries) the international interests of the shareholders rather than the national interest of the producing country. For the shareholders, in their capacity as producers and sellers of crude oil, were to a large extent selling crude oil to themselves. Thus a reduction in the price of crude, although it meant a decreased profit to the producing country under the 50/50 profit-sharing arrangement, did not necessarily mean a decreased profit to the shareholders, since what they lost on the producing swings, they could regain on the transport, refining and marketing roundabouts, in that the shareholders' transport, refining and marketing interests stood to gain the equivalent of what their producing interest had lost as the result of any reduction in the price of crude. Similarly, from the point of view of the level of production, it appeared to the producing country that, if a shareholder in a producing enterprise was already obtaining from other sources, at equivalent or better terms, most of the oil that he needed for the requirements of his refining and marketing affiliates, he had little incentive to increase the level of production in that particular producing country.

Such criticisms were more or less silenced during the first half of the 1950's by the fact that both prices and levels of production, and consequently the sums payable to the producing countries, continued steadily to increase. Whatever the theoretical disadvantages of leaving matters entirely in the hands of the oil companies, the producing countries, enjoying incomes in some cases more than ten times what they had been receiving before 1950, felt disinclined to quarrel with what appeared to be a lucrative bargain. But the very profitability of Persian Gulf oil— a profitability conferred by the fact that production costs, due to the high productivity of the wells, are very much less than in the Western Hemisphere—led 'independent' newcomers to outbid the established 'majors' in the continuing quest for new concessions. As a result, concessions were awarded, as in Iran, providing for local participation, and, as in the Neutral Zone, where a Japanese Company agreed to a 56 per cent/44 per cent profit sharing arrangement (covering refining and marketing as well as producing profits) in favour of the producing country. These favourable terms in respect of new concessions naturally caused some discontent in producing countries about the terms of the old concessions. The cautionary Iranian experience under

Mossadeq was sufficient to discourage precipitate action, but the coming end of the sellers' market for crude oil, heralded by two price reductions in February 1959 and August 1960, amounting between them to a reduction of the order of 15 per cent, encouraged a relatively responsible and respectable examination of existing concessions which found expression in various proposals for a greater share of control by the producing countries over the exploitation and disposal of their own oil resources. Of these proposals, three—two of which are identified with Sheikh Abdullah al Tariqi, Minister for Oil Affairs in Saudi Arabia, and the other with the Shah of Iran, are worthy of mention here.

(1) The 'hiving-off' of the operating company from its shareholders and its operation as a national entity, paying dividends to its shareholders but becoming responsible, as a national entity, for the production and disposal of oil with due regard both to the national interest and to the provision of a fair return to the shareholders who would, however, no longer be able to pre-empt oil produced in proportion to their shareholding at a price laid down by them, but who would have to obtain it, under long term contract or otherwise, as a result of negotiation. As a corollary to this 'hiving-off' process, the operating company, which would of course be free to acquire local shareholding, would acquire, either in conjunction with or separately from its foreign oil company shareholders, interests in overseas refining and marketing enterprises, as well as acquiring its own tanker fleet, in order to have an assured outlet for at least part of its production. (Tariqi.)

(2) The formation of a 'producers' cartel' consisting of representatives from the Governments of the major exporting countries, which would allot export quotas to each of its members in such a way as to avoid flooding the market and as to keep prices at a profitable level. (Tariqi and Perez Alfonso, the Venezuelan Minister for Oil Affairs.)

(3) Insistence that any proposed future changes in the export prices of oil should be submitted to and agreed by the Governments of producing countries before being put into effect by the oil companies. (The Shah of Iran.)

Implementation of any of these proposals would require a

revision of existing concessions. The first proposal, which is not dependent on any form of combination between the exporting countries, and which roughly represents the actual position of most large foreign enterprises operating in Western European countries or in the United States (e.g. English and German Ford in Europe, Shell Oil in the United States) would seem to be a fore-shortened view of a probable—or at all events possible —long-term trend of development. The second and third proposals pre-suppose the setting up of an international body representing the interests of the principal oil exporting countries. Such a body—the Organization of Petroleum Exporting Countries (O.P.E.C.)—was in fact set up during 1960 and its present (1961) membership consists of Venezuela, Iran, Iraq, Kuwait, Saudi Arabia and Qatar, who between them provide something over 80 per cent of the 'free world's' total oil imports.

There are various and obvious difficulties about the implementation of either the 'pro-rationing' or 'consultation' proposals. It seems probable that the most fruitful immediate result of O.P.E.C., from the point of view of the member-countries, will be seen, not in the specific implementation of either of these two proposals, but in the increasing tendency of the major oil companies, confronted with the vague threat represented by the mere existence of O.P.E.C., to deal with a buyers' market in crude oil by squeezing the profits of their transport, refining and marketing affiliates, in order to maintain the profits of their producing affiliates and, consequently, the profits of the producing countries.

The Development of International Air Routes through the Persian Gulf Area

THE FIRST INTERNATIONAL airline to operate in the Persian Gulf area was the German Junkers Company which, from 1924, operated a regular service from Berlin to Tehran through Russia. This service was later extended to Baghdad via Tehran, and operated until 1930, when it was discontinued.

From 1921 the British R.A.F. had been running a regular mail service between Cairo and Baghdad and, on 1 January 1927, the British Imperial Airways inaugurated a mail and passenger service from Cairo to Basra via Gaza, Rutbah Wells and Baghdad. In October 1925 Imperial Airways started surveying possible landing grounds on both sides of the coast of the Persian Gulf with a view to extending the service from Basra to Karachi. Eventually a route was laid out along the Persian coast of the Gulf, and a temporary transit agreement arrived at with the Persian Government; in April 1929, a Cairo-Karachi service was opened, taking five days for the trip, with main stops at Gaza, Baghdad, Basra, Bushire, Bandar Abbas and Charbah, and with intermediate stops at Amman, Rutbah, Ramadi, Lingeh, Jask and Gwadar. As the transit agreement with the Persian Government was a temporary and rather precarious one (after some renewals it eventually expired at the end of 1932) Imperial Airways continued their surveys on the Arabian shore and, in October 1932, their route through the Gulf was transferred to the Arabian side via Basra, Bahrain, Sharja and Gwadar. By this time longer 'hops' had become possible and fewer landing grounds and refuelling stops necessary.

Meanwhile, in 1930, the K.L.M. (Dutch) had started operating a regular service from Amsterdam to Batavia and Air Orient (French) from Paris to Saigon, via the Persian Gulf. In 1933 the Imperial Airways Eastern Service was extended from Karachi across India to Calcutta and from there to Bangkok and Singapore. At the beginning of 1935 this route was extended to Australia. In 1937 Imperial Airways (to become the British Overseas Airways Corporation in 1938) inaugurated a flying boat service from London to Karachi via the Persian Gulf with night stops at Habbaniyah and Sharja and intermediate stops at Basra and Bahrain.

By the time of the outbreak of war in September 1939, B.O.A.C., K.L.M. and the French Air Orient were all running regular services to the Far East via the Persian Gulf, B.O.A.C. with landplanes and flying boats, and the other two with land planes. Baghdad, Basra, Bahrain, Sharjah and Gwadar had all been developed as amphibious international landing grounds and refuelling points.

After the war revolutionary developments in passenger aircraft design and performance led successively to the abandonment of flying boats, to the cutting out of night stops and to the elimination of intermediate refuelling points. There was also a tremendous and progressive increase in the number of passengers and in the amount of freight and mail carried, and consequently in the number of airlines operating and in the number of services operated by each line. It became possible to fly straight over the mountains and deserts of Persia *en route* to and from the Far East (before the war this had been impracticable both politically and technically) instead of flying up and down the Gulf. Through traffic became concentrated on Baghdad, Basra, Bahrain and Tehran, which all became important international airports, servicing the ever increasing number of international airlines (B.O.A.C., K.L.M., Pan-American, T.W.A., Air France, S.A.S., Air India, Pakistani Airways, Luft Hansa, Ala Litoria, to name but a few) running to and from Europe and the East. In addition to through traffic there was an increasing volume of passengers, freight and mail leaving and entering the Persian Gulf area to and from Europe and the United States, mainly as a result of the oil companies' operations in and around the Gulf. International airports, mainly for the servicing of this oil companies' traffic, were established at Dhahran, Abadan and Kuwait. Apart from this there was an increasing volume of air traffic between the capitals of the Middle East and between the various States in the Persian Gulf area. This traffic was principally serviced by a number of national and regional airlines, in some of which the big international airlines had an interest (e.g. Middle East Airways, Iraqi Airways, Iranair, Air Jordan, Air Liban, Misrair, etc.), and by numerous regional airports. Gulf Aviation, a subsidiary of B.O.A.C., was established to carry air traffic up and down the Gulf on the Arabian side, from Kuwait to Musqat.

By 1961 there were seven international airports (Baghdad, Tehran, Basra, Abadan, Bahrain, Dhahran and Kuwait), about a dozen regional airports, scores of landing grounds, many of them constructed and maintained by the various oil companies operating in the area, and innumerable emergency landing strips in the Gulf area. The international airports served as essential links on the great trunk routes to and from the United States and Europe and the Far East, situated, as they were, half-way between the international airports of Cairo, Tel Aviv, Beirut, Damascus and Istanbul to the west and Karachi, New Delhi and Colombo to the east. Apart from their role as transit points, these airports, owing to the increasing economic importance of the Persian Gulf area, became increasingly important as starting and terminal points for passengers, freight and mail to and from Western Europe and the United States.

(Much of the pre-1940 information in this Appendix was derived from *Britain's Imperial Air Routes 1918 to 1939*, by Robin Higham, published in London in 1960 by G. T. Foulis & Co. Ltd. I also acknowledge with gratitude information provided by B.O.A.C and K.L.M.)

References to Texts of State Papers, etc., for Treaties and Other Transactions mentioned in the Text

THE REFERENCES ARE in order of date, with the page reference given in brackets. The reference given is the most easily assessible, and not necessarily the original, English text. In the case of Treaties the dates given are the dates of signature and not the dates of ratification.

I wish to acknowledge the assistance I have received from the following publications.

Collection of Treaties, Engagements and Sanads Relating to India and Neighbouring Lands. C. U. Aitchison. First published in Calcutta in 1866. References taken from Third Edition published in 1895. (Referred to as AITCHISON.)

Diplomacy in the Near and Middle East. J. C. Hurewitz. van Nostrand for Princeton University, 1956. (Referred to as HUREWITZ.)

The extent of my debt to these two publications is abundantly apparent. I also wish to acknowledge the assistance of the following publications:

Documents in British Foreign Policy, 1919–39, ed. E. L. Woodward and R. Butler, H.M.S.O., 1952.

Revue Egyptienne de Droit International, Cairo.

I wish to acknowledge the assistance of the London Library and Chatham House in providing me with access to these publications and to the originals of various British State Papers.

1801. 'Malcolm Treaty' between H.M.G. and Persia. 28 January 1801. HUREWITZ, Vol. I, doc. 27, p. 68 (p. 19).

1820. Treaty between H.M.G. and Trucial Sheikhdoms for Suppressing Piracy and the Slave Traffic. 28 January 1820. HUREWITZ, Vol. I, doc. 27, p. 68 (p. 13).

1834. Anglo-Russian Agreement on Persia (renewed in 1888). Parl. Papers Misc., No. 2 (1898), pp. 127–8. H.M.S.O. C–9088 (p. 20).

1838. Slave Trading Convention between H.M.G. and Trucial Sheikhdoms. AITCHISON, Vol. VII, p. 254 (p. 14).

1847. Slave Trading Convention between H.M.G. and the Trucial Sheikhdoms. AITCHISON, Vol. VII, p. 256 (p. 14).

1851. Slave Trading Treaty between H.M.G. and Persia. AITCHISON, Vol. VII, p. 147 (p. 14).

1853. Treaty of Peace in Perpetuity between H.M.G. and Trucial Sheikhdoms. 4 May 1853. HUREWITZ, Vol. I, doc. 61, p. 143 (p. 13).

1861. Slave Trading Convention between H.M.G. and Sheikh of Bahrain. AITCHISON, Vol. VII, p. 264 (p. 14).

1862. Anglo-French Declaration on Musqat. 10 March 1862. HUREWITZ, Vol. I, doc. 34, p. 168 (p. 17).

1865. Convention Relating to Telegraphic Communication between Europe and India—Great Britain and Persia. 23 November 1865. HUREWITZ, Vol. I, doc. 75, p. 169 p. 26).

1874. Slave Trading Convention between H.M.G. and Sultan of Musqat and Oman. AITCHISON, Vol. XI, p. 77 (p. 14).

1880. First Exclusive Agreement between H.M.G. and Sheikh of Bahrain. 22 December 1880. HUREWITZ, Vol. I, doc. 88, p. 194 (p. 23).

1890. Russo-Persian Railroad Agreement. November 1890. HUREWITZ, Vol. I, doc. 95, p. 207 (p. 30).

1891. Treaty of Friendship, Commerce and Navigation between H.M.G. and Sultan of Musqat and Oman. 20 March 1891. HUREWITZ, Vol. I, doc. 96, p. 208 (p. 17).

1892. Second Exclusive Agreement between H.M.G. and Sheikh of Bahrain. 13 March 1892. HUREWITZ, Vol. I, doc. 88, p. 194 (p. 23).

1899. Treaty between H.M.G. and Sheikh of Kuwait. 23 January 1899. HUREWITZ, Vol. I, doc. 100, p. 218 (p. 25).

1901. D'Arcy Oil Concession. 29 May 1901. HUREWITZ, Vol. I, doc. 102, p. 209 (p. 36).

1903. Baghdad Railroad Convention. 5 March 1903. Parl. Papers Baghdad Railway, No. 1, Cmd. 5635, pp. 37–48 (p. 86).

1907. Anglo-Russian Agreement on Persia. Parl. Papers 1907 Treaty Series, No. 34, Cmd. 3753 (p. 33).

1913. Anglo-Turkish Convention on Persian Gulf. 29 July 1913. HUREWITZ, Vol. I, doc. 108, p. 269 (p. 40).

1913. Bahrain Order in Council. 12 August 1913. *London Gazette*, 12 August 1913, Vol. LXXXII, p. 656 (p. 40).

1914. Agreement for Reorganizing the Turkish Petroleum Company by the d'Arcy Group, the Deutscher Bank and the Anglo-Saxon Petroleum Co. 19 March 1914. HUREWITZ, Vol. I, doc. 111, p. 276 (p. 88).

1914. Act of Parliament providing for H.M.G. shareholding in the Anglo-Persian Oil Co. 20 May 1914. Parl. Papers 1914, Vol. 54, Cmd. 7419 (p. 81).

1914. Anglo-German Agreement on Baghdad Railway. 15 June 1914. HUREWITZ, Vol. I, doc. 113, p. 281 (p. 40).

1914. Ottoman Promise of a Concession to the Turkish Petroleum Co. 28 June 1914. HUREWITZ, Vol. I, doc. 114, p. 286 (p. 88).

1916. Sykes-Picot Agreement. Documents in British Foreign Policy 1919–1939. 1st Series, Vol. 4, pp. 241–51 (p. 88).

1918. Denunciation of Tsarist Russian Privileges in Persia by the Soviet and Persian Governments. 26 June to 27 July 1918. HUREWITZ, Vol. II, doc. 17, p. 34 (p. 60).

1918. Armistice of Mudros between Great Britain and Turkey. 30 October 1918. Cmd. 53 of 1919 (p. 54).

1918. Anglo-French Declaration to Inhabitants of Occupied Enemy Territories in Turkey. November 1918. HUREWITZ, Vol. II, doc. 15, para. 4, p. 30 (p. 62).

1919. Anglo-Persian Treaty. Persia, No. 1, Cmd. 300 of 1919 (p. 56).

1920. Treaty of Sib between Sultan of Musqat and Oman and Imam of Oman. *Revue Egyptienne de Droit Internationale,* Vol. 13, 1957, p. 120 (p. 122).

1920. Anglo-French Oil Agreement. Cmd. 675 of 1920 (p. 89).

1921. Russo-Persian Treaty of Friendship. HUREWITZ, Vol. II, doc. 33, p. 90 (p. 60).

1921. Treaty of Friendship between Russia and Turkey. HUREWITZ, Vol. II, doc. 34, p. 95 (p. 52).

1922. Treaty between H.M.G. and Iraq. Parl. Papers 1925 Treaty Series No. 17, Cmd. 2370 (p. 65).

1923. Treaty of Lausanne. Cmd. 1929 of 1923 (p. 66).

1925. Turkish Petroleum Co. Concession in Iraq. 14 July 1925. HUREWITZ, Vol. II, doc. 44, p. 131 (p. 90).

1926. Tripartite Treaty between Great Britain, Iraq and Turkey. Parl. Papers 1926 Treaty Series No. 7, Cmd. 3488 (p. 68).

1927. Treaty of Jidda between H.M.G. and Amir of Nejd. 22 May 1927. Parl. Papers 1927 Treaty Series No. 25, Cmd. 2951 (p. 73).

1928. 'Red Line' Agreement between international Oil Companies. 31 July 1928. HUREWITZ, Vol. II, doc. 54, p. 161 (p. 91).

1930. Treaty between H.M.G. and Iraq. Parl. Papers 1931 Treaty Series No. 15, Cmd. 3797 (p. 115).

1933. Revised Agreement between Persia and Anglo-Persian Oil Co. 29 April 1933. HUREWITZ, Vol. II, doc. 58, p. 188 (p. 85).

1938. Saadabad Pact between Afghanistan, Iran, Iraq and Turkey. HUREWITZ, Vol. II, doc. 63, p. 214 (p. 105).

1940. Russo-German Negotiations for a Projected Soviet Sphere of Influence in the Near and Middle East. November 1940. HUREWITZ, Vol. II, doc. 68, p. 228 (p. 141).

1942. Tripartite Treaty between Great Britain, Russia and Iran. Parl. Papers 1942. Persia, No. 1, Cmd. 6335 of 1942 (p. 129).

1943. Declaration on Iran made by U.S.A., Russia and Great Britain at Tehran Conference. HUREWITZ, Vol. II, doc. 73, p. 237 (p. 131).

1946. Irano-Soviet Dispute before U.N. Security Council and the Proposed Oil Agreement. 2–4 April 1946. HUREWITZ, Vol. II, doc. 80, p. 261 (p. 146).

1947. Treaty of Portsmouth between H.M.G. and Iraq. Cmd. 7309 of 1948 (p. 192).

1950. Anglo-Iranian Oil Co. Supplemental Agreement. Parl. Papers 1951. Persia, No. 1, Cmd. 8425, pp. 19–22 (p. 166).

1950. Saudi-Aramco Agreement on Revision of Aramco Oil Concession. 30 December 1950. HUREWITZ, Vol. II, doc. 94, p. 314 (p. 172).

1951. Correspondence between H.M.G. and Persian Government and Relevant Documents covering the Oil Industry in Persia. Feb.–Sept. 1951. Cmd. 8425 of 1951 (pp. 155–156).

1951. Treaty of Friendship, Commerce and Navigation between H.M.G. and the Sultan of Musqat and Oman. Parl. Papers 1952 Treaty Series No. 44, Cmd. 8633 (p. 196).

1954. Iranian Oil Consortium Agreement. 29 October 1954. HUREWITZ, Vol. II, doc. 104, p. 348 (p. 209).

1955. Treaty between Turkey and Iraq (Baghdad Pact). 24 February 1955. Parl. Papers 1955 Misc. No. 5, Cmd. 9429 (p. 194).

1955. Special Agreement between H.M.G. and Iraq. (H.M.G's Adherence to Baghdad Pact.) 4 April 1955. Parl. Papers 1955 Treaty Series No. 50, Cmd. 9544 (p. 194).

1961. Exchange of notes regarding relations between the United Kingdom of Great Britain and Northern Ireland and the State of Kuwait. June 19 1961. Cmd. 1518 of 1961 (p. 264).

Notes

CHAPTER ONE

1. In fact a system of dual control developed, by the Government of India on the one hand and the Home Government on the other with the India Office, after 1857, acting as liaison between the Government of India and the Foreign Office. The Foreign Office appointed the Minister in Tehran and the various Consuls in the area, while the Government of India appointed the Political Resident (at Bushire) and the various Political Agents. The Political Resident, who was also a Consul General, as well as many of the Political Agents, who were also Consuls, thus had to serve two masters, who were not always in agreement.

2. The dispute with France over Musqat centred on British objections to the French extending the protection of their nationality and flag over some of the subjects of the Sultan of Musqat. On occasion this protection was used for the purposes of slave-trading and gun-running. The Hague Tribunal ruled that the French were only entitled to extend protection towards those to whom that protection had been granted before 1861, the year of the Anglo-French Declaration. In this dispute, the differing viewpoints between the Foreign Office and the Government of India became frequently apparent. While the Government of India was all for a strong stand against French pretensions, the Foreign Office, concerned with the wider implications of such a strong stand, insisted on moderation. Musqat, whose official status was, and remains, that of an independent sovereign State and not that of a protectorate, was, unlike the Arab Sheikhdoms of the Gulf, in Treaty relationship with the Home Government and not with the Government of India, and the British Representative there was a Consul. It appears in fact that the Anglo-French Agreement of 1861 was, by an oversight, not communicated to the Government of India until about twelve years after it had been signed. After 1904 a certain amount of friction between the British and French persisted in Musqat, mainly as a result of the arms traffic. Musqat was used as an entrepot for a flourishing arms traffic between the French-controlled port of Jibuti and the mainland of Persia and Baluchistan, on the other side of the Gulf, whence the smuggled arms found their way towards the North-West Frontier of India. Hence the concern of the Government of India. In 1914 the Sultan was prevailed on by the British to exercise something like effective control of the movement of arms and ammunition in and out of his ports.

3. The process of Russian colonization of Turkestan was assisted and accompanied by the construction of the Transcaspian Railway. Starting from Krasnodovsk on the eastern shore of the Caspian, it went to Ashkabad, on the Russo-Persian frontier, and thence eastward, eventually being extended as far as Tashkent.

4. See Note 1.

5. For a full account of the Persian claim to Bahrain see *Bahrain Islands— A Legal and Diplomatic Study of the British-Iranian Controversy*, by F. Adamiyat. The Persians claim that their right to the islands was recognized twice by the British, once in 1822 and again in 1869. The attraction during the nineteenth century was the pearl fisheries of Bahrain. After the establishment of the British protectorate, a British gunboat patrolled the pearl fisheries during the season to discourage poachers.

6. These disturbances mainly took the form of attacks on Persian residents of Bahrain inspired by Bahrain's Sunni religious leaders. (The Persians were Shias.) The British intervened to protect the Persians and induced the Ruler to deport some of the fanatical religious leaders.

7. Over Kuwait, as over Musqat, differences in view became apparent between the Home Government and the Government of India. The Home Government was reluctant to dispute with Turkey over the question of Kuwait, and resisted the Government of India's policy which was to support the Sheikh of Kuwait against his suzerain. The Home Government, as usual, got its way, and, in an Anglo-Turkish Agreement signed in 1913 (but never ratified) covering Anglo-Turkish relations along the Arabian shore of the Gulf, and also the question of buoying and lighting the Gulf and the Shatt-al-Arab estuary, the British recognized Turkish sovereignty over Kuwait.

8. This was in confirmation of the Anglo-Turkish Agreement on the subject. (See Note 7.) The question of the control of navigation on the Shatt has been an endemic matter of dispute between Iran and Iraq ever since.

9. The steamers on these two services were owned and operated by the British firm of Lynch Brothers.

10. The land line was operated by the Government of India through the Indo-European Telegraph Department. The sea cables were operated by the Eastern Telegraph Company.

11. In 1903 the German-owned Anatolian Railway Company received from the Porte a concession for the extension of the Anatolian Railway through Mesopotamia down to the headwaters of the Persian Gulf.

CHAPTER TWO

1. A Political Agent had already, in 1900, been installed at Bahrain. In 1904 a Political Agent was appointed to Kuwait, in 1908 to Sharja, and in 1910 to Mohammerah (Khorramshahr).

2. The practice of taking sanctuary, either in a mosque or shrine, or in some other place such as a Legation where the police cannot get at one, is a traditional Persian method of protest against oppression. It is known as 'bast' and those who practise it are 'bastis'. As late as 1961 certain National Front leaders sought sanctuary from arrest in the Senate building.

3. This Agreement, which was concluded with Russia by the Home Government and not by the Government of India, was most unpopular with the latter, who considered both that the Agreement had conferred far too much influence on Russia in Persia and also that the British sphere of influence was too small and should at least have been extended to cover the

province of Arabistan (Khuzistan) where the British Political Agent at Mohammerah was already in close touch with the powerful Sheikh Khazaal.

4. The British India Steam Navigation Company had, for many years, been the principal, if not the only, line of steamers trading regularly in the Gulf.

5. The rise of the Amir of Nejd had important implications for the British in the Gulf. His great enemy, ibn Rashid of the Shammar, was a Turkish protegé, and at the beginning of the century was predominant in the Peninsula. The successive defeats of ibn Rashid at the hands of ibn Saud greatly weakened Turkish influence, and particularly weakened Turkish ability to exert pressure on Kuwait (whose Ruler, in backing ibn Saud, was undoubtedly actuated by a desire to see this Turkish pressure reduced). But the rise of the Wahhabi ibn Saud alarmed the Rulers of the other British-protected Sheikhdoms on the Arabian coast, who had not forgotten Wahhabi depredations a century before. As early as 1906 the Government of India was anxious to come to terms with ibn Saud, both in order to offset Turkish pressure on Kuwait and to facilitate their duty of protecting the other littoral Sheikhdoms. In the course of conversations with a British Political Agent ibn Saud expressed his future intention of annexing al-Hasa and, anxious to avoid any hostile British reaction to this, offered to accept a British Political Agent there. But the Home Government, anxious to avoid embroiling themselves with Turkey over the affairs of the Persian Gulf, sternly forbade any interference in the affairs of central Arabia, and the (unratified) Anglo-Turkish Agreement of 1913 (see Note 7, Chapter One), specifically debarred H.M.G. from entering into an alliance with the Amir of Nejd.

6. ibn Saud's annexation of al-Hasa was, *faute de mieux*, recognized by the Turks who appointed ibn Saud Wali (Governor) of Nejd and al-Hasa.

CHAPTER THREE

1. But Treaties with the Rulers were almost invariably concluded in the name of the British Government and not in that of the Government of India.

2. As from the end of 1916, when the Lloyd George Coalition came into office, the war effort in the Middle East was directed by a Cabinet Committee of which the Foreign Secretary, the Secretary for India, and the Secretary for War were members. This arrangement continued until the beginning of 1921, when control of the British Mandated territories in the Middle East was transferred to the Colonial Office. Control of relations with the Persian Gulf Sheikhdoms continued to be exercised by the Government of India until 1946, when this control was transferred to the Foreign Office.

3. See *Wassmuss*, by Christopher Sykes (Longmans Green, 1936), Chapter Seven.

4. The Indian Expeditionary Force was sent to India by and remained under the control of the Government of India until February 1916 when control was transferred to the War Office in London, as a result of allegations of maladministration made by a Commission of Enquiry. The name of the force was then changed to Mesopotamian Expeditionary Force (M.E.F.).

5. Shortly before the capture of Baghdad a Cossack Brigade actually made contact with the advancing British forces.

6. This force was originally organized by the War Office independently of the M.E.F. Later it became attached to and was reinforced from the M.E.F. There was some controversy at the time about the wisdom of extending the operations of the M.E.F. to Persia and Sir Arnold Wilson attributes the British military weakness in Iraq at the time of the 1920 rebellion largely to this extension. The principal protagonist of this extension in the War Cabinet was Lord Curzon who was obsessed with the idea of a strong British presence in Persia as a safeguard first against German and later against Russian penetration towards India.

7. This force had been sent to Persia by and was responsible to the Government of India.

8. For reasons which will become apparent in a later chapter great importance was attached by the British War Cabinet to the British occupation of the whole of Mosul Vilayet.

CHAPTER FOUR

1. U.S.A. was not at war with Turkey.

2. The town and immediate surroundings of Mosul were occupied after the Armistice and in spite of Turkish resistance under a clause in the Armistice agreement which provided for the surrender of all Turkish garrisons in the various theatres of war.

3. After the war Mesopotamia became generally known by its Arabic name of Iraq and will be referred to henceforth as such.

4. Denikin was one of the leading White Russian army commanders.

5. One of the clauses in the Treaty stated that the U.S.S.R. 'unconditionally reject the criminal policy (of the West) not only as violating the sovereignty of the States of Asia but also as leading to organized brutal violence on the body of the peoples of the East'.

6. Cmd. 5974 of 1939, Annex I, pp. 50–51.

7. A 'Mandate' was a trusteeship awarded to a country by and exercised under the control of the League of Nations.

8. Only 69 out of 100 delegates attended and ratification was secured by 37 votes to 24 with 8 abstentions after the British High Commissioner (Dobbs) had warned the king that any further delay over ratification would mean its rejection by H.M.G. Even so, the Treaty was only ratified on condition that the Financial Agreement was amended and on condition that the Treaty would be regarded as null and void in the event of H.M.G. not securing sovereignty for Iraq over the Vilayet of Mosul.

9. See Sir Arnold Wilson's *Clash of Loyalties* (O.U.P., 1931), p. 22.

10. By the terms of the Treaty of Jidda ibn Saud recognized the *status quo* in Bahrain, which was a useful concession both for the Sheikh of Bahrain and for the British and a perennial source of irritation to Persia, which in that year began to advance the Persian claim (which has been persisted in ever since) to Persian sovereignty over Bahrain.

11. A quarrel arising between ibn Saud and Salim arising out of the disposal either of the captives or of the loot was to have the result of putting an

Notes

end to the traditional friendship between the House of Saud and the House of Subah when Salim became Sheikh of Kuwait little more than a year later.

12. See Note 11 *supra*.

13. For details of the Treaty of Sib and subsequent events see Chapter Ten.

CHAPTER FIVE

1. Cmd. 7419 of 1914.

2. *Middle East Oil and the Great Powers*, B. Shwadran (Praeger, N.Y., 1955), pp. 33–37.

3. It was subsequently maintained by Persia that the 16 per cent of profits basis was adversely affected both by the favourable price paid by H.M.G. for oil under bunkering contracts with the Royal Navy and also by the increasing incidence of British taxation.

4. Shwadran, op. cit., pp. 162–3.

5. The 1933 concession did not continue A.P.O.C's previous monopoly on the construction of pipelines to the Persian Gulf. This removed the principal obstacle to the exploitation of northern oil and in 1937 a concession covering the province of Khorassan was given to the American Amiranian Co. which eventually relinquished it without finding oil.

6. Shwadran, op. cit., p. 42.

7. Ibid., pp. 52–55.

8. Ibid., pp. 162–3.

9. And to the rights of the Sultan's Privy Purse for ever.

10. *Oil in the Middle East*, S. H. Longrigg (O.U.P. for R.I.I.A., 1954), p. 31.

11. Shwadran, op. cit., pp. 201–4.

12. Cmd. 675 of 1920.

13. A high-sounding device intended to ensure that U.S.A. should receive a substantial share of any war loot that was going.

14. Standard of New Jersey, Standard of New York, Gulf, Atlantic Refining, Pan American. Later, Gulf, Atlantic and Pan American sold their interests to Standard of N.J. and Standard of N.Y. Standard of N.Y. later became Socony-Mobil. The shareholders in Near East Development Corp. were thus reduced to two U.S. 'majors', Standard of N.J. and Socony-Mobil.

15. The first commercial production in Iraq came from what was known as the Transferred Territories in and around Khanaqin. This area, which was included in the d'Arcy concession, had been transferred from Persia to Turkey under the award of the 1914 Boundary Commission. It was subsequently provided that the terms of the d'Arcy concession should be honoured by the Iraqi Government in respect of the Transferred Territories, and the Khanaqin Oil Company, wholly owned by A.P.O.C., was formed. Small quantities of oil were produced until 1958 when it was taken over by the Iraqi Government under a provision in the concession which enabled them to do so if the production was under a certain minimum.

16. Shwadran, op. cit., p. 277.

17. *Kuwait and Her Neighbours*, H. R. P. Dickson (Allen and Unwin, 1956), p. 277.

18. Such anti-trust prejudices as may have caused the State Department to hesitate about the legality of the Red Line Agreement were presumably mitigated by the consideration that whereas Anglo-Dutch interests (Royal Dutch-Shell and BP) were both bound by the Red Line Agreement, there were already two major U.S. oil companies—Texas and Standard of California—which were not so bound (Texas had been an original member of the U.S. T.P.C. group but had withdrawn before the signature of the Red Line Agreement). Moreover it was open to any U.S. company already a partner in T.P.C. to sell its interest to another U.S. company and thus free itself from its obligations under the Red Line Agreement. This was subsequently done by Gulf and others with the result that eventually there were only two major U.S. companies—Standard of N.J. and Socony-Mobil—who were bound by the Red Line Agreement, and three—Gulf, Texas and Standard of California—who were not so bound.

19. Shwadran, op. cit., p. 290.

20. As a result of this partnership with Texas in Bahrain and Saudi Arabia the California Texas Oil Company (Caltex) was formed by which Texas's marketing organizations east of Suez were thrown into the partnership in consideration of Texas receiving a half share in the production of Bahrain and Saudi Arabia.

21. Shwadran, op. cit., p. 296.

CHAPTER SIX

1. The Capitulations were treaty arrangements arrived at between Persia and most of the Great Powers under which nationals of the latter enjoyed extra-territorial rights in Persia in that they were subject to the jurisdiction, not of the Persian Courts, but of their own Consuls. Capitulations in Persia were finally abolished by Reza Shah in 1927.

2. The repression of the Southern magnates also enabled the disbandment of the South Persia Rifles, the force which had been raised by the British during the war to keep order among the Southern tribes.

3. See Note 1.

4. By 1936 the Government had monopoly control of 33 per cent of all imports and 44 per cent of all exports.

5. Reza Shah's dislike of Great Britain's predominant position in the Persian Gulf was illustrated in 1927 when the Persian Government, on the strength of a short period of Persian occupation during the eighteenth century, officially laid claim to Bahrain and protested vigorously at the recognition of the British Protectorate by ibn Saud in the Treaty of Jidda. The timing of this claim, which has been persisted in ever since, was undoubtedly affected by the expectation that oil might be discovered in the archipelago.

6. By order of Shah Reza 'Persia' became officially known as Iran from 1935 onwards, and will be referred to as such in this book from this point. The name of the Anglo-Persian Oil Company was changed to Anglo-Iranian Oil Company. Under the present Shah both appellations are

officially permitted. The Persian world is 'Iran'. 'Persia' is derived from 'Fars', which is the name of one of the provinces of Iran and the Arabic name for the whole of Iran. Oddly enough the Iranian language is called by the Iranians 'Farsi'.

7. A ten-mile long narrow gauge railway from Tehran to Rey was constructed during the last years of the nineteenth century and is still (1961) in operation.

8. *Russia and the West in Iran*, G. Lenczowsky (Cornell Univ., 1949), p. 95.

9. The Yezidis are a small heretical Moslem sect living in the Jebel Sinjar on the border between Syria and Iraq. They are popularly referred to as 'devil-worshippers'.

10. Mr. C. D. (now Sir Charles) Belgrave.

11. Previously this route had run down the Persian side of the Gulf, but difficulties had arisen with the Persian Government in connexion with the contemporaneous dispute with the A.P.O.C.

12. For historical accounts of relations between Musqat and Oman and for discussions of the terms of the Treaty of Sib see (a) Sultanate and Imamate in Oman by J. B. Kelly (O.U.P. for R.I.I.A., 1959) and (b) The Question of Oman (Information paper No. 13 Arab Information Center, New York, Nov. 1960).

CHAPTER SEVEN

1. In 1945 nearly 3 million tons of oil was exported from Saudi Arabia and Saudi Arabia received nearly 5 million dollars in oil royalties.

CHAPTER EIGHT

1. Multiply barrels per day by fifty to obtain tons per year.

CHAPTER NINE

1. According to the Iranian Constitution a Minister cannot be a Majlis deputy. In practice this concession to Montesquieu's doctrine of separation between the Executive and Legislature has, in the absence of a strong Executive, or of carefully rigged elections, resulted in Majlises which see themselves either as a constitutional opposition or as rivals to the Government.

2. Under the 1933 Agreement 20 per cent of any increase in the Company's General Reserve accrued during the period of the Agreement was to be paid to Iran at the end of the Agreement. The Supplemental Agreement provided that 20 per cent of such increments should be paid to Iran annually.

3. See Cmd. 8425 of 1951. *Correspondence between H.M.G. and the Persian Government concerning the oil industry, Feb. 1951–Dec. 1951.*

4. See Cmd. 8677 of 1952. *Correspondence concerning Joint Anglo-American Proposals for the Settlement of the Oil Dispute.*

CHAPTER TEN

1. It is however conceivable that decreases in crude oil prices might make the fifty-fifty arrangement less rather than more profitable to the producing States than the six shillings a ton royalty which was being negotiated both in Iraq and Iran at the time of the announcement of the fifty-fifty agreement in Saudi Arabia. Also, the fifty-fifty arrangement implies that any 'community projects' carried out by the concessionary companies, in the way of schools, hospitals, roads, etc., are in fact paid for, to the extent of one-half, by the State, in that such expenses are deductible from the profits of the oil operation. Under the old flat rate royalty arrangement, any expenditure of this sort was borne entirely by the concessionary company.

2. In 1960 three of the I.P.C. partners withdrew from the Musqat and Oman concession and the concessionary Company was reconstituted with Shell holding 83 per cent and Gulbenkian 17 per cent.

3. Sheikh Khalifa died in October 1961, and was succeeded by his son Sheikh Issa.

CHAPTER ELEVEN

1. In June 1961 the 1899 Treaty which up to that time had regulated relations between Great Britain and Kuwait was replaced by a new Agreement which, in effect acknowledged Kuwait's sovereign independence and substituted the British Protectorate by an alliance with Great Britain. Immediately after the conclusion of this Agreement, General Qasim proclaimed Kuwait as part of Iraq, on the ground of it once having formed part of the Vilayet of Basra, and announced his intention of annexing it to Iraq. In accordance with the terms of the new Agreement and in response to a request for assistance from the Sheikh of Kuwait, British forces landed in Kuwait to repel what appeared to be a threatened Iraqi invasion. General Qasim, whose claim to Kuwait had been repudiated by most of the other member states of the Arab League (a repudiation which did not prevent Cairo from simultaneously condemning British 'aggression'), then announced that Iraq would pursue her claims to Kuwait by peaceful methods only. A Kuwaiti application to join the Arab League was opposed by Iraq, and a Security Council Resolution, proposed by Great Britain, and affirming the sovereign independence and territorial integrity of Kuwait, was vetoed by U.S.S.R. In the autumn of 1961 Kuwait was admitted to the Arab League, in spite of Iraqi objections, and the British force in Kuwait replaced by an Arab League force, consisting mostly of a Saudi Arabian contingent.

2. In February 1961 an attempt by Iran to use Iranian berthing masters, instead of Basra Port Authority, to berth and unberth ships at Abadan, led to a refusal by the Basra Port Authority to pilot vessels so berthed and unberthed up and down the Shatt and to the temporary cessation of oil exports from Abadan. In April 1961 the dispute was temporarily resolved by Iran waiving its right to the use of Iranian berthing masters.

CHAPTER TWELVE

1. BP was to receive from the other Consortium members (a) £32,400,000

Notes

in three instalments during the first year of the Agreement, and (b) a levy of 10 cents a barrel on all oil exported by the other Consortium members up to a total of 510 million dollars (£214 million).

2. See next paragraph below.

3. There was no statutory provision whereby Plan Organization was to receive any fixed proportion of the oil revenue, as had been the case with the Development Board in Iraq, which, before the Revolution was statutorily entitled to 70 per cent of the oil revenue. For the year AH 1340 (1961–2) the proportion was fixed at 55 per cent, the balance being divided between the general revenue budget and the N.I.O.C.

4. In April 1961 Sharif Emami, who had succeeded Dr. Iqbal as Prime Minister in the autumn of 1960, resigned and was succeeded by Dr. Amini who, as Minister of Finance in General Zahedi's government, had negotiated the Consortium Oil Agreement in 1954 and who had subsequently been appointed Ambassador to Washington. Summarily dismissed from this post in 1959 he had been an outspoken opponent of the Iqbal and Emami Governments and his appointment by the Shah as Prime Minister represented a clean break with the immediate past and an attempt to appease the mounting discontent which was demonstrated both in widespread strikes and in a revival of political activity by the National Front. Dr. Amini prevailed on the Shah to dissolve the Majlis, announced that he would take serious steps to combat corruption and implement land reforms and introduce long overdue measures of currency control and import restrictions. It remains to be seen whether these measures will be effective in saving the régime from the alternatives of a military coup or a National Front government, either of which might well be a prelude to communism.

Bibliography

A List of Books read, re-read, or consulted while writing
The Persian Gulf in the Twentieth Century

Adamiyat, F. *Bahrein Islands—A Legal and Diplomatic Study of the British-Iranian Controversy.* Praeger (N.Y.), 1955.

Aitchison, C. U. *A Collection of Treaties, Engagements and Sanads Relating to India and Neighbouring Countries.* Vols. VII & XI, Calcutta, 3rd ed. 1895.

Belgrave, Sir Charles. *Personal Column.* Hutchinson, 1960.

Bell, Lady (ed.). *The Letters of Gertrude Bell* (2 vols.). Benn, 1927.

Browne, E. G. *The Persian Revolution of 1905-9.* C.U.P., 1910.

Bullard, Sir Reader. *Britain and the Middle East from the Earliest Times.* Hutchinson, 1951.

Council on Foreign Relations (U.S.). *Middle East Dilemma. The Background to U.S. Policy.* 1953.

Curzon, Hon. G. N. *Persia and the Persian Question* (2 vols.). Longmans Green, 1892.

Dickson, H. R. P. *Kuwait and Her Neighbours.* Allen & Unwin, 1956.

Dickson, W. E. R. *East Persia, A Backwater of the Great War.* Arnold, 1924.

Eden, Sir Anthony. *Full Circle.* Cassell, 1960.

Finnie, David H. *Desert Enterprise—The Middle East Oil Industry and Local Development.* Harvard University, 1958.

Fontaine, P. *La Guerre Froide des Petroles*, ed. Je Sens. Paris, 1953.

Ford, Alan W. *The Anglo-Iranian Oil Dispute of 1951-52.* California University, 1954.

Foster, H. A. *The Making of Modern Iraq.* Williams & Norgate, 1936.

267

Frye, Richard N. *Iran* (2nd ed.). Allen & Unwin, 1960.

Glubb, Sir John. *War in the Desert*. Hodder & Stoughton, 1960.

Graves, Philip. *The Life of Sir Percy Cox*. Hutchinson, 1942.

Gupta, S. N. *Iran. An Economic Study*. Indian Institute of International Affairs, New Delhi, 1947.

Hamzavi, A. H. *Persia and the Powers—An Account of Diplomatic Relations 1941–46*. Hutchinson, 1946.

Hay, Sir Rupert. *The Persian Gulf States*. Middle East Institute, Washington, 1959.

Hoskins, H. L. *British Routes to India*. Longmans Green, 1928.

Hourani, A. H. *Minorities in the Arab World*. Royal Institute of International Affairs, 1947.

Howard, H. N. *The Partition of Turkey. A Diplomatic History 1913–1923*. Oklahoma University, 1931.

Hurewitz, J. C. *Diplomacy in the Near and Middle East—A Documentary Record*. Vol. I, 1535–1914. Vol. II, 1914–1956. van Nostrand for Princeton Univ., 1956.

Ionides, Michael. *Divide and Lose*. Bles, 1959.

Ireland, P. W. *Iraq; A Study in Political Development*. Cape, 1937.

Kedourie, E. *England in the Middle East. The Destruction of the Ottoman Empire, 1914–21*. Bowes, 1956.

Khadduri, M. *Independent Iraq; A Study in Iraqi Politics since 1932*. O.U.P. for R.I.I.A., 1951.

Lambton, A. K. S. *Landlord and Peasant in Persia*. O.U.P. for R.I.I.A., 1958.

Laqueur, W. Z. *Communism and Nationalism in the Middle East*. Routledge & Kegan Paul, 1956.

Lenczowski, G. *Russia and the West in Iran, 1918–1948*. Cornell University, 1949.

Lesueur, Emile. *Les Anglais en Perse*. La Renaissance, Paris, 1922.

Lloyd, Seton. *Twin Rivers; A Brief History of Iraq from the Earliest Times to the Present Day*. O.U.P., 1945.

Lockhart, Lawrence. *The Fall of the Safavi Dynasty and the Afghan Occupation of Persia*. C.U.P., 1958.

Longhurst, Henry. *Adventure in Oil. The Story of BP.* Sidgwick & Jackson, 1959.

Longrigg, S. H. *Four Centuries of Modern Iraq.* Clarendon Press, 1925.

— *Iraq 1900 to 1950.* O.U.P. for R.I.I.A., 1953.

— *Oil in the Middle East. Its Discovery and Development.* O.U.P. for R.I.I.A., 2nd., 1961.

Main, E. *Iraq from Mandate to Independence.* Allen & Unwin, 1935.

Mikesell, R. F. and Chenery, H. B. *Arabian Oil; America's Stake in the Middle East.* North Carolina University, 1949.

Miller, W. *The Ottoman Empire and its Successors, 1801-1927* (4th ed.). C.U.P., 1936.

Millspaugh, A. C. *Americans in Persia.* The Brooking Institute, Washington, 1946.

Motter, T. H. W. *The Persian Corridor and Aid to Russia.* Department of the Army, Washington, 1951.

Nakhai, M. *La Petrole En Iran,* ed. J. Felix. Bruxelles, 1938.

Owen, Roderick. *The Golden Bubble.* Collins, 1957.

Philby, H. St. J. *Arabia.* Benn, 1930.

— *Arabia of the Wahhabis.* Constable, 1938.

— *Arabian Days.* Robert Hale, 1948.

— *Arabian Jubilee.* Robert Hale, 1952.

— *Forty Years in the Wilderness.* Robert Hale, 1957.

Royal Institute of International Affairs. *The Middle East in the War* (ed. George Kirk). 1952.

— *The Middle East. A Political and Economic Survey* (ed. Sir Reader Bullard), 3rd ed. 1958.

Ronaldshay, Lord. *The Life of Lord Curzon* (3 vols.). Benn, 1928.

Said-Ruete, R. *Said Bin Sultan.* Alexander-Ouseley, 1929.

Sanger, R. H. *The Arabian Peninsula.* Cornell University, 1954.

Shah of Iran, H.I.M. the. *Mission for my Country.* Hutchinson, 1961.

Shuster, Morgan. *The Strangling of Persia.* The Century Co., New York, 1912.

Shemari, Samir. *The Oil of Kuwait*. Middle East Research and Publishing Centre, Beirut, 1959.

Shwadran, B. *The Middle East, Oil and the Great Powers*. Praeger (N.Y.), 1955.

Sykes, Christopher. *Wassmuss*. Longmans Green, 1936.

Sykes, Sir Percy. *A History of Persia* (2 vols.). 3rd ed. Macmillan, 1958.

Van der Meulen, D. *The Wells of Ibn Saud*. Murray, 1957.

Williams, K. *Ibn Saud*. Cape, 1933.

Wilson, Sir Arnold. *The Persian Gulf*. Allen & Unwin, 1928.

— *Loyalties—Mesopotamia 1914-17*. O.U.P., 1930.

— *Mesopotamia—A Clash of Loyalties*. O.U.P., 1931.

— *South West Persia*. O.U.P., 1941.

Wood, A. C. *A History of the Levant Company*. O.U.P., 1935.

Index

271

Index

272

Index

Index

Index

Persian Bank Mining Rights Corporation, 79

Persian Gulf, extent, 1–2; importance in eighth century, 2; piracy in, 11–13; defence of British interests in, 42, 43; and oil after 1947, 139; Iranian interests in, 206; navigation in, 239–42

Persian Gulf Command (U.S.), 143

Persian-Turkish war, 10

Petra, 73, 74

Petroleum Concessions Ltd., 96

Petroleum Developments (Qatar) see Qatar Petroleum Company

Philby, Hilary St. John Bridger, 69–70, 178, 179

pipelines, defence of, 42; monopoly of, to Persian Gulf, 80, 83, 84; I.P.C. constructs, to Mediterranean, 92; from Damman to Ras Tanura, 95; Iraq's dependence on Mediterranean, 119, 168, 189; Trans-Arabian, 172, 182; Kirkuk-Haifa, 192; I.P.C. pumping station destroyed, 200, 220, 223; importance of Mediterranean outlet, 217

piracy, 11–13, 197

Pirate Coast see Trucial Coast

Pishevari, Jaafar, Prime Minister of Azerbaijan, 145, 146, 147, 148

Plan Organization (Iran), 210, 211, 226

Portsmouth, Treaty of, 1947, 192

Portugal, 3–7

Qailani, Rashid Ali al see Rashid Ali al Qailani

Qais, Island of, 4

Qajar dynasty, 9, 18, 61

Qashgai, 37, 45, 61, 99, 148

Qasim, General Abdul Karim, Prime Minister of Iraq, 203, 205

Qasr-e-Shirin, 80

Qatar, 22, 76, 95, 120–1, 136, 176–7, 183–4, 206, 222, 223

Qatar Petroleum Company, 136, 173, 177

Qazvin, 127

Qishm, 8, 13

railways, Persian Gulf to Tehran, 30; Dharan to Riadh, 182; see also Berlin-Baghdad Railway

Ras al Kheima, 7, 13, 197

Ras Tanura, 95, 172

Rashid Ali al Qailani, Prime Minister of Iraq, 124, 126, 168

Razmara, General Ali, Prime Minister of Iran, 153, 154, 155, 162

Red Line Agreement, 91, 93, 95, 96, 171, 179

refugees, 198

Reuter, Baron Julius de, 30, 79

Revised Agreement with A.P.O.C., 1933, 82–3, 84–6, 166

Reza Khan, Shah of Persia, 61, 84, 101, 102, 103, 104, 127, 128, 141, 142

Riadh, 38, 69, 73, 107, 112

Robertson, Field-Marshal Sir William Robert, 50

Roosevelt, Franklin D., President of the U.S.A., 129

Royal Air Force, 71, 72, 115, 124

Royal Dutch-Shell Group, 67, 87, 88, 90, 209; see also Shell Petroleum Company

Royal Navy, defends East India Co.'s interests, 10; policing duties of, 11

Russia, interest in Persian Gulf port, 18; alliance with France, 28; influence in Persia, 30, 31; in north Persia, 44; advance from Caucasus, 47; revolution, 50 (after 1917 see U.S.S.R.)

Russo-Japanese War, 31

Russo-Persian Treaty of Friendship, 1921, 60, 83, 100, 148, 150, 211

Russo-Turkish Armistice, 1917, 54

Russo-Turkish Treaty of Friendship, 1921, 52

S.I.R.I.P., 244

Saadabad Pact, 1937, 105

Sadr, Sayyid Mohammed as, Prime Minister of Iraq, 192

Safavi dynasty, 5, 9, 18

Said, Sultan of Musqat, 16, 17

Said bin Taimur, Sultan of Musqat and Oman, 96, 121, 136, 178, 197

Said Halim Pasha, Grand Vizier, 88, 89

Said, Mohamed, Prime Minister of Iran, 144

Saida, 172

Salar-ed-Dowla, 36

Salim, Sheikh of Kuwait, 74, 75

Salman bin Hamad al Khalifa, Sheikh of Bahrain, 184

San Remo, Treaty of, 114, 115

San Remo Conference, 1920, 63

Saqar, Sultan bin, Sheikh of Sharja, 12

Saud, King of Saudi Arabia, 173, 178, 179, 182, 193, 195, 196, 201, 225

Saudi Arabia, oil concessions in, 94–5, 96, 111; production of oil in, 110; disapproval of Iraqi policy, 125; and World War II, 131–3; oil in, 1940–1954, 171–3; use of oil revenues by, 181–2; attracted by Nasserism, 194; in the 1950's, 195–6; and the Buraimi oasis, 196; British reactions to penetration into Trucial Coast, 198; and Suez incident, 200; relations with Iran, 206; and continental shelf

Index

279

Index

DATE DUE